THE SCIENCE OF THE GREATER JIHAD

Essays in Principial Psychology

THE SCIENCE OF
THE GREATER JIHAD

Essays in
Principial Psychology

CHARLES UPTON

SOPHIA PERENNIS

SAN RAFAEL, CA

First published in the USA
by Sophia Perennis
© Charles Upton 2011

Series editor: James R. Wetmore

For information, address:
Sophia Perennis, P.O. Box 151011
San Rafael, CA 94915
sophiaperennis.com

Library of Congress Cataloging-in-Publication Data

Upton, Charles, 1948–
The science of the greater Jihad: essays in
principial psychology / Charles Upton.

p. cm.
Includes bibliographical references.
ISBN 978-1-59731-128-1 (pbk: alk. paper)
1. Transpersonal psychology. 2. Psychology and religion.
3. Psychology, Religious. I. Title
BF 204.7.U68   2011
150.19'8—dc22   2011017818

CONTENTS

PREFACE

As a psychologist, I am an amateur, which means: somebody who does it because he loves it. I've written this book on "principial psychology" not as a therapist, but as someone with a practical interest in how psychology relates to the spiritual Path. I received a traditional Catholic education, and I have been on the Sufi path for over 20 years, as well as a student of comparative religion and metaphysics and mythopoesis for almost 45. Consequently this book is based most directly upon Sufi "ontological psychology", supplemented with concepts taken from Scholastic Philosophy, Kabbalah, Buddhism, and the Vedanta, as well as insights drawn from the poetry of William Blake. I took the "counterculture course" proposed by, and to, my generation, and learned what you can learn about the human psyche by that route; as Blake put it: "The road of excess leads to the palace of wisdom" and "If the fool would persist in his folly he would become wise." I've practiced yoga, Reichian exercises; I've experienced Reiki, Shen therapy, bodywork; along with many other San Francisco poets I studied the Jungians in the 1970's, and I absorbed the Traditionalist/Perennialist critique of the Jungians in the 1990's; I took a two-year tour-of-duty through the New Age, during which I learned what the psychics know, and what they don't know; in that context I participated for a while in group "dreamwork"—not in the Freudian sense of that term but as part of the "magical populism" of the New Age, which included lucid dreaming, certain practices which could be described as "Neo-Shamanism", and even various rather ill-conceived attempts to apply psychic power to social change. And I've also learned, in the course of these undirected but wide-ranging studies, things that I was only able to absorb by living through many, many situations where I absolutely had to figure out what people were up to, and what I myself was up to, or be destroyed. I learned psychology (or whatever I am calling by that name) according to the "sink or swim" method—and I did finally come to love it. I offer this book only as a set of pointers and suggestions to practicing therapists who already understand their craft as an element of the spiritual Path, and whose "hand's-on" expertise in dealing with clients on a professional basis will hopefully allow them to put to good use what is useful and discard what is erroneous in my rather abstract treatment of the subject—the actual practice of which has been, for me, the Sufi path itself.

What amazing beings we are, we humans! By our physical nature we are one with the whole animal world; by the Image of God within us, we are higher than the angels. When the Eternal Spirit and this earthly flesh meet in us, we become host to a synthesis of all the worlds, God-appointed stewards of His creation, bearers of the Trust. And when this exquisite synthesis goes wrong, or fails of completion, what a tangled web we weave! That's when we call out in our desperation, if we are not entirely lost, for a physician of the soul, someone who can help us not to keep on wounding ourselves with every gesture, betraying ourselves with every step. I only hope that this book may be of some use to those who aspire to become such physicians, and equally to those who are destined to seek their help.

Half of these essays are entirely new; the others are drawn, often slightly revised, from various of my other books: *The System of Antichrist: Truth and Falsehood in Postmodernism and the New Age*; *Hammering Hot Iron: A Spiritual Critique of Bly's Iron John*; *Reflections of Tasawwuf: Essays, Poems and Narrative on Sufi Themes*; *Knowings, in the Arts of Metaphysics, Cosmology and the Spiritual Path*; *Shadow of the Rose: The Esoterism of the Romantic Tradition*; and *Findings in Metaphysic, Path and Lore*. Between them they make up almost the entire *praxis* of such *theoria* as I have been able to articulate. If you are on a traditional spiritual Path, or believe you can get somewhere following a non-traditional one, or traveling as a freelance, I hope this book will prove useful in your quest.

CHARLES UPTON, SEPTEMBER 1, 2010

INTRODUCTION

If contemporary psychology has largely been reduced to behaviorism and psychopharmacology—if interest in the human quality and
the intrinsic *meaning* of psychological experience has begun to
wane—this is due in part to the fact that the psyche, taken in isolation and outside of its proper context, is ultimately unintelligible. In
other words, the attempt to understand the psyche in psychic or
psychological terms alone is doomed to failure.

The progressive recognition of the therapeutic ineffectiveness of
bare psychic introspection, or of the attempt to peer into the psyche
of another using the techniques of speech-based psychotherapy
alone, has led to a frustration with the self-enclosed and circular
nature of subjective experience and a quest for some level of scientific objectivity when it comes to understanding and solving psychological problems. Unfortunately, this objectivity has been sought
largely on the material level, in anatomy, physiology, biochemistry
and genetics. True and useful things can be certainly learned
through such studies, but just as the psyche in itself provides no
Archimedean point that would allow us to deal with psychological
problems through psychology alone, so to approach the psyche
via the body is inherently reductionist and thus of only limited
value; since material reality is more contracted and circumscribed
than psychic reality, true and stable objectivity in psychological
matters cannot be attained by material means alone. Only an understanding of the psyche in the context of a reality that is subtler and
more extensive than the psychic domain can provide such objectivity. This subtler reality, this higher objectivity, is the metaphysical
order.

We normally think of "objectivity" as applying almost exclusively
to material facts and "subjectivity" to the inner world of consciousness. But the inner world has its own objectivity. Not only is the
individual psyche part of the landscape of the psychic plane, which

objectively exists whether or not we are aware of it (as Huston Smith has remarked, "the brain breathes thoughts like the lungs breathe air"), so the psychic plane itself is embedded within the spiritual or intelligible or metaphysical plane, just as the material universe is embedded within the psychic plane.

In relation to the human form, the metaphysical plane represents a quasi-absolute objectivity, whereas the material plane is only relatively objective, given that it is ever-changing and intrinsically limited in terms of our experience by the diverse and mutable views of it held by subjectively-limited sentient beings. And although our views of the metaphysical plane are also subjectively conditioned, this does not affect the intrinsic objectivity of that plane, since it witnesses us from "above", just as we witness, also from above, the material plane. The difference between these two witnessings, however, is that the material plane, being insentient, cannot participate in our witnessing of it, cannot know that it is being seen, whereas we *can* know that we are being witnessed by the metaphysical plane. Our participation in the metaphysical or Spiritual plane is based only secondarily upon our perception of it; our primary mode of participation is by virtue of its perception of us. As the *hadith* of Muhammad expresses it, "Pray to God as if you saw Him, because even if you don't see Him, He sees you". Neither our view of ourselves nor other people's view of us make up our true reality; it is God's view of us, a view characterized by absolute objectivity, that constitutes us and creates us: whether or not we ever fully become aware of it, who He knows us to be is who we really are.

WHAT IS PRINCIPIAL PSYCHOLOGY?

Principial Psychology, elements of which are to be found in the various spiritual ways embraced by the great world religions and wisdom traditions, is based on a "pneumatic anthropology" that, in its simplest form, sees the human being as composed not of body alone, or of body plus soul/psyche, but as essentially tripartite: body (*soma*), soul (*psyche*) and Spirit (*Pneuma* or *Nous*). And although pneumatic psychology definitely includes methods useful in healing mental illness, its goal is essentially positive. Its proper use is not simply to overcome psychic pathology but to bring the individual into a state of "ideal normalcy"; consequently its primary role will not be to help the psyche "adjust" to social norms, or to reach integration and stability in its own terms without regard to any higher reality (which is considered to be intrinsically impossible and thus foolish and wasteful to attempt), but to conform the psychic substance to the archetypal Principles of the spiritual world, specifically to the eternal archetype of the human form. If such conformation is successful it will also effect a balanced adjustment to society—if, that is, the society in question is essentially traditional, and thus reflective in itself of the spiritual Principles. If such a society is not based on these Principles, however, if it is essentially profane, then the conformation of psyche to Spirit will place the individual at odds with society rather than adjusting him to it. Human spiritual integration does not conform us to the system of collective passion, egotism and delusion upon which profane society is based, but frees us from it definitively [see *Revelations*, chap. 18].

Principial Psychology may be defined as is any body of psychological theory and practice that exists as a integral element of a traditional spiritual Path, where the salvation of the soul, the realization of God or the attainment of Liberation stand in place of the Jungian goal of "individuation" and the Freudian one of social adjustment—a Path in the context of which even Maslow's "peak experiences" represent only one element among many, and not necessarily the most important one. The soul is not to be conformed to society nor "conformed to itself", nor is it to define itself as in quest for some ultimate *personal* experience; it is to be conformed to God, according to the norms, the doctrines, the methods and the graces given by God, and in line with His command. This, according to Principial Psychology, is the ultimate value and point-of-orientation according by which all psychological states and conditions are to be judged, the ultimate goal that all acts of healing, balancing, insight, challenge, therapeutic stress, stabilization, and inner synthesis, either applied to the soul from without or spontaneously experienced by it, exist only to serve. As such, Principial Psychology cannot function effectively as a generic psychotherapeutic method outside the bounds of a *particular* traditional Path. The Principial

Psychology expressed in the Eastern Orthodox Christian *Philokalia*, in Sufi literature and practice, in terms of the Ashtanga-(eight-fold) Yoga of Patanjali or the Noble Eight-fold Path of the Buddha will necessarily exhibit great differences, since their several points of departure, as well as their methodologies, are very different. Yet they do have certain elements in common—a fact which justifies, in my opinion, the definition and elucidation of Principial Psychology as such, if only to emphasize the fact that traditional psychology, from that of the first Shamans to that of the Scholastic philosophers of the Middle Ages, was never considered as anything other than the work of spiritually perfecting the human form—until, that is, the day when we began to collectively forget what it means to be human: the dawning of the modern age.

Principial psychology is essentially a form of *faculty psychology* like that of the medieval Scholastics, which was based largely on the *De Anima* of Aristotle and is well represented by the *De Anima* of St. Thomas Aquinas, and the *De Anima* of Francisco Suarez. Unlike Jerry Fodor's faculty psychology, as presented in his book *Modularity of Mind*, it is not a reductionist view of the brain/mind as divided into a number of partially closed neurological systems fulfilling different functions (however valid this view may be in its own terms), but an account of the major faculties the *soul*, not merely the brain, of their interaction, their correct hierarchicalization, and the various disorders, inversions and "psychic knots" to which they are subject. These primary faculties of the psyche, unlike this or that neurological sub-system, can be directly correlated with specific cosmological/metaphysical principles, and legitimately seen as hierarchically descended from them. According to traditional pneumatic anthropology, the world of the soul or psyche exists as the intermediary term between our human incarnate selves in this world and the metaphysical Principles upon which the cosmos, both psychic and material, is woven. It is this soul, and the plane of reality it inhabits, which both separates the *intelligible* or *spiritual* realm of the Principles from the material realm of the senses—thus allowing for the existence of the world we experience—and facilitates a two-way communication between them. The Spirit is inviolable and the body subject to inevitable death. Only the soul can be

lost or saved, depending in part upon whether it conforms itself to
the body, and consequently decays as the body decays, or to the
Spirit, thus participating as far as its capacity may allow in the
Spirit's inviolability and eternity.

In order to conform our psyche to its spiritual archetype, we need
to be able to distinguish between the psychic and spiritual worlds,
not simply theoretically but in the most concrete and practical of
terms. And the most effective way of making this distinction—
perhaps the only way—is to follow the norms of one of the great
wisdom traditions, a tradition that is rooted in the Principial world
and can thus objectively represent the presence of that world in
our lives. Initially we need to conform ourselves to these norms
"whether we like it or not"; in doing so, we will come to see quite
clearly the difference between our spiritual center, which wills to
conform itself to the Principles, based either on a direct intellective
intuition of them, or on a submission to the authority of Revelation
by means of the "virtual intellection" known as *faith*, and the part of
us that "likes" this or that, that sometimes likes to obey, sometimes
to disobey, and sometimes simply wants to remain mired in ambi-
guities and contradictions so it doesn't have to choose. The psychic
world is the realm of preferences; the spiritual world, of certainties.

The conscious conformation of our psyches to the norms of the
Spirit, in the knowledge that such conformation will entail what the
Prophet Muhammad called "the war against the soul", is the essence
of the Spiritual Path. On its higher levels, this Path is based on the
practice of contemplation, which might be defined (at least in terms
of one of its many facets) as the act of witnessing the psyche, and its
many changes, in the objective light of the Spirit.

Contemplation cannot effectively be practiced, however, in the
absence of *piety* and *morality*—otherwise it will degenerate into a
quest for various psychic states considered to be "spiritual", and so
lose its objective nature. Contemporary psychology, and society,
look upon piety and morality as the most subjective and contingent
of realities, as elements of mere "social belief-systems" that have little to do with the way the psyche *really* operates, and so work only
to muddy the waters. But the fact is that piety and morality, if they
are true virtues and not the counterfeit, ego-based forms of these

virtues proposed by profane and degenerate religion and society, are factors of a true, though limited, spiritual objectivity. Piety recognizes the existence of a real spiritual world and its precedence over nature, society and the human psyche; morality recognizes that objective spiritual Principles can appear within, and affect, the psychic and material worlds in the most concrete of terms, and that the practical consequences of the rejection of these Principles are uniformly negative.

Much of contemporary psychology has no practical access to, and almost no theory of, such principial objectivity. In a great deal of "conventional" modern psychotherapy (psychoanalysis in particular), the *therapist* is made to stand in for the lost objective factor—a role that he or she can rarely fulfill in any stable and ongoing way. The therapist represents the "reality principle" as opposed to the disordered subjectivity of the client; the client reveals his secrets, while the therapist simply listens and witnesses. The impassivity of the therapist, apart from whatever insights he or she might impart, is what allows the client to exhaust his psychic "projections" upon the therapist—a process known as "transference"—to become aware of them, to withdraw them, and thereby to attain a certain level of objective self-understanding; at least that's the theory. This theory breaks down, however, when we consider the phenomenon of "counter-transference"—the fact that the therapist himself is often affected by the projections of the client and starts to project back, producing a situation of tangled ambiguity and "boundary problems" in the face of which any true objectivity flies out the window. The person in need of psychotherapy may, if he or she is extremely lucky, encounter a therapist who has personally realized a level of real spiritual objectivity, and who can therefore incarnate the "reality principle", at least partially, in such a way that the client may be able to reach a degree of objective self-understanding with the therapist's help. But if the client is unlucky enough to encounter a therapist whose degree of realized objectivity is actually less than his—or someone educated in a postmodern academia mired in theories that "officially" deny the existence of objective reality—then he is in danger of losing whatever spiritual objectivity he might already possess. And it is the progressive recognition of this depressing fact (leaving aside the limits placed upon psychotherapy by the health insurance companies) that is at least partially responsible for the progressive abandonment of *psychology* per se, and its replacement by behaviorism and psychopharmacology, therapies which do not even recognize the existence of the psyche as an independent dimension of reality, but which—in line with the materialistic assumptions of our profane technocratic society—see consciousness as a mere epiphenomenon of material processes, if they do not deny the existence of human consciousness altogether. It is in hopes of proposing a viable alternative to this darkened and contracted view of the art of psychology, an alternative that is more in line with what has come to be known as Transpersonal Psychology, as well as the Integral Psychology of Ken Wilber, that I have attempted to define what I call Principial Psychology.

1

THE TRIPARTITE HUMAN PSYCHE IN FALL AND RESTORATION

The tripartite nature of the human microcosm—Spirit, soul and body—which is directly correlated with the tripartite nature of the created macrocosm—the Celestial/Intelligible/Spiritual plane, the psychic/imaginal plane, and the physical/sensual plane—is reflected on a lower level within the soul or psyche itself. In line with this truth, we can say that the human soul is made up of three primary faculties: the rational mind, the affections, and the will. The rational mind is the psychic reflection of the Intellect; the will is symbolically related to the body, given that it manifests most visibly and concretely as voluntary motion; and the affections are, as it were, the symbol of the psyche as a whole appearing *within* the psyche. The soul is also host to That which transcends it, the Spiritual Intellect, the *Nous*. In the original, unfallen soul as God created it, the rational mind turns to the Intellect for its first principles; the will obeys the directives that the rational mind derives from those principles; and the affections empower the will to obey the rational mind both constantly and willingly.

In the fallen soul, however—the soul as conditioned by and identified with the *ego*—the Spiritual Intellect is veiled; consequently this hierarchy is inverted. The affections are now attracted to inappropriate objects (a state symbolized in Genesis by Eve's eating of the forbidden fruit) without regard for what the rational mind—in its unfallen state—directs; the will follows these wayward affections by intending and enacting what they have suggested (symbolized Eve's offering of the forbidden fruit Adam, who also ate); and the rational mind (somewhat like the Serpent in the garden) is pressed into the service of the will, both to suggest to it various ways and methods by which it might transgress, and also to justify and *rationalize* those transgressions. Thus the fallen soul is hierarchicalized (in descending order) as Affections/Will/Rationality; the affective/sensual suggestion to sin appears as an impulse that is immediately acted upon, often in almost complete unconsciousness. Temptation to sin on the other hand, not when we impulsively give in to it but when we at least initially resist it (since if we do not resist an impulse we will not recognize it as a temptation), is hierarchicalized Affections/Rationality/Will: the suggestion first appears to the affections, is next "entertained" by the rational mind which will produce arguments for and/or against it, and is finally—unless the temptation is successfully resisted—enacted by the will, either mentally or physically [see *extraverted active imagination* below]. Karmic culpability only arises when the action enters the third stage; only the will can sin.

But what exactly is this "ego" that defines the "fallen" soul? The ego, in the sense in which I am using the word, is not the conscious personality as it was for Freud and Jung, but rather our attachment to obsessive self-definition, which is inseparable from our act of defining who other people are and what the world is. When the presence and providence of God are veiled for us, self-definition becomes obsessive and fixed; we begin to believe—unconsciously, but nonetheless effectively—that we are self-created; consequently it becomes impossible for us to see that God is continuously re-creating us and the world we live in, and thus to appreciate the uniqueness of each moment. We lose the ability to let the world and other people reveal themselves to us, nor are we really very interested in learning anything new or surprising about ourselves. Life stagnates, and we turn to the various passions, like lust and avarice and anger, in a self-defeating attempt to overcome this stagnation. Furthermore, the knowledge and experience that are necessarily excluded by our fixed definitions of self and world begin to form a large "unconscious mind"—the *unconscious* being simply all the things about ourselves and the world, and the higher worlds, that we don't want to be conscious of, individually or collectively, because we don't want to be conscious of God. Plato's prescription for dealing with this "unconscious" was *anamnesis*—"remembering" (or, more literally, "not-not-remembering"). All knowledge is virtually present to us; the need is to actualize it, to return to all we once knew before "heedlessness", what the Muslims call *ghaflah*, expelled us from Paradise.

Furthermore, the knowledge and experience excluded by the ego is, paradoxically, inseparable from the ego, a part of the ego; it lies under the sign of obsessive self-definition. The ego is like an iceberg, with a relatively small conscious apex and a large unconscious base. And since it is impossible to take responsibility for things we are unconscious of, and consciously place them in the hands of God, our unconscious becomes chaotic and unruly; it appears as the realm of the passions. Sufi psychology names this unconscious ego (comparable in some ways, according to Sufi teacher Javad Nur-bakhsh, to the Freudian *id*) the *nafs al-ammara*, the "soul commanding to evil".[†] If the rational mind is cut off from the Intellect, if the affections rule the will and the will dominates the rational mind instead of serving it, this is entirely due to the fact that our obsessive self-definition has relegated most of our psyche, and most of our potential experience of both this material world and the higher subtle worlds, to the unconscious realm. Every psychopathology of whatever description (excluding of course those conditions obviously based on physical causes) ultimately springs from the fact that the ego, not the Spirit of God, has taken possession of the human center of the psyche, the spiritual Heart. Nor does the fact that this or that mental illness is reflected in physiology and brain chemistry prove that physiology and brain chemistry are the necessarily the causes of it. When we are frightened by an inner or an outer event—

---

† The ego, to define it more completely, is the principle of passion and delusion that leads to *sin* on the moral plane and *error* on the noetic one. It is made up of the *nafs al-ammara*, largely but not entirely identifiable with the Freudian *id*; of certain aspects of the Freudian *ego* considered as obsessive self-definition; and of those aspects of the Freudian *superego* that Wilhelm Reich termed "compulsive morality", and which in Sufi terms appears both as the *nafs al-lawwama* or "accusing *nafs*", the obsessively troubled conscience, and as the "bewitching *nafs*" which tempts the soul to spiritual or intellectual pride.

the sight of an automobile accident, for example—our heart-rate increases. Does this mean that our increased heart-rate really caused the automobile accident?

So the inversion of the hierarchy of psychic faculties and our bondage to the ego are two ways of talking about the same condition. We speak of the "fallen" soul—but where exactly did it fall from? Was there ever a "time" when the faculties of the soul were not inverted, at least partially, when there was no "unconscious"? We speak, in more of less mythic terms, of the Golden Age or the Garden of Eden; and we idealize (or at least we used to) the paradise of childhood and/or the "oceanic experience" of life in the womb. But the fact is that, according to our sense of linear time, no lost paradise is in evidence. Obsessive self-definition was less a problem for us in childhood, but our ability to make rational decisions, control our impulses and consciously submit our lives to God was also less developed (if, in fact, it is any better developed even now!). So we are forced to conclude that if there indeed was a "fall", it was a fall from Eternity into time, not necessarily a fall from an earlier and better time. In God we were all perfectly as He knew us and created us to be; and given that Eternity is an aspect of God, we are all, in one sense, still there. But when time supervened—when, due to the exclusionary nature of obsessive self-definition, experience ceased to be global and, having become partial, necessarily also became sequential (just as a darkened room after sundown can no longer be seen all at once, but only as a sequence of partial views according to where we shine our flashlight)—the soul fell; the proper hierarchy of the psychic faculties was inverted. "When" or even "how" this happened may ultimately fall under those questions which the Buddha classed as "tending not to edification": the true question is, not how we got into this prison, but how we can get out again. The answer to this question, this plea, is the spiritual Path, the quintessential expression of God's "particular mercy", *al-Rahim*. In the course of walking this Path all necessary questions will be answered, while all unnecessary and barren questions will be happily forgotten.

In the earlier stages of the spiritual Path—those known as "the lesser mysteries"—the goal is to return the soul to its original nature as God created it, thus re-establishing its proper hierarchy, where the rational mind obeys the Intellect, the will obeys the rational mind, and the affections obey the will. The soul is "edified", built up as a solid *edifice* with a wide foundation of strong character supporting a "pinnacle" of exalted consciousness. Such edification represents the re-ordering of the soul in its *active* mode, the return of its ability to act in line with spiritual principles. The human soul is also capable, however, of operating in *receptive* mode—as in the case of memory, for example, as well as in the *active* or *objective imagination*, which is poles apart from subjective fantasy. When the affections are receptive they regain the ability to reflect the Intellect directly, without the mediation of either the rational mind or the individual will—an ability that defines the whole *imaginal* aspect of spiritual contemplation, as well as the contemplation of spiritual beauty in nature, art, and the human body. When the will is pacified through obedience to the rational mind, and the rational mind correctly re-oriented in obedience to the Spiritual Intellect, the turbulence of the affections subsides, until the emotional substance becomes like a still lake on a windless day, capable of reflecting the Sun not as a mass of separate and ephemeral points of light, but as a single unified form.

The rational mind, the will and the affections are the three primary faculties of the human psyche. The psyche, however, is also host to a number of composite faculties. Chief among these are *memory* and *imagination*, both of which take three distinct forms: passive, active and transcendental, which are related to the three *gunas* or modes of *Prakriti* (universal Substance) in Hinduism: *tamas*, *rajas* and *sattwa*. Active imagination may be further divided into introverted and extraverted modes.

In *passive memory*, the action is hierarchicalized Affections/Will/Rationality, directly in line with the fallen condition of the soul. The affections suggest an impression, the will immediately follows it, and then thought elaborates it. Passive memory—nostalgic reverie—is ultimately based upon the attraction of the affections to the subtle form of material nature, upon the longing to return to our "mother", our maternal origins in the natural world, apart from the knowledge of the rational mind and the resolution of the will. (People addicted to passive memory will see all life in terms of it, even defining human experience itself as the process of "making memories".) Such memory becomes an almost necessary "recreational activity" to the soul eaten up by the rational willfulness of modern life, based upon the enslavement of the rational mind to the will, according to which the soul is always trying to put the affections to work to fuel this or that obsession. The crepuscular and putrescent poetry of Georg Trakl is the quintessential expression of this state. In one way it can be looked at as the subtle revenge of the repressed affections upon the willfulness that has repressed them. Our emotional nature, tired of being exploited and drained by our ambitions and obsessions, undermines them by periodically "unplugging" our rationality and will—but as René Guénon pointed out, "bourgeois sentimentality" is nothing but the opposite face of bourgeois rationalistic voluntarism. And to the degree that passive memory is simply a falling back upon "This World" as a protective matrix (however much we may also unconsciously fear this World), it progressively destroys the virtue of *vigilance* that makes contemplation of eternal realities possible. This unconscious quest for security, or for unconsciousness *as* security, along with the vices of curiosity and ruthless ambition, is what defines the soul's conquest by the power of "This World", the system of collective egotism and illusion. It is better to relate to the natural world through labor, or even through danger, than it is to take it as a kind of vacation resort; if we understand the natural world as rigorous as well as beautiful, then it will not become for us "the darkness of This World" (a darkness enforced by the Ego/World complex because it doesn't want us to see or believe in anything beyond its horizon or outside its control), but rather the ensemble of the Names and Signs of Allah—a support for contemplation, not a substitute for it.

When William Blake said "Memory is Eternal Death", he was referring to passive memory. Existence ruled by time and becoming is always passing away into Hades, into the kingdom of ghosts; indulgence in such ghostliness makes us moribund, nearly transforming our souls into ghosts themselves even before physical death, and all but guaranteeing that we will leave much of our human reality behind, in ghostly form, after it. Nor is passive memory really free of willful rationality just because it has the power to temporarily detach us from it; it remains bound to voluntaristic rationality just as the shadow is bound to the solid object. As such it remains under the inverted hierarchy of Affections/Will/Rationality that characterizes the fallen soul *per se*.

The state of passive memory is well analyzed by William Blake in his poem *Tiriel*.

Depending upon whether our memories are pleasant or unpleasant, passive memory will call up feelings of nostalgic longing on the one hand, or of regret and/or revulsion on the other. And passive memory, whether pleasant or unpleasant, is the emotional expression of that state of soul characterized by Kierkegaard, in *Sickness unto Death*, as "despair of necessity"—not that one despairs that necessity is absent, but rather that necessity, seen not in eternal terms as Necessary Being but in temporal ones as irrevocable fate, is the basis of one's despair. Both pleasant and unpleasant recollections, when under the power of passive memory, generate despair; the classic poetic expression of the conscious recognition of such despair (which, while acutely painful, may also represent a real chance to wake up, to begin the struggle for our freedom) is Francis Thompson's poem *The City of Dreadful Night*.

Active memory is something higher than passive memory. It is the willful use of the rational mind to access this or that item of factual information (*true* information, not fantasy) by employing the affections, putting to use their power of *sympathy*. Active memory is hierarchicalized Will/Affections/Rationality: the intent to remember something employs the affections as its "search engine", after which the rational mind fixes the results as conscious knowledge. Active memory thus represents a partial redress of the fallen condition of the soul, which is hierarchicalized Affections/Will/Rationality; it is a step toward edification.

In searching the past, active memory is looking not for potentials but for *facts*, for things already actualized; consequently it is operating, imperfectly but validly, in the realm of Necessary Being. Insofar as facts inhabit the past, they are alienated from the metaphysical order, which subsists in the eternal present; but insofar as they are actualities, not mere potentials or possibilities, they partake of that order—given that, according to the Scholastic philosophers, God is both Necessary Being and Pure Act. Insofar as history is *over*, it is *finished*; insofar as it is *finished*, it is *perfect*. It is no longer subject to becoming. Thus an understanding of past events is a real approach to the intuition of eternity, which is the metaphysical sense. And this is even more true of the study of physical laws and mathematical axioms, which are the same in all places and times; this is why Plato considered the study of mathematics as the best preparatory course for an understanding of metaphysics.

Transcendental memory draws upon realities situated beyond the hierarchy of the psychic faculties; it may be seen as the higher octave of the active memory. In terms of the spiritual Path, the transcendental memory is a higher function than the search for objective facts—which is, nonetheless, good preparatory training for it, since the essence of the Path is to overcome egoic subjectivity and reach Objective Truth. In the traditional terminology applicable to the spiritual Path, transcendental memory is *recollection*, whose highest form is *the remembrance of God* (*dhikr; japam; mnimi Theou*). To remember God is to recognize Him as the One Absolute and All-encompassing Fact, of which all other facts are mere reflections— which is why the true facts of any situation, past or present, are one mode of the actual presence of God in that situation. The remembrance of God is "memory" in the sense that it recalls, or calls-back, a forgotten Reality—forgotten, however, not in the past, but in (or beneath) the present. A memory we are searching for will have as its content some past event, but the actual form of it already lies below the surface of consciousness, in this very moment.

The remembrance of God invokes pre-Eternity, which is often experienced as nostalgia for a lost Paradise—not the natural paradise of passive memory, however, but the celestial Paradise of the Eternal Human Form. To remember that we were once united with God in pre-Eternity is to begin to remember that pre-Eternity is not fundamentally past, but present. God is here; Eternity is now. (The Kabbalists say, "what is here is elsewhere; what is not here is nowhere". This can be paraphrased, in temporal rather than spacial terms, as: "What is real now always was and always will be real; what is not real now never will be, and never was". In light of this, William Blake's "alchemical" demand, "what can be destroyed must be destroyed!", makes perfect sense.)

To the degree that we recognize God as present in this moment, we begin the process of "withdrawing projections". *Projection* is the tendency to falsely see what is really in oneself as being in some thing, person or situation in the outer world, or as the world as a whole. But since God is infinite and absolute, and since "the Kingdom of Heaven is within you", the realization of His presence cuts all ties with memory and anticipation; what has been, is now, and so the past is obliterated—*as past*, that is—not by forgetting it but by *remembering* it, given that all things are present in God. Furthermore, what *will* be is here already as well, and so the future too is obliterated: all that could ever be desired (by the Heart) or feared (by the ego) is here in the One Presence.

The remembrance of God thus effects the recollection of the human form. The human being immersed in becoming, bound to the wheel of birth and death, is *dismembered*—not spatially but temporally; the dismemberment of Osiris and his reconstitution by Isis is a symbol of this condition, and the Power which overcomes it. He leaves the past strewn with his experience, the future littered with his intent. But when the Presence of God is remembered in the present moment, and this remembrance stabilized, then the scattered limbs of the remembrancer magically reassemble themselves, like the dry bones in Ezekiel's vision; in the words of Rumi (addressed to God) from one of his Quatrains, "When You return, *everything* returns." Detachment from past and future, when this is where the bulk of our identity has been placed, is experienced as annihilation, the Sufi *fana*. And the return of our psychic self-projections out of past and future, when complete, is experienced as the Sufi *baqa*, subsistence in God—subsistence as the integral human form residing in the eternal present, that reality the Sufis refer to as *al-insan al-kamil*, the Perfect Man. The return of those projections is legitimately symbolized by the Resurrection of the Dead—at which point, in Blake's words, "the Daughters of Memory [the Muses] become the Daughters of Inspiration". This is the realm of Tantra, the dimension in which our passions and obscurations (our fears and desires, our revulsions and our longings, our *projections*), rather than being suppressed or cut off, undergo a *metanoia*, until they are revealed as the very substance of God's universal manifestation, which is equally the *Shakti* or Power of Attention by which we contemplate Him.

When active memory culminates in the remembrance of God and passive memory is consequently overcome, the nostalgic longing and/or revulsion of passive memory are transformed into *gratitude*—gratitude for the Mercy of God. And this transformation takes place, precisely, through the medium of *disgust*. Disgust is one of the most unpleasant feelings we can experience, but also among the most hopeful signs of *catharsis*, of spiritual purification.

Passive imagination, like passive memory, is hierarchicalized Affections/Will/Rationality; its other name is "fantasy". (Here we can see how the *passions* of the fallen soul are directly related to *passivity*, and hence how deliberate, principled action, even though it may have certain negative consequences, is still a real step toward redemption.) Our affections are attracted by this or that set of impressions within the subtle realm; our will is appropriated by them and engages with them; our thinking mind (largely mediated by unconscious speech) elaborates them, forms them into articulate images; this is what it is to *fantasize*. Passive imagination is like passive memory except that it deals with things which have never existed in the material world, and may never come into this world— with possibilities, that is, not necessities.

Passive imagination has to do not with facts but with potentials. We may never intend to bring these potentials into the real world, opting to indulge in them as if they were a world in themselves, but nonetheless they are always pressing for incarnation, which is why fantasies of lust or anger often lead to lustful or violent actions. And if we indulge in potentials which we never intend to realize, our lives become unreal; thus passive imagination may be accurately compared to sexuality when divorced from either reproduction or contemplation, both of which represent the actualization of the potentials inherent within it. (The resistance of passive imagination to the concrete realization of potentials is analyzed by William Blake in *The Book of Thel*.)

Passive imagination, since it has to do with Possible Being rather than Necessary Being, exists on a lower ontological level than passive memory. It shuns actuality, both practical and metaphysical, and thus tends to replace it. It is a parasite on reality. It can give one a sense that so much is possible, that one's life and one's soul are so rich in potential that one can take one's own sweet time in realizing this potential, since one is virtually immortal. The drawbacks of this illusion are analyzed in the Japanese Nō play *Kantan* and the Simon and Garfunkel song "Hazy Shade of Winter".

Passive imagination, of course, is also subject to nightmare, to the apprehension of negative potentials; the rich, inviting contemplation of what we would like to see happen, or simply to see, is inseparable from the fearful contemplation of what we are afraid might happen, or what we are terrified of ever witnessing, even on the imaginal level. The irresponsibility that positive passive imagination feeds is always eventually compensated for by the creeping insecurity that invites negative passive imagination; if we are not fulfilling our duties, we may legitimately fear that life will deal us a serious blow. Passive imagination (especially in its positive form) is analyzed by Kierkegaard in *Sickness unto Death* as "despair of possibility"—not the despair that nothing is possible (which would be his "despair of necessity"), but the despair that hides itself in the fantasy of possibility itself. Yet despair of necessity often underlies despair of possibility. The false hope which likes to say "everything is possible!", while not taking even the first step toward realizing the possibility at hand, is usually nothing but a denial of an underlying feeling that "nothing is possible", that if one were to take the concrete steps necessary to realize a given potential, one would inevitably find the door of reality slammed in one's face.

Active imagination is a step above the "infra-psychic" fantasy world of passive imagination. It is hierarchicalized (like consciously resisted temptation, its negative partner) as Affections/Rationality/Will; consequently it too is a partial step toward edification. It takes two forms. In *introverted* active imagination, we consciously interact with the symbolic images our psyche presents us with, interrogating them, challenging them, in order to reach greater psychological (and even sometimes spiritual) insight. The affective substance of the soul receives the imprint of an inner symbolic image; the rational faculty interrogates this image and thereby transforms its evocative aura of hidden significance into conscious knowledge; the will then intends to existentially realize the psychospiritual consequences of the knowledge thus gained. This is one of the major tools in the psychoanalytic method of Carl Jung and his school. In its *extraverted* form, active imagination represents the process of bringing potentials out of the imaginal realm and into concrete physical manifestation in this world. The affections "attract" and "entertain" the potential in question, the rational mind turns this potential into an effective plan; and the will carries it out.

Transcendental Imagination, like transcendental memory, draws upon realities that exist beyond the psychic hierarchy. It is the Eternal Imagination of William Blake, in line with which he characterized the Holy Spirit as "an intellectual fountain". Ibn al-'Arabi speaks of two discrete levels of the world of imagination, *the alam al-mithal.* The lower arises from the stored impressions of sense experience; the higher (*al-Malakut*) receives direct impressions from the Intelligible Plane of the eternal Archetypes or Platonic Ideas (*al-Jabarut*), and clothes them in imaginal form. That the lower form of imagination draws upon the impressions of past sense experience shows the hidden identity or affinity between passive memory and passive imagination. That the higher form of imagination emanates directly from the Intelligible Plane, and thus represents the closest, the most fully *incarnate* relationship (in the subtle sense) between the human psyche and the world of metaphysical principles, mediated not by abstract rational discourse but by the concrete imaginal reverberation of direct Intellection, establishes the identity between Ibn al-'Arabi's higher imaginal plane and Blake's Divine Imagination or Poetic Inspiration. These two levels of imagination, however, are not entirely discrete, given that an inspiration emanating from the higher level must clothe itself with the substance of the lower one; we could not imagine Wisdom as a beautiful woman if we had never seen beautiful women. It is true that the archetype of feminine beauty exists on a higher plane than the material, and that all feminine beauty in this world is derived from it. Yet if this archetype were to attempt to manifest directly in this world in the absence of any memories of feminine beauty, or the present contemplation of this beauty in human form, it would be unrecognizable and thus unintelligible. Dante's Beatrice was a ray of

Divine Beauty whose proper home was Paradise—yet if he had never seen her, however briefly, in this world, he could never have recognized her in her Celestial environment. (Herein, incidentally, may lie the truth behind Thomas Aquinas' problematic assertion, which seems to deny the reality of direct Intellection, that knowledge can reach the soul only through the senses.) Nonetheless, while the *ta'wil* (exegesis in the sense of "return-to-source") of the higher imagination leads to the plane of the eternal metaphysical principles, the *ta'wil* of the lower, unless it carries some of the higher along with it, leads only to the darkness of the material world, cut off from the more elevated levels of the Ontological Hierarchy and thus virtually non-existent. (For the best introduction to Ibn al-'Arabi's doctrine of the imagination, see *Imaginal Worlds* by William Chittick. We should also note that Ibn al-'Arabi posits a third level of imagination, the universal, which is simply to say that all the worlds, celestial, psychic and material, spring from and constitute the Universal Imagination of God.)

Transcendental imagination is supremely active; it is not our action, however, but that of God, Who impresses directly upon the affective substance of our soul in its *quintessential* state the truths He wishes us, not to merely fantasize about or think about, but to *realize*. When the affective layer of the psyche is polarized and differentiated into various specific emotions, it cannot receive the impressions of the transcendental imagination. When, however, it returns to its undifferentiated state through the virtue of *apatheia* or spiritual impassivity, which may be represented as the resolution of the Four Elements or four primal emotional qualities [see Chapter II] into their common source in the Aether, which is their Quintessence ("emotions" being specific determinations of the affective substance that are on their way to becoming "impulses", "motives" or "motivations" in their interaction with the will), it becomes receptive to impressions emanating not from the surrounding psychic environment but directly from the Spiritual or Intelligible Plane. Passive imagination is *passive*, not receptive; it is not properly intentional. Active imagination is indeed active and intentional, but only on the individual plane, although the symbols it individually interacts with may also have their transcendental aspect. Transcendental imagination is activity per se, the union of a given truth eternally actualized in the Mind of God with the active willingness of the human subject to both receive and *conceive* (not simply remain passive to) that truth. When the Virgin Mary said, in Luke 1:38, "Be it done unto me according to Thy Word", she was opening not only her psyche but her body itself to the transcendental imagination of God.

As we have seen, passive imagination is ontologically lower than passive memory because it deals with unrealized potentials, not actualities. Likewise active imagination is ontologically lower than active memory, but it is spiritually higher, in the sense that contemplation of Necessity via memory, though higher than the entertainment of Possibility via imagination, is not always fertile for us in spiritual terms since it is an attribute of God, not of the human psyche, and consequently may sometimes have a paralyzing effect on our spiritual lives. A contemplation of the eternal Truth as Necessary Being alone, complete in an eternal Past ruled by the Ancient of Days, will—unless our own future becomes spiritually pregnant with it, unless Possibility is activated by it—make spiritual progress *impossible*. In one sense, Necessary Being is God Himself, Who alone cannot not be. In relation to the human ego, however, Necessary Being is transformed into the despair of necessity, the bonds of fatality and *karma*. Likewise, though Possible Being is not what *must* be but only what *might* be—merely contingent, not absolute—in relation to the human ego it may, God willing, be transformed into the virtue of *hope*. We may certainly hope that one of the things that *might* be is our own realization of God. To the degree that we are immersed in the possibility of becoming, not the Necessity of Eternal Truth, only the manifestation of that Necessity as a *concrete possibility* in our own lives can offer any hope of liberating us. So we might say, paraphrasing the Eastern Fathers, that "Necessary Being becomes possible being so that possibility might become Necessity." What only "might be" is perpetually uncertain and unreliable—and yet the other meaning of the word "might" is precisely *power*. The *mighty* one is he who has the power to actualize possibilities, to transform possible being into Necessary Being; hence "With God, all things are possible."

Active memory and transcendental memory are respectively an approach to, and an arrival at, Eternity through the past; active imagination and transcendental imagination are an approach to and an arrival at Eternity through the future—or rather, they are the future in the act of approaching us, and becoming present to us *as* Eternity, beyond fear and desire. When the pre-eternity of Memory and the post-eternity of Imagination are united in the eternal present, this is Eternity per se, in which the remembrance of God as Eternal Actuality and the self-revelation of God as the Mercy of Possibility are one and the same.

When transcendental Memory and transcendental Imagination unite, the Divine Intellect is unveiled; when the Divine Intellect is unveiled, the fallen soul is edified, its inverted hierarchy of faculties set right—or rather *up*right. The faculties are correctly hierarchical-ized along the *axis mundi* and consequently oriented to what the Sufis call the *Qutb*, the Pole of the Spiritual Intellect, both cosmolog-ical and personal—the reality that T.S. Eliot called "the still point of the turning world", and which appears in the person of the spiritual Master. We become edified, upright, righteous human beings—*tzaddikim*. (The Hebrew letter *tsade* symbolizes, among other things, "the north"—the quarter of the Pole.) Rationality serves Intellection directly; will serves Intellection indirectly by obeying the dictates of reason; the affections empower the will to so serve, thus purifying the rational mind as well and opening it more fully to Intellection; they also gain the power to directly reflect spiritual Intellection on the plane of the psyche, just as a mirror reflects light. This is the completion of the "lesser mysteries" which, in the context of the spiritual Path, is the proper object of Principial Psychology. Beyond this, beyond psychology, beyond the psyche itself, lie the "greater myster-ies" which constitute the final union of the soul with God.

TOWARD THE GREATER MYSTERIES

As we pointed out above, when the will is pacified in submission to God, the turbulence of the affections is stilled, until the emotional substance becomes like the surface of a calm lake on a windless day, capable of directly reflecting a true image of the Sun of the spiritual Intellect, without the mediation of the rational mind; this is the station the soul enters when contemplating the Divine Beauty, where Beauty and Truth are one. When the will submits to God via obedience to the dictates of the rational mind, itself in obedience to the *Nous*, this stillness or *hesychia* remains imperfect. But when the will submits to God directly through the open Eye of the Heart—directly through the *Nous*, the Uncreated Intellect—the stillness of the affections becomes mirror-like and perfect.

One of the major controversies in Scholastic Philosophy took place between those who believed that the intellect is the highest faculty of the soul, and those who assigned this position to the will. The first party—Albert the Great, St. Thomas Aquinas, Godfrey of Fontaines and their disciples, who primarily followed Aristotle—believed that spiritual knowledge is the highest good; the second party—St. Bonaventure, Duns Scotus, William of Ockham and their school, who mostly followed St. Augustine—believed that love and moral choice are highest.

But (as should be obvious), a spiritual knowledge that is not expressed in terms of sound moral choices and a loving disposition is far from complete, while a will that operates in the absence of spiritual knowledge will not know what to choose, just as a love cut off from such knowledge will not know what to love. The limitation of the first condition is expressed in the saying "paper cakes do not satisfy hunger", that of the second by the proverb "the road to Hell is paved with good intentions". We cannot know what is right and wrong in moral terms unless we know what is true and false in metaphysical terms; but if our metaphysical knowledge does not win the submission of our will and the loyalty of our affections, it remains barren and impotent.

Given the importance of Aquinas in Roman Catholic theology one would have thought that the notion of the primacy of the intellect would have totally permeated the doctrines of the Church. Yet in many ways the primacy of the will remains a strong principle in traditional Catholicism, especially in moral theology and the theology of the sacraments. Temptation may affect one's mind and emotions, but sin is not present until the will gives its assent to this influence. Someone who believes erroneous doctrines is said to be in *material* heresy, which is only virtual, but if he or she continues to assert these errors in the face of scripture and tradition and the necessary conclusions of reason, then the heresy is said to be *formal*—that is, actual—because it has passed over into the will. One of the conditions necessary for the valid administration of a sacrament is a proper intent on the part of the minister; this intent is not vitiated by wrong ideas as to the nature and requirements of the sacrament, however, but only by a rebellion of the will against the sacrament after its true nature is known. Lastly, in the case of exorcism, the process can only be successfully completed when the will of the exorcist, in submission to the will of God, goes head-to-head against the demon, and when the exorcee—whatever errors or sufferings or horrors his thoughts, feelings and imagination might subject him to—chooses, with his naked will, to reject evil and accept the Good.

So in this sense the will would seem to be primary. And yet the intellect, from another point of view, would appear to be the higher faculty, since it relates us to unchanging, eternal realities, not to the partialities and contingencies we must deal with when called upon to choose between alternatives. This apparent conflict stems in part from the ambiguity of the Scholastics as to the real nature of the *intellect*. Aquinas did posit the distinction between *Intellectus* (*Nous*) and *ratio* (*dianoia*); nonetheless, since he maintained, following Aristotle, that *Intellectus* does not possess the independent power to intuit the Intelligibles, only the ability to "make sense" out of sense data, he had little concept of pure intellectual intuition. But as soon as we accept Plato's teaching that *Intellectus* or *Nous* does possess the power to intuit first principles directly, just as the eye perceives light, then we can clearly distinguish *Intellectus* from *ratio* or *dianoia*, the discursive power that argues from premise to conclusion. And as soon as we do this, the conflict between the primacy of the intellect and the primacy of the will simply disappears. Certainly the will in obedience to God is higher than mere discursive thought—but how can the will choose to reject temptation or oppose the power of the demon *against* the enticements of the feelings and *against* the rationalizations of the thinking mind unless it intuits the truth of a Reality higher than feeling, higher than thought? For the will to choose the Good it must *know* the Good—and when the soul is in a condition where the will is ill-advised to obey the rational mind since *ratio* is in confusion or rebellion, its only recourse is to obey God directly. It can do this in one of two ways: either by following the norms laid down by divine Revelation *whether or not it understands them*, or by conforming itself to God directly through the Eye of the Heart, the *Nous*. When the individual rational intellect is not conformed to the *Nous*, as in the case of temptation or material heresy or demonic possession, then the will—as long as it obeys the Will of God—*is* higher than the rational intellect. But in order for it to obey the Will of God beyond the discursive mind it must intuit the reality of God through the theological virtue of Faith, and Faith is *virtual Intellection*—"the presence of things hoped for, the evidence of things not seen." When the individual will conforms itself to the Will of God through Faith, then virtual Intellection becomes actualized; we see not "through as glass, darkly", but "face to face". *Ratio* when conformed to *Intellectus* is higher than a *voluntas* in rebellion against such a conformed *ratio*—but *voluntas*, when submitted to *Intellectus* or obedient to Revelation is higher than a *ratio* that is in error because it is veiled from *Intellectus* and/or not in line with Revelation. (As Frithjof Schuon writes, "Revelation is the Intellection of the macrocosm; Intellection is the Revelation of the microcosm"). Feeling also, when conformed to Intellection, is higher than rationality and will when they are not so conformed; it is a way of knowing in itself. But in a soul whose *ratio* is in error and whose *voluntas* is in rebellion, feeling will not be a reliable guide; nonetheless God can reach it, and inform it, if He so wills.

As we have seen, in the case of the normally-hierarchicalized soul, *voluntas* is subordinate to *ratio* as *ratio* is to *Intellectus*, and so in this sense intellect is certainly higher than will. And in the case of the soul in extremity, where the affections are poisoned and the rational mind darkened, but where "man's extremity" is nonetheless "God's opportunity", the will, if conformed directly to the Intellect, effectively *is* the Intellect: this is the doorway to the Greater Mysteries. The power of the will is certainty, and certainty is the very presence of Truth. So we can say that while the obedient will is higher than the darkened intellect—just as the enlightened intellect is higher than the rebellious will—in no case can *voluntas* be higher than *Intellectus*; the human will only becomes one with the Intellect in submission to God *through* the Intellect. The will is always the servant—the Uncreated Intellect, the Master; in human terms, the intellect has precedence over the will because the true intellect is paramount in its actualization, while the true will is paramount only in its self-sacrifice. In God alone are Will and Intellect perfectly one, because His Will is perfectly conformed to His Knowledge: whatever He wills, He wills by *knowing* it. This is what Meister Eckhart means when he says that God's Knowing is higher than His Being—though from another perspective His Knowing and His Being are certainly One without a second: there are no divisions in God.

In the words of the Holy Qur'an, *Allah need only say to something "Be!" and it is.* On the face of it this seems to say that God is essentially Will, given that His Will is sovereign over all existence. But the Qur'an also calls Him *Witness over all things.* And if Allah is presented as saying the word "Be!" *to* a thing, this indicates that He has Knowledge of it *before* it possesses being, before He has called it into existence. So in Islam as well as in Meister Eckhart's Christian gnosis, God as Absolute Knower has precedence over God as Divine Will.

Islam posits three levels of relationship to God: *islam, iman* and *ihsan. Islam* is submission of the will to the divine Law; *iman* is the faith that grows out of this submission—which, given that faith is virtual intellection, begins to teach the *mumin* the truths of Allah; *ihsan* is excellence, beauty, perfection, at which point we pray to God as if we see Him, because we know that even if we don't see Him, He sees us—and to know that we are known is to know the Knower. Here the submission of the will to God is shown as a preliminary step to the knowledge of God. Yet this submission is not simply the root cause of this Knowledge, this *ma'rifa*, but also, in a sense, the essence of it. Whatever knowledge we may possess as individual knowers must always be partial, even if it is given by Allah, but submission to God is total because to be submitted to God is the true nature of all things—of all things *in* God; and if someone does not submit to and conform himself to the object of his knowledge, but rather rebels against it by wishing it to be other than it is, then how can he know it? Thus the perfect submission of the will to God is none other than the perfect knowledge of God, which is ultimately not our knowledge, but His. As the Sufis say, as long as we are identified with ourselves we cannot not know God; when we are no longer identified with ourselves, then God knows Himself in us.

But in all this talk about the intellect, the feelings, the will, who exactly is the human person? In my opinion, the center of the human individual is the will: what we *really* intend (which we are not always conscious of) is who we really are. The human being centered in the Uncreated Intellect is to a large degree beyond individuality. The human being centered in the feelings has not yet attained individuality. The human being who is one with his intent is one with himself.[†] To be identified with your thoughts doesn't necessarily put you at one with your will or your feelings; to be identified with your feelings doesn't automatically put you at one with your will or your thoughts. But if you are one with your will, then you have a stable point from which to deal with, and integrate, both your thoughts and your feelings—which is necessary for human wholeness; the one who is cut off from the Uncreated Intellect or the rational mind or the feelings cannot be called a complete human being. The Uncreated Intellect is higher than the will because it is higher than individuality—but unless the will is submitted to the Intellect, the Intellect has not been attained.

The Intellect is the highest; the will is the crux; the feelings are the harvest.

---

† The theology of the will was suppressed to a degree by the Protestant Reformation. Luther, and Calvin even more so, granted no spiritual significance to human will: man was saved by Grace through Faith—or simply by predestination—not by works. (The truth is, Grace and Faith are the spiritual powers that call for works and ensure that they will be fruitful.) One of the greatest ironies of the Protestant ethos, however, is that the very people who denied the spiritual efficacy of works gave us the "work ethic". Why is this? The reason is simple: to deny the spiritual efficacy of the will does not do away with it but simply turns it over to the Devil, whose only ethic is *success*; the will obedient to God is thus transformed into self-will. But the crucial role of the will in the spiritual life could not have been forgotten unless it was already beginning to be identified with self-will in the popular mind, and was thus already partly alienated from Grace. Perhaps Frithjof Schuon's lack of any adequate theory of the will can be put down to his Lutheran background.

2

LOVE AND KNOWLEDGE ON THE FIELD OF SPIRITUAL COMBAT

*A Comparison of the Sufi Teachings
of Javad Nurbakhsh and Frithjof Schuon*

INTRODUCTION

The observance of one's initiatory vows and a receptivity to the *baraka* one's lineage and spiritual Master make up the operative reality of the Sufi path. Yet an understanding of "pure" metaphysics may also be of use on that path, as long as we realize that ideas alone, without practice, guidance and submission, can never alchemize the soul, even if the mental substance becomes receptive enough to catch a few lightning-like flashes from the spiritual Heart. To acquire a speculative knowledge of the eternal metaphysical principles can be a great support on the path (as well as a great distraction)—yet the operative essence of the path is not the fleeting intuition of changeless realities, but the progressive, methodical and *permanent* removal of the subjective, psychic obstacles to the manifestation of objective Love and Truth. When the will is submitted to God, the soul is pacified; when the soul is pacified, the Eye of the Heart opens. Thus Sufism may be legitimately seen, on one level, as an operative, principial psychology—the science of the operation of metaphysical principles on the plane of the human psyche, and of our conscious cooperation with them.

In the words of the Qur'an (41:53), God says *We will show them Our signs on the horizons and in themselves, till it is clear to them that it is the truth. Suffice it not as to thy Lord, that he is witness over every-thing?* In other words, God absolutely transcends the division between inner and outer reality; His Love, His Knowledge and His Command appear equally in the realm the psyche and the realm of outer circumstances. Yet the "horizons" do not only symbolize outer, material reality; they also represent the Truth of God as it dawns upon us from beyond the horizon of the subjective, psychic domain—in other words, the reality of metaphysical objectivity.

Being and knowing are ultimately One, which is why ontology (the science of being) and epistemology (the science of knowing), are inseparable. And psychology, especially in relation to the spiritual Path, is necessarily an aspect of epistemology. A spiritual state or station is always the reflection, or effect, of an objective meta-physical reality—a Name of God.

If we concentrate on ontology alone, without reference to our spiritual state—that is, without watching how the truths we witness are reflected in and affect our own souls—then our knowledge of God will remain purely mental or abstract. But if, on the other hand, we attempt to witness and understand our psychic states without simultaneously recognizing them as reflections of objective realities, if we take them as entirely subjective—which postmodern philosophy and culture teach us to do—then we are ignoring Allah, and taking the *nafs* or unconscious ego as our god. The *nafs* can hide just as cunningly inside narcissistic self-intoxication, masquer-ading as asceticism or the love of God, as it can behind abstract mental knowledge, masquerading as gnosis. If the passional soul, the *nafs-al-ammara* is to be flushed from its hole, the army of meta-physical knowledge and the army of psychological self-understand-ing must meet, in a pincers movement, on a field whose center is the Heart, *al-Qalb*. The Arabic root QLB or QBL embraces a range of meanings that include turning around, turning toward, overturning and returning; according to the *hadith*, "The hearts of the children of Adam are as if between the two fingers of the Infinitely Compas-sionate. He turns each however He wishes. O God, O Turner of hearts, turn our hearts toward obedience to You." The Heart is part and parcel of the subjective psyche because it is always turning, this way and that. It is open, on one side, to the realm of contingency and becoming, but it is also the objective presence of God within the psyche, by which it may be seen that the Heart's turning is ultimately from God Himself. Self-understanding is the seed of objectivity, just as objectivity is the basis of self-understanding. If "He who knows himself knows his Lord," then he who knows his Lord also thereby knows himself.

Everything in the postmodern world works to tear apart epistemology and ontology, knowing and being—and only a sacred, *ontological psychology* can stitch them together again. Sacred psychology is the science of how the human soul is conformed, not only theoretically, but practically and existentially, to spiritual Truth. As such, it takes fully into account the conscious and unconscious barriers to such conformation, in the three realms of thought, feeling and will. It is, in other words, also an *operative epistemology*, in which Knowledge and Being are united—at which point, in the words of St. Thomas Aquinas, "the Knower becomes the Thing Known". And the fire which melts down the separation between Knowledge and Being, and recasts them in One Form, is Love. It is this sacred psychology that Dr. Javad Nurbakhsh, who always speaks in terms of the classical science of Sufism, presents in every one of his books.

I: KNOWLEDGE OF GOD

The ways of knowing God are three: philosophy, theology, and *gnosis* or intellection; gnosis may be expressed—given that the gnostic is commanded to express it—in terms of metaphysics and/or theosophy. *Philosophy*—true philosophy—is speculation on the nature of being and the ways of knowing it, as well as the on cosmological laws and the ethical consequences that flow from such speculation—which is why philosophical knowledge must include self-knowledge; as the Delphic Oracle taught the philosophers of Greece, *know thyself*. *Theology*—at least as the word is used in western Christendom—is rational speculation on the truths that God has revealed to us in Scripture, which is from a Source far above rational knowledge. *Metaphysics* is the science of first principles or eternal truths, ultimately based on that direct perception of spiritual Truth that the scholastic philosophers call "intellection" and

some of the Church Fathers, gnosis—a knowledge that is sometimes, but not always, inspired by revealed scripture. *Theosophy* is
the articulated wisdom flowing from intellection or gnosis directly,
from the immediate witnessing of Divine Reality. It often embraces
a metaphysical cosmology as well, having to do with the relationship between God and His own Self-manifestation as the celestial,
psychic and material universes, including the spiritual, psychic and
physical aspects of our Human Form. The Human Form is the center and epitome of God's Self-manifestation in this world, and also
the ladder that leads from the manifest universe back to its Divine
Source. Philosophy and theology give us knowledge *about* God;
only *gnosis* (in Arabic, *ma'rifa*) opens us to knowledge *of* God,
where God Himself is both the Knower and the Known. (NOTE: In
Eastern Orthodox Christianity, the word *theoria* denotes a way of
being and knowing that is much closer to *theosophy* or *gnosis*, as I
have defined them, than the "theology" of the western church. In
the west, theology is essentially speculative; in the east, it is both
speculative and operative.)

According to Dr. Nurbakhsh, the stage below true Sufism but
above rational or theoretical or particular knowledge is gnosis,
ma'rifa, knowledge of God, while the flower and essence of Sufism is
the Love of God, which is not other than the perfection of knowledge. Knowledge has to come before Love, since in order to love
anything you first have to know it. And Love is the final fruit of
Knowledge of God, since to know God is to love Him. Furthermore,
as Maimonides said, "Love is the highest form of Knowledge," since
Love delights to dwell upon its Object; to live in intimacy with
Someone is to know Him well.

In *Sufism: Meaning, Knowledge and Unity*, in the chapter
"Ma'refat, Knowledge of God," Dr. Nurbakhsh has this to say:

> According to some Sufis, ma'refat is comprehension or knowl-
> edge of "the thing itself," of essential knowledge. In this essay,
> however, the word is used to mean true knowledge of God.
>
> A drop of spray cannot engulf the sea nor can the part compre-
> hend the whole; thus, without doubt, man cannot know God in a
> way that befits Him. The best proof of this is God's own saying,

"They measure not God with His true measure" (*Koran* VI:92; XXXIX:67); and, as the Prophet has said, "we have not known Thee according to Thy true measure."

Of course, with Divine help and grace, one may know God's attributes, at least to the extent of one's capacity. However, no-one can know god's Essence, his very Self, through his own limited selfhood. As 'Ali has said, "I know God by God; I know 'other-than-God' by God's light." (Nurbakhsh 1981, p. 44)

Imagine a ladder. The lowest rung is a theoretical knower who depends on the particular intellect, and the highest is a perfect Sufi. The knowers can be found between these two levels.

The more the knower depends on himself and his own knowledge, the lower the rung he occupies, but as he moves away from himself and his own knowledge, submitting more and more to God, he approaches the highest step. In reality then, the perfect knower and the perfect Sufi are one and the same. (Ibid., p. 66)

In the words of Frithjof Schuon, "Knowledge only saves us on condition that it enlists all that we are, only when it is a way and when it works and transforms and wounds our nature, even as the plough wounds the soil" (Schuon, 1954, pp. 144–145).

Rational or particular knowledge is the Arabic *'aql* and the Latin *ratio*. *Ma'rifa,* on the other hand, is *gnosis*, based on the transcendent faculty known in Latin as *Intellectus* and in Greek as *Nous*, and called by both Sufis and Eastern Orthodox Christians "The Eye of the Heart". The knowledge of the Heart does not proceed logically or imaginatively from premise to conclusion. It is immediate, like sense perception, except that it perceives not temporal events but eternal realities. It knows these realities just as the eye knows light.

We westerners have over-developed our rational, mental intelligence at the expense of every other way of knowing; but rationality which denies the higher forms of knowing upon which it is based ultimately breaks down. This is why, in postmodern times, we have become obsessively cerebral, without necessarily any longer being able to think. We are addicted to words and images; we need more of them every day, faster and faster, in order to suppress our awareness of the devastating effects of our addiction to words and images. This is why theosophy and metaphysics can imbalance the postmodern western soul, if they are taken on the purely mental level—which they will be, initially, especially if we approach them through books. Thus Dr. Nurbakhsh emphasizes the development of the spiritual virtues and the purification and awakening of the spiritual Heart, over and above the explicit study of metaphysics. If gnosis results from purification, it is known for what it is, a gift of God. If metaphysical principles are first understood on the mental level, and then allowed to sink toward the Heart in hopes that they will be realized, the result will be very uncertain: first, because the study of metaphysics can be intoxicating to those open to it; it can produce quasi-spiritual states which, since the principles in question are solidly understood on the mental level—the level of the particular intellect, of the kind of knowledge that can be acquired through memory—may be mistaken for stations of spiritual *gnosis*, which they certainly are not; second, because the vast gulf between even a good mental understanding of metaphysics and the dark, habitual mindset of profane secular society is a standing temptation to intellectual pride; and third, because the Heart must be purified in any case for a mental understanding of metaphysical principles to give way to true *gnosis*.

Yet if the mental level is not fed with lore about God, it will necessarily feed itself on something else—on *everything* else. If our minds are secular, profane, and therefore dissipated, they will exist as a veil concealing the Knowledge and Love of God. And God only knows whether the cold intellectual pride of the person with a purely mental understanding of metaphysics, or the demonic dissipation of the person whose mind is fed on the jagged, vicious images of secular culture, is the greater barrier.

Sufis have always maintained that union with God cannot be attained through books; nonetheless Sufis, including Dr. Nurbakhsh, have always written books. According to one story, a Sufi was in the habit of going out at night with a powerful lantern which he placed in the middle of the crossroad, where it attracted swarms of moths. He himself, however, went off to the side of the road, where he pursued his own studies by the light of a single candle. Though his light was faint, it was sufficient—and he was certainly not troubled by moths!

This story points to the possibility of occupying the mind with the lore of God so as to weaken its ability to distract the Heart from the contemplation of God. Lore-knowledge is not in itself the stable witnessing of Reality in any degree, and it can certainly become a serious distraction in itself. But under the right circumstances, God willing, it can support the witnessing of Reality by luring the mental substance away from its worldly dissipation, and concentrating it upon at least the reflected light of spiritual Truth.

And this is true to an even greater degree of the study the Qur'an. To listen to the recitation of the Book is even more powerfully recollecting than the study of metaphysics, since it is addressed to all levels of the human being, body, soul, Heart and Spirit. Awash in the abrupt and lightning-like periods of those Divine verses and signs, the wandering dog of the attention is brought swiftly to heel.

> *The Qur'an heats you to white heat.*
> *Its verses pound you*
> *on the anvil of your own nothingness*
> *Till you assume the shape of the Book.*
> *It does this without your knowledge.*

II: STATES AND STATIONS
FROM THE STANDPOINT OF KNOWLEDGE

Dr. Nurbakhsh teaches that Sufism is a school of humane conduct, concentration upon God and forgetfulness of self. He defines the spiritual Path (insofar as it can be systematically defined) in accordance with classical Sufi authorities, as made up of *states* and *stations*. Spiritual states are gifts of God; spiritual stations are acquired through our own efforts—with the proviso that all things, ultimately, are God's gifts, that even our own existence can in no way be attributed to us, any more than we can claim it as a personal achievement. Our existence is a free gift of His Existence to our essential nothingness. Spiritual states can be thought of as announcements of potential stations, while spiritual stations are, in one sense, states which have become crystallized, so that they form a permanent part of the human character.

The sacred psychology of spiritual states and stations makes up a great part of the science and lore of Sufism. But if we are essentially nothing, then who is experiencing those spiritual states and acquiring those spiritual stations? And if the practice of Sufism is based on forgetfulness of self, doesn't its expression in terms of the psychology of states and stations work against that forgetfulness? If I have acquired a particular station or am experiencing a particular state, and I know it—since unconscious states are not states at all, and unconscious stations, things that no-one could attempt to acquire through conscious effort—doesn't this build up my sense of separate selfhood rather than doing away with it?

This certainly would be true, except for the fact that states and stations are actually unveilings of the Names and Qualities of God, as well as intimations of God's hidden Essence, unknowable in Its fullness by anyone but God Himself. States are temporary unveilings of Reality, or unveilings which, though they may be long-lasting, have not yet alchemized the substance of our soul (i.e. our intellect, feelings and will), while stations are intimations become *certainties*: Whatever we really know about Reality compels us; we become the servants, the slaves of it because we are forced to take it into account. More than mere subjective experiences, then, states and stations are also objective realities. They affect and transform our psychic subjectivity because they come from beyond it, and above it. They dominate that subjectivity, just as an event of great joy or terror will snap us out of subjective daydreaming (in terms of states), or as, when driving a car, we have to take into account the objective layout of the city streets (in terms of stations). If they weren't objective aspects of the One Reality, states and stations would be nothing but the fantasies of the lower self, the *nafs*.

It is said that the realized Sufi is beyond states and stations. What does this mean? In subjective terms, it means that his ego-attachments and identifications, the knots and blockages in his psychophysical system, have all been burnt out. Wherever there is such an ego-knot, a spiritual state or unveiling supervenes to undo it. When that knot is untied, the state is finished with and does not return again; that particular "place" in the soul is now a station, a permanent trait of one's character. For example, neurotic fear (an ego-knot), burnt out by *states* of ecstatic love, becomes the *station* of courage and equanimity. But when a state keeps returning in such a way that a given ego-knot gets tighter instead of looser, as with any addiction, you can be sure that no matter how ecstatic or apparently enlightening the state appears to be, it is not really a spiritual state but a demonic fantasy of the *nafs*.

In objective terms, the realized Sufi is beyond states and stations because, in his case, the objective truth that God is the Only Being has been unveiled. When there is no-one there to be the subject of states and stations, how can they occur? Paradoxically, however, it is precisely the objective Truth of God, during the process of dawning upon us, that affects the soul with spiritual states and stations. What else could have the power? Illusion cannot enlighten itself. Reality (God) seems to dawn upon illusion (me), but it can't really do so without dispelling the illusion of my separate selfhood. Reality can only truly dawn upon Reality, and it has in fact already done so, from all eternity. Spiritual stations, therefore, are the qualities of God, not the qualities of man. It is said that the human soul is "qualified by God's qualities"; yet it is only God who is ultimately the subject and ground of these qualities; the human soul is only the mirror of them. If this is not clearly enough understood, one may become a connoisseur and collector of spiritual states and virtues, which will ultimately turn out to be nothing but the fantasies and pretensions of the *nafs al-ammara*, the "ego which commands to evil."

III: KNOWLEDGE AND LOVE

Dr. Nurbakhsh speaks of the relationship between love and knowledge in these terms: "In discussing Intellect and Love from the point of view of Sufism, what is usually meant by intellect is reason or the particular intellect. But, in fact, the perfection of Divine Love manifests itself as the Universal Intellect; the perfection of Love is the same thing as the Universal Intellect." (Nurbakhsh, 1978, p.27) The particular intellect seeks to acquire knowledge, but whatever knowledge comes to us by Love is given, not acquired.

Nothing is more certain than that it is impossible to become a friend of God through metaphysical "knowledge" acquired from books and other forms of hearsay. It can sometimes, or for some people, even be an impediment on the Path. As Lao Tzu reminds us in his *Tao Te Ching*: "In the pursuit of knowledge every day something is acquired; in the pursuit of Tao every day something is dropped" (Feng and English, 1972, chap. 44). Nonetheless, the fact that Shah Nimatullah, the founder of the Nimatullahi Order, of which Dr. Javad Nurbakhsh was Pir until his death in 2008, wrote a commentary on the doctrines of Ibn al-'Arabi, is good evidence that under the right circumstances metaphysical lore can be highly useful, given that a spiritual Master writes only to instruct others. And the example of Ibn al-'Arabi himself, "the Pole of Knowledge," illustrates the truth that profound metaphysical knowledge, like that found in his densely-packed *Fusus al-Hikam* (*The Bezels of Wisdom*) is in no way essentially opposed to Divine Love, as manifested in the beautiful metaphysical/erotic poems of his *Tarjuman al-Ashwaq* (*The Interpreter of Ardent Desires*)—though we need to remember that the capacity to express metaphysical ideas or compose beautiful poems on divine subjects has little to do with one's true spiritual station. And some of the greatest Sufis, known and unknown, never wrote a word.

The famous Ibn Sina (Avicenna) however, a central figure in both Muslim and Western Christian philosophy, may illustrate the opposite possibility, at least according to one perspective. After his death, the Sufi master Ala al-Dawla al-Simnani saw the Prophet in a dream, and asked him: "What do you say on the subject of Ibn Sina?" The Prophet replied, "He is a man whom God caused to lose his way in knowledge." Likewise the Sufi Baha al-Din al-Amili also dreamt of the Prophet, and asked him about the post-mortem condition of Ibn Sina. The Prophet answered: "Ibn Sina wanted to reach God without me, so I touched his chest and he fell into the fire." (Nasr, 1978, p.194)

So acquired knowledge is certainly a two-edged sword, even if touched by the light of the Universal Intellect. It is equally certain, however, that the following two statements can never be made in objective sincerity: "I know God quite well; I simply don't love Him," and "I love Him with all my heart, but I don't really want to know Him." Since, according to the Qur'an, all things return to Allah— this being true of philosophical discourse as well as of human souls—we must nonetheless remember that no statement about God that contains the word "I" can be entirely sincere either, in the ultimate sense, because "I" is precisely the veil of God—unless that "I" be recognized as God Himself, as in Meister's Eckhart's teaching, "my truest 'I' is God." And without "myself," the argument between Love and Knowledge has no place to hang its hat, given that the separation between the two is nothing but an illusion of the ego. In Rumi's words, from the *Mathnawi*: "Now," said the Friend, "since thou art I, come in: there is no room for two I's in this house."

When attempting to describe the Nimatullahi Sufi path as I have experienced it from my own limited perspective, I often call it "apophatic *bhakti*," two words which can probably best be translated as "love for the inconceivable."

The usual reaction to the juxtaposition of these two words is surprise, followed by either delight or bewilderment. Most people who are interested in mysticism know that the *bhakti-marga* in Hinduism is the path of love, as opposed to the path of knowledge, *jñana-marga*, and the path of action, *karma-marga*. But the usual idea of *bhakti* is that it requires a formal object, an image of God as the Friend, the Beloved, the one with the beauty-mark, the dark entangling tresses, and the bewitching eyes. Hafiz:

> If that Shirazi Turkish maid
> Would take my heart into her hand
> I'd give Bokhara for the mole on her cheek,
> Or Samarkand.

The idea that the path of *bhakti* can take one beyond form, that the greatest Beauty is the beauty of the Invisible—*Layla*, or Black Night—is a novelty to many people. I remember an exchange I had with Dr. Ralph Austin at one of the Berkeley conferences of the Ibn al-'Arabi Society. I maintained that the greatest beauty is invisible; he, that beauty, as a mode of *maya*, has entirely to do with the world of manifestation. All I could tell him was that, by all *sane* criteria, he was right.

As I have already pointed out, to approach mysticism with the mind is dangerous. Mystical ideas can be so fascinating to those sensitive to them that they can sometimes produce glimpses of the

Truth which take a person beyond himself, beyond his real stage of development. In the words of Frithjof Schuon, "A cult of the intelligence and mental passion take man further from truth. Intelligence withdraws as soon as man puts his trust in it alone. Mental passion pursuing intellectual intuition is like the wind which blows out the light of a candle" (Schuon, 1954, p.132). Nonetheless, metaphysical ideas can sometimes clarify our experience by furnishing the mind with concepts accurate enough to prevent less accurate concepts from distorting that experience and veiling it. There is nothing more unfortunate, and ultimately unnecessary, than for a state of spiritual unveiling to run up against a mass of mental scruples which maintain that such things can't really happen.

The writers of the Traditionalist School—René Guénon, Ananda Coomaraswamy, Martin Lings, Titus Burckhardt, Marco Pallis, Leo Schaya, Rama Coomaraswamy, Wolfgang Smith, Seyyed Hossein Nasr, Whitall Perry, Joseph Epes Brown, James Cutsinger, William Stoddart, Frithjof Schuon, Huston Smith *et. al.*—are often identified with the doctrine that knowledge is higher than love. And this characterization is partly justified. As Martin Lings puts it (whose voice and personality radiated love, whether he knew it or not), speaking of the spirituality proper to our time, which he terms "the extreme old age of the macrocosm": ". . . the esoterism in question could not be other than what the Hindus call *jñana-marga,* the way of knowledge, or, more precisely, of gnosis. It was fated to be so, for such a way presupposes a perspective of truth rather than love, and it is objective regard for truth which characterizes the wisdom of old age." (Lings, 1987, p. 77)

I believe the Traditionalists exalt knowledge above love because they often limit love to a passionate and sentimental *bhakti,* clearly inferior to a sober, elevated and all-comprehensive *jñana.* Frithjof Schuon, however, maintained that "Perfect love is 'luminous' and perfect knowledge is 'hot'. . . .In God Love is Light and Light is Love" (Schuon, 1954, p.148), and taught that "The way of love—methodical *bhakti*—presupposes that through it we can go toward God; whereas love as such—intrinsic *bhakti*—accompanies the way of knowledge, *jñana,* and is based essentially on our sensitivity to the divine Beauty" (Schuon, 1991, p.118). "Where there is Truth, there is also Love", Schuon wrote. "Each Deva possesses its Shakti; in the human microcosm, the feeling soul is joined to the discerning intellect, as in the Divine Order Mercy is joined to Omniscience; and as, in the final analysis, Infinitude is consubstantial with the Absolute." (Schuon, 1986, p.194)

Nonetheless, the doctrine that *jñana* is higher and more complete than *bhakti* surfaces again and again in the writings of Schuon and others of his school. And although this doctrine may generate an unwarranted bias against love in some people, I believe that there is a sense in which it is intrinsically true, though to understand exactly how it is true requires a "revisioning" of what *bhakti* and *jñana* really are.

To begin with, they aren't absolutely bound to spiritual temperament, though this will always be an important factor. It is possible for *jñana* and *bhakti* to coexist within the same individual, depending upon whether he or she is in a state of or contemplative "sobriety" or ecstatic "drunkenness". Furthermore, some contemplatives may pass through a station that could be called "bhaktic" and arrive at one that is "jñanic", as in the Sufi doctrine of "sobriety after drunkenness"; *jñana* itself could be described, in the words of St. Augustine, as a kind of "sober inebriation." According to the Vedanta, devotion to God may open out, in the course of the spiritual Path, into a permanent contemplative realization in which God is the *atman*, the absolute Witness (cf. the Qur'an, 41:53). And we should remember that Shankaracharya himself, the greatest exemplar of *jñana* in Hinduism, wrote devotional songs.

C. F. Kelley, in *Meister Eckhart on Divine Knowledge*, distinguishes between a bhaktic, or affective, or "relational" mysticism, such as that of Francois de Sales or St. John of the Cross, based on "a gazing at, a looking at" its Divine Object (Kelley, 1977, p.15), and the *jñanic* mysticism of Eckhart, who could say: "My truest 'I' is God." But "relational" is not always equivalent to "affective." Those of *jñanic* temperament will tend to see the subject/object duality of relational mysticism as inseparable from *bhakti*, as when Sri Ramakrishna—in whom, however, the distinction between *bhakti* and *jñana* was almost certainly transcended—said, "the devotee wants to eat sugar, not become sugar." The knower is one with Knowledge, but the lover must remain in polarity with the Beloved for Love to exist. But *advaita* (non-dual) *bhaktas*—a definition which probably includes most Sufis—tend to have the opposite perspective: that it's really *jñana* which cannot exist without the subject/object polarity, because in the way of Knowledge the Knower must soberly contemplate the Known, while in the drunkenness of Love all separation between lover and Beloved is swept away in Union. However, as Dr. Nurbakhsh reminds us, perfect Love is identical to the Universal Intellect.

In the words of Sri Ramana Maharshi, the paramount *jñani* of modern times, "*Bhakti* is love for God with form; *jñana* is love for God without form." This indicates that *jñana* cannot purely be limited to the perspective of knowledge as opposed to love, and would seem to imply the correlative, that *bhakti* cannot be reduced to a perspective of love as opposed to knowledge. What I have named "apophatic *bhakti*" above, Ramana Maharshi apparently calls *jñana*. But if *bhakti* and *jñana* are not simply equivalent to love and knowledge, then what are they? To put it simply, *bhakti* is not strictly love as opposed to knowledge, but rather a *passion for God*, while *jñana* is not strictly knowledge as opposed to love, but rather serenity, sobriety and completion. It is important to note, however, that the bhaktic passion is "passionate, not passional," a distinction William Blake epitomized when he wrote, in *Auguries of Innocence*:

> *To be in a Passion you Good may do*
> *But no Good if a Passion is in you.*

Bhakti, according to this definition, is the principle of relational mysticism, which is inseparable from a passionate desire both to know God *and* to unite with Him in love. Wherever there is duality there is passion, since the two must strive to become One, and by so striving continue to assert their twoness. But when the "two" in question are the human soul and the Divine Reality, before which that soul is effectively nothing, the passion of this nothing to embrace that Reality in love, as well as encompass It in knowledge, is infinitely inflamed and infinitely frustrated at the same time, dissolving in ecstasy and returning to separation again and again, until it learns to temper its spiritual hunger, to submit to the will of the Beloved, to want whatever He wants even more than it desires union

with Him on its own terms. This, incidentally, is the esoteric meaning of the "beloved Lady hard-to-attain" in the traditions of the
troubadours and the *Fedeli d'Amore,* where the Lady symbolized,
and sometimes actually incarnated, the principle that all willful
attempts at Union ultimately violate true love. God cannot be possessed or seduced, but must simply be obeyed, whether Her answer
in a given spiritual moment be a sweet Yes, a bitter No, or a coy Not
Yet.

Jñana, then, would be the principle of "trans-relational" or
advaita mysticism, in which God is both the Witness and That
which is Witnessed. The *jñanic* gnosis is not cerebral as opposed to
feeling-centered, but serene and complete as opposed to fragmentary and passionate, which is why Schuon, as we saw above, can distinguish between methodical *bhakti,* which expresses itself in
relational mysticism, and intrinsic *bhakti,* which is inseparable from
jñana. Furthermore, when Schuon writes "What is 'love' at the start
will appear as 'Knowledge' in the result, and what is 'knowledge' at
the start will appear in the result as 'Love'" (Schuon, 1954, p.148), the
context permits the interpretation that he is speaking not only
about two different individuals, a "knower" and a "lover," but also
about the final spiritual destiny of thought and feeling within the
same soul.

In *Survey of Metaphysics and Esoterism,* Schuon expresses the difference between a "bhaktic" consciousness which contemplates the
Divine Object and is finally absorbed into It, and a "jñanic" one
where the Divine Subject takes precedence, placing the second perspective higher than the first. He says:

> [when] the perception of the Object is so intense that the con-
> sciousness of subject vanishes, the Object becomes Subject, as is
> the case in the union of love; but then the word "subject" no
> longer has the meaning of a complement that is fragmentary by
> definition; it means on the contrary a totality which we conceive
> as subjective because it is conscious. When we place the emphasis
> on objective Reality—which then takes precedence in the relation
> between the subject and the object—the subject becomes object
> in the sense that, being determined entirely by the object, it

forgets the element consciousness; in this case the subject, inasmuch as it is a fragment, is absorbed by the Object inasmuch as it is a totality, as the accident is reintegrated into the Substance. But the other manner of seeing things, which reduces everything to the Subject, takes precedence over the point of view that grants primacy to the Object: if we adore God, it is not for the simple reason that He presents Himself to us as an objective reality of a dizzying and crushing immensity—otherwise we would adore the stars and nebulae—but it is above all because this reality, a priori objective, is the greatest of subjects; because He is the absolute Subject of our contingent subjectivity; because He is at once all-powerful, omniscient and benefic Consciousness. (Schuon, 1986, pp.39–40)

[in] the infinite and absolute Subject whose Object is on the one hand its own Infinitude and on the other its Universal Unfolding, there is no scission into subject and object on any ontological plane whatever....for in this case the Subject is not a complementary pole, it is simply That which is. If we nonetheless term it "Subject," it is to express that *Atma* is the absolute Witness, at once transcendent and immanent, of all things. . . . (Ibid., p.39)

In describing this shift of emphasis from the human subject contemplating a Divine Object into which he or she is ultimately absorbed, and the "transformation" of this Object into the Absolute Subject, the *atman*, Schuon is not simply presenting different spiritual perspectives; he is also, and necessarily, talking about successive stages in the spiritual Path. And it is only in terms of this development from relational to *advaita* mysticism, starting from the subject/object duality, moving though absorption in the Absolute Object, and culminating in the realization of the Absolute Subject which, in contemplating the universe, gazes on nothing but Itself, that *jñana* is higher than *bhakti*. In terms of permanent spiritual stations, *jñana* comes after *bhakti*, but in terms of temporary spiritual states, they can alternate. Sometimes God is "the other" in terms of my consciousness; at other times the human form—still, for sake of convenience, designated by my name—appears in the mirror of God's consciousness.

The practice of remembrance of God through invocation of His Name, central to Sufism (as *dhikr*) and Orthodox Christian Hesychasm (as *mnimi Theou*, usually in the form of the Jesus Prayer), and common as well in Hinduism (as *japa-yoga*), encompasses both *bhakti* and *jñana*. On the bhaktic level, I invoke God's Name, hoping He will unveil His presence. On the jñanic level, God speaks His own Name within me. The human form *is* God's Name in a sense; through the eyes of the human being who remembers Him, God names all things in manifest existence as aspects of Himself.

In the Vedanta, this development is presented in terms of four stages of realization: 1) *The universe is unreal, Brahman is the Real* [where the universe includes the human subject, which still "exists", though it is recognized as an illusory—in Buddhist terms, devoid of self-nature, in Sufi terms, too "poor" to claim self-existence]; 2) *There is only Brahman* [both the human subject and the universe it perceives are annihilated]; 3) *I am Brahman* [the "place" of the human subject is now "occupied" by the Witness, the *atman*]; and 4) *All this is Brahman* [the Witness witnesses all things as Itself]. And this development, far from being a motion away from love and toward knowledge, is actually a motion toward the union of love and knowledge, since in Brahman, the Divine Essence, love and knowledge are One. In the words of Ramana Maharshi, "Imperfect *jñana* and imperfect *bhakti* are different; perfect *jñana* and perfect *bhakti* are the same."

In one sense, it is impossible for "me", who am nothing, to love God, Who is more than everything, any more than a gnat can make love to an elephant. There is no equality between the terms, no "middle ground"—unless the spiritual Master, as a living representative of the Logos, is in fact that ground. As Dr. Nurbakhsh says in one of his poems, "The Beloved is alive/ And the lover is dead." Nonetheless, on the Path of Love many images of the Beloved are generated, a new one in each *waqt*, each present moment of spiritual time; and as the *Shaykh al-Akbar* ("greatest of Sufi shaykhs") Ibn al-'Arabi teaches, God is willing to accept the worship paid to this momentary "God created in belief" as if it were actually He. But it is not actually He, except in essence; and as the lover comes to realize this, his love expands into the Absolute Transcendence of God until all sense of the lover's psyche or personal identity is burned away; the moth (*psyche* in Greek) is consumed in the flame of the candle. This is the Sufi *fana*. But the candle, the Absolute Witness, still remains as Witness to the universe, which is none other than He— and what should He see in the foreground but the little human identity, still there, still composed of body, speech and mind, essentially unchanged, except for the fact that it is no longer "me." This is subsistence-in-God, the Sufi *baqa*. Ibn al-'Arabi says of this station, referring to "divine gifts that . . . stem . . . from the Essence:

> [they] can result only from a Divine Self-revelation, which occurs only in a form conforming to the essential predisposition of the recipient of such a revelation. Thus, the recipient sees nothing other than his own form in the mirror of the Reality. He does not see the Reality Itself, which is not possible, although he knows that he may see only his [true] form in it. . . . If you have experienced this [in the spirit] you have experienced as much as is possible for created being, so do not seek to weary yourself in any attempts to proceed higher than this, for there is nothing higher, nor is there beyond the point you have reached aught except the pure, undetermined, unmanifested [Absolute]. In seeing your true self, He is your mirror and you are His mirror in which He sees His Names and their determinations, which are nothing other than Himself. (Austin, 1980, p.65)

Meister Eckhart says exactly the same thing: "The eye through which I see God, and the eye through which He sees me, are the same eye."

The entire story of the path leading from relational mysticism through annihilation in God to the unveiling of the Absolute Witness is told in the famous *hadith* of the Prophet Muhammad (peace and blessings be upon him): *Pray to God as if you saw Him*— relational mysticism—*because even if you don't see Him*—annihilation in God—*He sees you*—subsistence before the face of the Absolute Witness.

Dr. Nurbakhsh, seemingly in opposition to the Traditionalists, places Love above Knowledge. The Sufi, as God's perfect lover—or rather, as the *locus* where the Beloved, the Lover and Love are recognized as none other than God Himself—is on a higher station than the gnostic or *arif* who has learned mystical secrets through direct unveiling, and stored them in his heart like precious jewels, just as the *arif* is on a higher station than the academic or religious scholar, limited to the particular intellect, who has gained all his or her knowledge through hearsay. As Nurbakhsh says in one of his poems, "Where love is, there are no secrets." But where all secrets are revealed, knowledge too must be perfect: "In reality . . . the perfect knower and the perfect Sufi are one and the same." (Nurbakhsh, 1981, p. 66)

So if both perfect knowledge and perfect love describe the perfect Sufi, is not the language of love enough, for those who have ears to hear it? Why speak of spiritual knowledge, with all its dangers of intellectual pride and mental greed, if Love is both *tariqa* and *haqiqa*, both the Path and the Goal? The reason is that gnosis is the only guarantee of objectivity; and without objectivity, love (or what passes for love) will inevitably be narcissistic and self-referential— under the power of the commanding *nafs*. Unless Divine Love is perfectly objectified—which does not mean "transformed into a mere object" but rather "freed from the limiting subjectivity of the one witnessing it"—then the lover, at least to a degree, will be in love with his or her own reactions to God, not with That One alone. One may temporarily lose oneself in intoxication, ravished by the beauty of the Beloved, only to return to the painful sobriety of (apparent) self-existence, over and over again. The only way out of this vicious cycle is the intoxicating sobriety of gnosis, in which Love is purified of the emotional reactions, the whining and pleading of the drunken lover, by being recognized as *al-Haqq*, the Truth. In the words of Frithjof Schuon, "The love of the affective man is that he loves God. The love of the intellectual man is that God loves him; that is to say, he realizes intellectually—but not simply in a theoretical way—that God is Love." (Schuon, 1954, p. 149) In the words of Hujwiri, from his *Kashf al-madjub*,

> Intoxication is to imagine that you have undergone annihilation, while in reality your own attributes remain. Thus, it is a veil. Sobriety, however, is a vision of your subsistence at the same time

when your attributes have been annihilated. Thus, it is true unveiling.... The sobriety of heedlessness is the greatest of veils, while the sobriety of Love is the most manifest unveiling." (Nurbakhsh, 1985, pp. 73–74)

The element of gnosis doesn't necessarily require a sophisticated philosophical mind—though the most sophisticated philosophies, or theosophies, that we possess are those produced by gnostics, by *arifs*. All we need is the firm certainty that God is objectively real; the knowledge that we are absolutely dependent upon Him, instant-by-instant, for our very existence; the intuition that God sees and knows us, in this very moment, infinitely better than we can know either ourselves or Him; the perception that God's knowledge of us is in fact our essential reality; and finally the realization that what we call "me" is fully objective to that Divine Witness within us, Who (in Eckhart's words) is "our truest 'I'", given that "he who knows himself knows his Lord." Once this truth is realized, all philosophical and metaphysical speculation becomes unnecessary.

IV: THE SUFI DOCTRINE OF THE *NAFS*

If Sufi doctrine is made up both of a metaphysics capable—up to a point—of alchemizing the psyche, and an operative psychology based on objective metaphysical principles, then the understanding of "pure" metaphysics must always be complemented by an understanding of the psychic "knots" or barriers which, in a given individual, in a given place and time, or in terms of the human form itself as conditioned by the inherent limits of the material and psychic worlds, prevent those metaphysical principles from being understood intellectually, loved on the level of the affections, and submitted to on the level of the will. An understanding of these psychic knots, both in general terms and also as they specifically appear, both habitually and momentarily, in the case of an individual soul—particularly one's own—is called "gnosis of the *nafs*." The word *nafs* means "soul", most usually in the sense of the unconscious ego. The Sufi idea of the *nafs* is close to the Freudian concept of the *id*, except for the fact that Freud's *ego* is also an expression of the *nafs*, as are certain unconscious and obsessive aspects of his *superego*; blind and compulsive moralism is just as much a product of unconscious egotism as is blind and compulsive vice. (There is, however, a higher "gnosis of the *nafs*" by which the soul is completely objectified, and becomes the site of the total Divine Manifestation; see below.)

In the course of the spiritual Path, the *nafs* is purified and refined. Various Sufis have spoken of different stages of this purification, some referring to three stages, others to as many as seven. Dr. Nurbakhsh speaks of four stages. According to his teaching, the *nafs* first appears as "the commanding *nafs*", the lower passional soul which rules us on the basis of our own whims, desires and self-will, until we submit instead to God's rule and become true *Muslims*. Next appears "the accusing *nafs*," the troubled conscience, which recognizes the evil of the commanding *nafs*, struggles against it but is ultimately powerless to overcome it. This is followed by "the inspired *nafs*," which begins to have intimations of higher realities and is able to know and follow what is good for it. And the final development is the "*nafs*-at-peace," the individual self in perfect submission to the Will of God. Some authorities identify the *nafs*-at-peace with the Heart; at any rate, it opens onto the Heart, which is only firmly established as Heart when the Spirit, *Ruh*, has finally conquered the *nafs* and subdued it—when the *pneumatic* humanity gains power over and subdues the *psychic* humanity.

The work of subduing and refining the *nafs* is also the work of developing the virtues. Every virtue is the expression of a metaphysical principle existentially actualized within the soul, and one of the simplest and most powerful images of this actualization is the system of the "six stations of wisdom" in the teachings of Frithjof Schuon. In *Stations of Wisdom*, Schuon presents this doctrine in terms of the six discrete dimensions—the passive and active aspects of the will, the affections and the intelligence respectively, in their highest mode of operation. On the level of the will, purity and detachment are intrinsically paired with spiritual combat against the passions; on the level of the affections, peace and the contemplation of spiritual beauty are intrinsically paired with the fervent desire to be united to the Beautiful; on the level of the intellect, discrimination between the Real and the unreal is intrinsically paired with complete identification with the Real.

The Six Stations of Wisdom comprise an unsurpassed and radiant image of the spiritual virtues as emanations of the Real addressed to our particular human faculties. Yet this image has a tendency to remain in a sort of ideal or aesthetic suspension, far above the vicissitudes of actual psychophysical life. That some have been capable, God willing and with the help of initiatory method and *baraka,* of realizing these virtues I have no doubt. Yet Schuon's understanding of the *nafs-al-ammara,* the actual psychic tendencies which would militate against their realization, leaves something to be desired. In terms of a general critique of the modern world, his analysis of the collective *nafs* is of the highest value; yet as he himself admitted, he was no psychiatrist. For example, his presentation of spiritual combat as the active aspect of the spiritual will, whose passive aspect is detachment, is theoretically profound; yet for actual advice on how to carry on such combat, Nurbakhsh's *The Psychology of Sufism* is of greater value, in my opinion, given that it is understood that such combat cannot be learned from books, and is rarely effective without competent spiritual guidance.

Once upon a time the prophet Muhammad (peace and blessings upon him), after returning with his warriors from battle, said to them: "Now we return from the lesser holy war to the greater holy war". "What is the greater holy war?" they asked. "The war against the soul", he replied. When the Prophet defined the greater *jihad* in these terms, he laid one of the essential foundation stones of Sufism.

All spiritual traditions recognize that one cannot contemplate Absolute Truth without a progressive victory over the distracting desires of the ego, which include everything from lust and anger at the lower end of the spectrum to the simple assertion of one's independent existence at the other. The "enemies" of the singer in the psalms of David are one representation of this egoic soul. In Christianity it is called the "old Adam," and is sometimes symbolized as the dragon slain by St. George. The Buddhists portray it as the mass of *klesas* or psychic impurities, and often use the image of a mad, drunken monkey to dramatize its effect on human consciousness. Sufism however, with its doctrine of the *nafs,* may well possess the most sophisticated psychology of the passional soul ever developed, according to which the *nafs* is seen not only as a beast to be conquered, but also as a deceiver to be outwitted, a resource to be tapped, a servant to be enlisted, and ultimately as a manifestation of the Wisdom of God—just as, in one Christian icon of St. George, the princess rescued by the knight from the dragon ultimately binds the now docile beast with a blood-red cord tied about her waist, and leads him home.

The *nafs*, from one perspective, is the entire "natural" human psyche, which, like an iceberg, is composed of a relatively small visible portion—the conscious ego—and a much larger invisible mass—the "unconscious." But the concept of the *nafs* in Sufi psychology differs from that of the soul or psyche in most other psychological or religious doctrines in that the psyche only "constellates" as the *nafs al-ammara*, the "soul commanding or inciting to evil," after one has committed one's life to the spiritual Path. Before then the psyche will produce pleasant or unpleasant, constructive or destructive effects. It may be "maladjusted" in social terms or relatively better-adjusted; it has certain virtues, certain vices, certain potentials, and various tendencies which are not well-formed enough to clearly belong to either camp. But when God has become the conscious center of one's life, then—as in a time of civil war—the various citizens of the psyche are forced to take sides. The commanding *nafs* only reveals itself as "commanding" when we have begun to disobey it.

Since the *nafs* in its first stages represents all that comes between us and God, all that perverts our will so that we do not obey Him, or darkens our intellect so that we cannot intuit His Reality, a war without quarter against this *nafs* becomes imperative—the "war against the soul." But from another point of view, things are not quite so simple.

The position of humanity in the hierarchy of being is unique, a position which Islam defines by saying that we are both *abd*, God's abject slave, and *khalifa*, God's fully-empowered representative. In a certain sense, we bear the responsibility for the maintenance of the cosmic order. As it says in the Qur'an, *We offered the Trust to the heavens and the earth and the hills, but they shrank from bearing it and were afraid of it. And man assumed it* (33:72). The Trust is our essential duty to act as mirrors for God in the created universe—and while we are in the grip of the *nafs*, which causes us to believe that we are self-created, and therefore that we have the right to be self-determined, we cannot fulfill this function. But we can't literally destroy this *nafs*, nor can we conquer it. We can't conquer it because the "we" in question is itself part of the *nafs*, the part that is entirely capable of perverting spiritual struggle so as to build up an apparently separate identity instead of annihilating it. Nor can we destroy it, because the *nafs* is created by God Who wills its existence, and a war against the Will of God is lost before it begins.

So is God then a tyrant and deceiver, who has put us in a hopeless double-bind by commanding us, on pain of hellfire, to kill the ego—something which He knows to be impossible because He Himself opposes it? Certainly, the tyrannical and deceiving *nafs* will tend to falsely represent Him in these terms. Nonetheless, it is true that God has commanded us, in one sense, to struggle against the current of His Self-manifestation in order to reach Him, just as a salmon must swim upstream against the current of the river to reach its Source.

The *nafs* is the trace in our nature of God's original creation of the universe, of his command *kun*, "be!", addressed to all the things that have come into being. If we follow this current, which is the "natural man" or "old Adam" within us, we will live only to express ourselves, to develop and enhance our existence, and end by burning ourselves out in dissipation and flight from God, like sunlight that becomes ever dimmer in its flight from the Sun. What could be more "natural"? This is, in fact, what the whole cosmos is doing, according to the theory of an expanding universe originating in a "big bang." It is simply following the law of entropy, dissipating itself, burning itself out in order to manifest on the material plane certain possibilities latent within the Divine Nature, and thereby fulfilling its function, as expressed in the famous *hadith qudsi* in which God says: "I was a hidden Treasure and longed to be known, so I created the universe that I might be known". But in a negative but no less lawful sense, the expanding, entropic universe is precisely "the heavens and the earth and the hills" in flight from the Trust. The universe is God's manifestation; the power which manifests the Divine Nature—in Hindu terms, *Vidya-Maya*—also necessarily veils It by appearing to be something other than Him—*Avidya-Maya*.

The universe outside humanity, though it does indeed mirror God, mirrors Him in a fragmentary way, as does a human psyche when in the grip of the *nafs*. The material universe, composed of whirlpools of galaxies and throngs of living species and swarms of elementary particles, of energies and their fields, and the human consciousness made turbulent by passions and attachments, are like a lake on a windy day. The light of the Sun reflected in such a lake appears as a million dancing sparks of light. But when the wind sinks, and the lake becomes calm, then the Sun is reflected as a single unified form. This ability of the human spiritual Heart to reflect God in His entirety—and on the basis of this perfect mirroring to contemplate the material universe as ultimately composed of nothing but the "signs" of Allah—is the Trust which That One has laid upon us. It is the reason why He created us in the first place, and why He has sent prophets and avatars to instruct us and religious revelations to enlighten and save us. The soul which has become calm like a lake on a bright and windless day is the "*nafs*-at-peace," which is also sometimes identified with the spiritual Heart. The Heart in Sufism is not quite the fullness of the *atman* or Divine Self of Vedantic Hinduism (which is perhaps better translated by the Sufi term *sirr*, "secret", just as *sirr al-sirr*, "the Secret of the secret", may refer to the Absolute Essence as It is in Itself, beyond even the divine act of witnessing, the reality that the Hindus call *Brahman*), but is more like what Jung was groping toward in his concept of the "Self archetype"—the "central" point of the psyche where it is intersected by a ray of the Spirit radiating from Allah, the Absolute Witness, the Divine Self. (In the Qur'an 41:53, which we have already quoted above, Allah is identified as the Absolute Witness: *We will show them Our signs on the horizons and in themselves, till it is clear to them that it is the truth. Suffice it not as to thy Lord, that He is witness over everything?*) The Heart is thus the border between the realm of psychic multiplicity and that of Spiritual Unity. As it is said in the *hadith qudsi*, "Heaven and earth cannot contain Me, but the heart of my believing slave can contain Me."

In another sense, however, even the *nafs*-at-peace remains under

Divine Wrath, since it still manifests a trace of separate existence. The ego, no matter how submissive, cannot attain Union with God. When a young man told the Sufi woman saint Rabiʿa that he had never committed a sin, her answer was: "Alas, my son, thine existence is a sin wherewith no other sin may be compared." On the other hand, if we continue to battle against and suppress the *nafs*, how can it ever become the *nafs*-at-peace? Initially the *nafs* must be fought against; later, as the Path unfolds, it is to be instructed and trained; ultimately it is to be enlightened, at which point it becomes identical with the spiritual Heart. In terms of the human psyche, God can only be known through the *nafs-at-peace*, this being a limited and subjective form of knowing, but the *nafs* can be known in its entirety only through God. In other words, the realization of the *atman*, the indwelling divine Witness, before whose Eye the human psyche is purified of all subjective self-involvement, transforms the soul, the psyche, the *nafs* from a self-referential obscurity into a total and unified manifestation of all levels of Being, as Witnessed by That which is Beyond Being. This is the higher "gnosis of the *nafs*" we alluded to above.

God has two mercies: *Rahman* (equivalent in some ways to *Avidya-Maya*), His general mercy, by which He creates the universe, and *Rahim* (closely equivalent to *Vidya-Maya*), His particular mercy, by which He leads all things back to Himself. *Rahman* is general because it says "yes" to everything; *Rahim* is particular because it says "yes" to beliefs and actions which bring us closer to God and "no" to beliefs and actions which drive us further away. By *Rahman*, God grants the wish of all possible things to be actualized; He bestows upon them the life and reality they long for. The joy of sexuality and the fear of death are the measure of the depth of this longing. But the desire for separate existence, which begins as a mercy, ends under the sign of wrath: departing from God, or rather from the knowledge that God is the only Reality, created beings end up in the outer darkness, subject to evils and sufferings of all kinds, and they cry to God for relief. In response to this cry, God unveils *Rahim*, which manifests in terms of religions, and sacred laws, and prophets, and saints, and the spiritual Path. All creation cries to be saved, and *Rahim* mercifully dawns to show the Way back to God, the sovereign Good, the only Reality. The mercy of creation is general because it encompasses all things. The mercy of divine revelations such as the Qur'an is also general to a degree because it is addressed to an entire community—yet within it are the seeds of a particular mercy, one addressed to "myself" alone and only fully manifest as *tariqah,* the spiritual Path. And even though the work of this Path is the conquest of the *nafs,* the annihilation of "myself," nonetheless, without the appearance of "myself", the spiritual crisis which heralds the dawn of God's particular mercy, and ultimate the return of all creation to Him, could not take place. Though revelations are given to whole religious communities, no community as a whole ever became a saint.

Religion is God's wish that we abandon attachment to His general and creating mercy, and commit ourselves to His particular and saving mercy. Only humanity is confronted with this choice. The animals, the plants, the minerals are fixed under *Rahman.* The angels made their choice in pre-eternity, and those who have retained angelic status remain rapt in the contemplation of God. Only humanity can consciously choose, by God's grace, to shift our center-of-gravity from *Rahman* to *Rahim,* this choice being the essence of the spiritual Path. We are required, in other words, to break identification with one of God's mercies and avail ourselves of the other, which means that, according to the doctrine of Ibn al-'Arabi, we must stop living on the basis God's *will* to send us out into creation, manifest as our God-given instincts—a will that is essentially nothing but God's perfect fulfillment of our own desire—and grant His *wish* that we abandon our own desire and return to Him—a wish which is nothing but His compassionate response to our own cry for help. In terms of the spiritual psychology of the Sufi way, we must purify the Heart so that the army of the Spirit may take possession of it from the army of the *nafs.* All this is epitomized in the passage from the Qur'an, *There is no refuge from God but in Him* (9:118).

The *nafs,* then, being the product of God's *Rahman,* is not evil in essence, though it is certainly the *source* of evil, which is why it is said in the Qur'an, *I seek refuge in the Lord of Daybreak from the evil of that which He created* (113:1–2). And in a larger sense, we can say that if God had not by His general mercy created the universe, His particular mercy would have no field of operation, just as a salmon, though it must fight against the current to swim upstream, would have no river to travel in if the water were not flowing downstream. And just as that fish, even though he is fighting against the current of the river, is also using it, so the goal of the alchemy of the Sufi path is to transmute the *nafs* from a mortal enemy into an obedient servant—not, of course, a servant of oneself (that is, of *itself*), but rather of one's Lord. This is why it Sufis say that first you have to repent—thus transforming the commanding *nafs* into the "accusing *nafs*" or remorseful conscience, the field of the greater *jihad*—after which you will eventually have to repent of that repentance: the goal of war is not war without end, but victorious peace. This is the point at which the accusing *nafs*, the sign of the struggling ascetic, is transformed into the *nafs*-at-peace, the sign of the lover of God.

The war against the soul, against the commanding *nafs*, is a total war, and the enemy, even though in essence he is a product of God's mercy, is effectively merciless, profoundly destructive and infinitely more powerful than the puny "spiritual" ego that wants to be wise or good or even self-annihilated by its own efforts and on its own terms, without God's help and the grace of one's spiritual Master. To fight the commanding *nafs* on the basis of one's self-will is doomed to failure, if for no other reason than that the self-will of the spiritual ego is itself an aspect of the commanding *nafs*—the aspect personified by the Sufis as Eblis, the Muslim Satan. Nonetheless, this impossible battle still has to be fought. The *nafs* must try to annihilate itself, try to attain God, simply because the spiritual traveler has to begin somewhere, and at the beginning of the spiritual Path the traveler is all *nafs*. This hopeless attempt at self-transcendence has the effect of transforming the primitive passions of the commanding *nafs*, based on the struggle for security, pleasure and power, into self-criticism and spiritual aspiration: the accusing *nafs*. The very energy of the lower passions is tapped for the purpose of traveling the spiritual Path. This transformation does not take place by self-will, however, but by the grace of God—yet insofar as we still believe we are self-determined, we must make full use of this fundamentally illusory self-determination, or no progress will be made. Dr. Nurbakhsh explains it in these terms, according to the paradox of free will and predestination: At the beginning of the Path, if the aspirant claims that everything happens by God's will he is an unbeliever; he must exercise his own free will and assume full personal responsibility for carrying out his spiritual duties. But if at the end of the Path he still claims to possess free will, he is again an unbeliever, since the goal of the Path is to witness how everything that happens is by God's will, since none other than God exists. (cf. Nurbakhsh, 1996, p.80)

According to the *hadith qudsi*, God's mercy takes precedence over His wrath—which, in terms of the individual, means that submission is higher than struggle; the accusing *nafs* is superseded by the *nafs*-at-peace. Thus the goal, and one might say the "environment" of the greater *jihad* is peace, submission, surrender—and absolute submission can only be made to the Absolute itself; this is indicated by the fact that the Arabic words *Islam*, "submission," and *salaam*, "peace, surrender" (which is a Name of God), are from the same root. The ultimate end of submission is not simply submission of the will or the affections to God, but submission of one's very sense of separate existence. In Sufi terms, this is *fana*, annihilation-in-God, whose seemingly-opposite but actually complementary aspect is *baqa*, subsistence-in-God. To subsist in God is to know oneself as absolutely contingent upon the Absolute. It is to come to the end of self-determination and self-definition. In *fana*, the ego is killed; in *baqa*, it is realized that the ego need not be killed since it has never existed in the first place.

The saying of Jesus, "he who seeks to keep his life shall lose it, but he who loses his life, for My sake, shall find it," refers to precisely the same reality. When in the Qur'an Allah says, O *men! Ye are the poor in relation to God, and God is the Rich to whom all praises are due*, He is attributing all Being to Himself, and none at all to us—except *His* Being. The ego, then, is fundamentally a mis-perception; in Vedantic terms, it is nothing but an identification of the Absolute Witness with the body, or the will, or the feelings, or the mind. When the Absolute Witness is unveiled, this identification is broken—it was never there: a realization which Ramana Maharshi taught his students to demonstrate to themselves by attempting to witness the essence of ego, and thereby discovering that there is no ego to be witnessed. This is the essence of the Sufi doctrine that, in reality, only God exists. In the words of the Qur'an, *all is perishing except His face.*

<h2 style="text-align:center">V: THE REMEMBRANCE OF GOD
ON THE FIELD OF SPIRITUAL COMBAT</h2>

The Invocation of the Name of God, the Sufi *dhikr* or *zekr* (closely related to the Platonic *anamnesis*), is essentially the practice of remembering God and forgetting oneself. It should always be emphasized, however, that the Invocation of God's Name—in Sufi terms—can't be effectively practiced on one's own initiative; it can only be conferred through a valid initiation. In the words of Dr. Nurbakhsh, "One can recite the words of zekr heard from anyone, but zekr itself can be bestowed only by a perfect master." (Nurbakhsh, 1979, p. 34)

In regard to this, Ramana Maharshi tells the following story: A king once asked a sage why he couldn't simply practice a form of the Invocation he had discovered in a book. The sage responded by turning to a nearby guard and shouting, "Seize the king and bring him to me!" Not surprisingly, the guard did not move. "Seize him!" repeated the sage. The guard remained frozen. Enraged, the king roared to the guard, "On the contrary, seize this so-called wise man and bring him to me!" The guard obeyed instantly. "Explain yourself or lose your head!" roared the king. "Certainly, Your Majesty", the sage replied. "I was merely illustrating a point. The Invocation is effective only if it has authority behind it; if the would-be practitioner attempts to command it on his own non-existent authority, it will remain inert. Only the King can allow, and command, his subjects to approach him; *they* have no authority to demand that *he* approach them. The Invocation is the servant of God, not man—and of the spiritual Master who is God's representative."

The *hadith qudsi* quoted above—"Pray to God as if you saw Him, because even if you don't see Him, He sees you"—can also be taken to refer to three distinct levels of the *dhikr*. To begin with, "I" am speaking God's Name, struggling to remain conscious of Him, or asking Him to reveal His Presence—to "me." The "God" I am dealing with on this level is what Ibn al-'Arabi called "the God created in belief." He is inseparable from my ego; in a way He is a projection of it; contemplating Him on this level is the same thing as contemplating myself: this is the meaning of "*as if* you saw Him." Nonetheless, as Ibn al-'Arabi points out, God still accepts the prayers we make to our image of Him, even if that image is an illusion—because, in another sense, it really *is* Him. God, as the Essence of all forms, is indeed worshipped—though in a veiled way—through the worship paid to idols, even if the idol is our own ego. According to Shankaracharya, the ego, even though it is the veil over the Self, is also a sign of the Self. It is true that those who worship God in the form of their own egos experience Him as Wrath; but if they were to allow that Wrath to take them beyond the level of personal and religious idolatry, it would be revealed as a face of Mercy.

At a later stage of the *dhikr,* the one represented by "even if you don't see Him," we realize that our image of God is really only the projected shadow of our ego, and begin to encounter God as He is. At this point the words of Abu Bakr apply: "To know that God cannot be known is to know God." The limited, egotistical "knower" is bewildered, neutralized; the unknowability of God consumes all our attempts to know Him in the fire of Knowledge itself; this is *fana,* annihilation in God. Here we are no longer invoking God's Name, but God is invoking His own Name within us. The Name no longer refers to a separate Object as perceived by a separate subject; God and His Name are One.

To catch a glimpse of the reality of God by forgetting yourself—or to remember God so completely that the individual self is forgotten for a moment—is to realize that you are seen more fully and more penetratingly by Him than you could ever see yourself. *Remember Me, and I will remember you* (Qur'an 2:152). And such Remembering in reality begins not with you, but with Him: *It is We who have sent down the Remembrance.* (Qur'an 15:9) To remember God until God is known as the only Rememberer is to become the mirror of Allah, and realize the Supreme Identity.

This is the final stage of remembrance, the stage of "He sees you." The limited subjective selfhood is first forgotten (*fana*) and then transformed into the object of God's remembering, an object which is fundamentally none other than God, since That One witnesses only Himself. This is the stage of "subsistence in God" (*baqa*), which implies one's subsistence as a Name of God, with no independent self-existence other than His. And though it is the third and final stage of remembering, it is also virtual, and effective, from the beginning, because it is the Truth.

According to Dr. Nurbakhsh, "Sufis must confirm, seek and see only the Absolute Being and not think about anything else" (Nurbakhsh, 1996, p. 27). But he also says, "To attain God one must wage spiritual combat *(jehad)* with the *nafs*, and Sufis devote most of their time to this combat. . . ." At this point one might ask, if the essence of the path is to remember God and forget the ego-self, how can the Sufi spend most of his time in spiritual combat against the ego-self, the *nafs*? If you have declared war on someone, you had better pay very close attention to what he's up to.

One answer is that the decision to seek only the Absolute will necessarily bring up everything in one's soul which knows that it must die if the Absolute is ever actually found. Thus the practice of attention is largely the practice of becoming aware of distractions. In his chapter on *mohasebeh* (self-examination) from *In the Paradise of the Sufis*, and in *The Psychology of Sufism*, in the chapter on the *nafs*, Dr. Nurbakhsh makes it clear that attention to the states of one's ego is the necessary complement to concentration upon Absolute Being. Since the ego does not really exist, to be aware of it is to detach from it, to deny it the food it lives on, which is identification, whereas to be unconscious of it is to identify with it, and consequently to remain lost in the illusion of selfhood.

So at the very least we can say that the purpose of *dhikr* is not to build a fantasy-palace of spiritual comfort with walls so thick that the clamoring of the *nafs* is drowned out, leaving the soul in a state of complacency and self-satisfaction which is mistaken for spiritual peace; such an attempt is itself a deception of the *nafs*. The true practice is to be simultaneously aware of the Divine Name, which (in virtual terms) is God's real Presence within the soul, and of the reactions of the *nafs* to one's awareness of that Presence. In this simultaneous awareness, however, there is no essential division; to divide one's attention, giving part of it to God and another part to the *nafs*, would be to set up the *nafs* as a partner with God, this being the sin of *shirk*. In God's Presence, the attention is not divided but unified, since He is the One, the Real. God's presence is ultimately the Witness, and the Witness encompasses all that is witnessed, with no essential division between them. In that Presence, if we fully embrace it through self-forgetfulness (in the positive sense of sacrifice of one's self-concept, not the negative one of psychological repression, which is nothing but the self-imposed division of attention between what is acceptable to the ego and what is not), then the egoic patterns and deep feelings which arise are not something ultimately other than God, something that we always have to keep a separate lookout for, but are progressively revealed as realities which move like waves through the depths of the Divine Nature. They constitute what Frithjof Schuon calls *maya-in-divinis*, the prefiguration of contingent being within, and as, Absolute Being. And Dr. Nurbakhsh was undoubtedly referring to these realities, in terms of the Divine wrath experienced by the *nafs* in the process of being transformed into the action of God—and simultaneously being revealed as always having been that action—when he said that in the sea of Unity we should expect to encounter sharks from time to the time, since the perfection of the Ocean requires the existence of such creatures.

The purpose of *dhikr*, then, is not to let us rise above the *nafs* through identification with metaphysical Truth conceived of as a spiritual ideal, but rather to transmute the *nafs* on its own ground, so that it no longer veils that Truth. Spiritual idealism wants to rise, let us say, from the earth of materialistic "ordinary life", first through the water of spiritual devotion and then through the air of metaphysical understanding, till it reaches the fire of identification with the Absolute; this is the very path taken by the *nafs* when it tries to "spiritualize" itself. Dr. Nurbakhsh, however, presents the purification and transmutation of the *nafs* as a motion in the opposite direction:

> The wayfarer's progress at the spiritual level of the *nafs* is downward. This is to say at first, the commanding *nafs* is governed by a fiery nature. When it descends from this fieriness to become the

blaming *nafs*, it becomes governed by airiness. Once it has descended from airiness and become the inspired *nafs,* it becomes governed by wateriness. Once it has descended from this watery nature and become the *nafs*-at-rest, it becomes governed by earthiness, gaining stability, whereupon it becomes characterized by humility, dignity, meekness and submissiveness. (Nurbakhsh, 1992, p. 67)

Remembrance of God transmutes the soul: will, feelings and thought. Because it is a constant and never-ending practice performed under vow of obedience, it pacifies and strengthens the will, thus accomplishing the first two of Schuon's stations of wisdom: detachment from all that is other than God, and combat against all that would distract one from the presence of God.

Because it is a Name which refers to and makes present a real Object, the invocation of the Divine Name transmutes thought. As Dr. Nurbakhsh puts it, "The Sufi is attentive to the Name itself, as well as to its meaning or significance. This is necessary since human beings have the habit of being attentive to a concept by means of words. Thus, when a word is remembered, the corresponding concept tends to rise in one's awareness. Attention to the Name alone . . . is a kind of idol-worship" (Nurbakhsh, 1979, p. 20). In the course of *dhikr*, by which we remember that God *Is*, ordinary dissipated thought is transmuted into the question, "*if* God is, then Who and What is God?" The asking and answering of this question continues, constantly changing, in the light of God's presence, until "I-and-You" is transcended. In Sufism this spontaneous asking-and-answering, on a level deeper than discursive thought, where question and answer are not successive but simultaneous, is termed *fikr*, contemplation. In the words of Ruzbehan Baqli, "Thought for the ordinary man is plunging in the sea of illusion, while contemplation for the elect is being immersed in the ocean of understanding." (Ibid., p. 56)

On the level of feeling, remembrance of God brings to consciousness the psychological knots or habitual patterns of psychophysical tension of which the *nafs* is composed. We have created these psychological knots to prevent ourselves from feeling our true feelings.

These patterns of tension operate on the level of the emotions by making us either dissipated and manic, or congealed and depressed, or both. On the level of the will, they make us lazy and/or driven; on the level of thought they render our minds formless and chaotic, but also filled with hard fixed ideas—all for the purpose of hiding from us what we really feel, and what we might really know. They are very good at what they do.

One of the primary ways that *dhikr* cuts through this mass of *ghaflah*, this "heedlessness," is by alchemizing the emotions. The practice is to use whatever emotions the *dhikr* brings up—fear, anger, sorrow, elation, mellowness, shame, disgust—any and every emotion which arises in a given moment, to deepen and empower the *dhikr*. Thus "the obstacles become the Path." In *dhikr*, the will is dedicated to constancy of practice and the intellect to attention. Once this dedication is established, the emotions rise and offer themselves to be transmuted. Initially they appear as distractions; ultimately they become food and fuel.

Emotions are energy; remembrance is attention. In tantric terms, emotion (on the level of pure contemplation) corresponds to an aspect of *Shakti*, and attention to a manifestation of *Shiva*. Attention invokes energy; energy empowers attention; the Union of attention and its energy is Liberation. Dr. Nurbakhsh describes this Liberation as follows: "The baqa corresponding to inner fana [annihilation in God's Essence, as opposed to outer fana, annihilation in His Acts] is one in which the very veils that are the temporary essence and attributes of the disciple's self are removed. Here, God neither veils the creation, nor does the creation veil God. The veil has been totally removed, and duality transformed into Unity." (Nurbakhsh, 1979, p. 24)

The emotional and psycho-physical knots are the fuel; the remembrance is the fire.

The practice is to feed the fire. Feed those knots to the *dhikr* and it will burn brighter and hotter, bringing more and more psycho-physical knots smoking and bubbling to the surface.

Behind these knots of the *nafs* are true feelings, which are not to be confused with those so-called "positive" emotions, or habits of auto-stimulation, that one is habitually using to distract oneself from emotional pain. These surface emotions are still part of the *nafs*; they are nothing but our way of avoiding the encounter with our psycho-physical knots, and are also a direct expression of these knots. Behind these knots of habitual self-avoidance are the true feelings themselves, the ones we may have spent a lifetime trying to stay unconscious of by distracting ourselves, creating false identities (which involve us with false situations in order to maintain and validate themselves) and generally polishing up our character-armor— notably *fear, hurt, anger* and *sadness*. No matter: feed them all to the *dhikr*. Posit them not as shameful vices or terrible illnesses or impenetrable barriers to God, but as elements of fervor, of longing for union with the Beloved. [NOTE: Depression, mania and panic are not feelings, but psycho-physical strategies for avoiding feelings. In depression we hide from them in a kind of auto-sedation; in mania we fly over the top of them; in panic we fight and/or flee them.]

On the level of the *nafs, fear* is the denial that all things must return to Allah because they are without self-identity, and He the only Reality. On the level of the Heart, it is vigilance in allowing no sense of self-existence to intrude upon the Presence of God. The fear of the *nafs* is transmuted into the vigilance of the Heart by means of Awe before God.

On the level of the *nafs, hurt* is the disappointment of expectations, the feeling of being teased, seduced or rejected by the person or situation we hoped to be united with. On the level of the Heart it is devotion to God as Beloved, whatever His actions may be, in the realization that, though He can never belong to us no matter what we do, we already belong to Him; it is to place ourselves in God's hands, "like a corpse in the hands of a washer of the dead." The hurt feelings of the *nafs* are transmuted into the Heart's submission to God's actions by the practice of accepting, in humility, all events *as* God's actions, and thus ultimately recognizing all events as veils and manifestations of Mercy: If God's Mercy has precedence over His wrath, then His wrath is necessarily a servant of His Mercy. Because God is the Sovereign Good, every way He moves us, every way he turns our Heart, is good for us; the experience of Divine Wrath is based on our resistance, not His intent.

Anger on the level of the *nafs* is the false arrogation to oneself of absolute power over circumstances, which is continually being frustrated, since we are not God; on the level of the Heart, it is God's righteous anger against this very arrogance, His overpowering demonstration that omnipotence is His alone. On p. 47 of *The Psychology of Sufism*, Dr. Nurbakhsh identifies Satan with the human ego, the *nafs*. Satan is the one who cannot be and yet desires the prerogatives of being, which is why he must make his living as a thief. Thus the word *kun*, ("be!") is not only the word of creation, but also the word of exorcism. The anger of the *nafs* is transmuted into the Heart's righteousness through swift obedience to God's command.

Sadness on the level of the *nafs* is the feeling that one is lost in an empty world, and that there is nothing beyond this world; on the level of the Heart it is the ability to repose deeply in Being. The sadness of the *nafs* is transmuted into the Heart's repose by means of nostalgia for Eternity, longing for a distant Paradise, which culminates in the witnessing of the infinite generosity and abundance of God as present in this moment.

These four primal emotions are alchemized by God's grace consciously received and cooperated with, a transmutation that occurs on the border between God's real action and the apparent action of the *nafs*—in this case most likely the *nafs-e mulhama*, the "inspired nafs", which lies between the accusing *nafs* and the *nafs*-at-peace on the scale of spiritual development (see Nurbakhsh, 1992, pp. 56–58).

This bare *schema* of the emotions and their transmutation certainly does not exhaust the subject. Every realized Sufi—and I am not among their number—will speak of the matter, if he or she is commanded to do so, in a different and unique way. My view is based on my own spiritual states, not yet free of subjectivity, plus the teachings of those wiser than I, and my own speculation on both that teaching and those states.

It is important to understand that fear, hurt, anger and sadness are not only subjective reactions but also objective realities; they represent forces operating on the psychic plane, beyond their momentary appearance in this or that individual—forces that are themselves reflections of metaphysical principles located on the spiritual plane. The ultimate metaphysical roots of fear, hurt, anger and sadness are to be found on the level of the fundamental Divine

Attributes; those who have a clear vision of these *hypostases*, as well as a vision of the nature of the *nafs* in light of them, will be able to deal with these primal emotions from a standpoint of transcendental objectivity.

From one perspective, the most fundamental divine *hypostases* are the Absolute and the Infinite. According to Frithjof Schuon,

> In metaphysics, it is necessary to start from the idea that the Supreme Reality is absolute, and that being absolute it is infinite. That is absolute which allows of no augmentation or diminution, or of no repetition or division; it is therefore that which is at once solely itself and totally itself. And that is infinite which is not determined by any limiting factor and therefore does not end at any boundary....
>
> The Infinite is so to speak the intrinsic dimension of plenitude proper to the Absolute; to say Absolute is to say Infinite, the one being inconceivable without the other....
>
> The distinction between the Absolute and the Infinite expresses the two fundamental aspects of the Real, that of essentiality and that of potentiality; this is the highest principial prefiguration of the masculine and feminine poles [Schuon, 1986, pp. 15–16].

According to Schuon, the Absolute is related to God's Transcendence, since it excludes, as non-existent, all that is other than Itself, and the Infinite to His Immanence, since there is no place where It is not. Yet it is equally possible to conceive of the Absolute vis-à-vis the relative, manifest world, as that Reality by virtue of which the very relativity of that world becomes apparent, and of the Infinite in and of itself, as a transcendent property of God alone, independent of formal manifestation—given that relativity, while virtually endless on its own plane, is composed of nothing but boundaries: only God is Infinite. Therefore we can say that the ultimate root of *fear* is the *transcendent Absolute*; of *hurt*, the *immanent Infinite*; of *anger*, the *immanent Absolute*; and of *sadness*, the *transcendent Infinite*. Before the transcendent Absolute, manifest existence has no "rights"; it is as nothing; it is already annihilated. In the presence of the immanent Infinite, all expectations are frustrated; closure cannot be made; to either possess or reject the loved object is impossible, since She is simultaneously beyond one's grasp and at the root of one's desire. Before the immanent Absolute, one's self-will is broken; God's Will alone prevails, because only what He Wills has the power to be. In the presence of the transcendent Infinite, all that can be desired lies beyond, and draws us beyond, all that can be seen or known in the realm of formal existence. The practice, then, is to recognize *fear* as the presence of the truth that only God exists, and submit to being annihilated; to recognize *hurt* as the presence of the truth that God exceeds and violates all one's expectations, and allow oneself to be passively moved in accordance with His Will, "like a corpse in the hands of a washer of the dead"; to recognize *anger* as God's command to us to cut the throat of self-will, instantly, and stand in wait for the dawning of God's Will, equally ready to actively cooperate with it, or to renounce action entirely if that be His wish; and to recognize *sadness* as a call from God to let what is dying in us die completely, and to rest, undying, in the depths of the Divine Nature, renouncing all longing for future solace and accepting instead the influx of present Mercy, in the realization that, while *all is perishing except His Face,* nonetheless *Wherever you turn, there is the face of God.*

Due to these correspondences with the metaphysical order, any feelings which go to feed remembrance instead of distracting one from it may be progressively transmuted into, or unveiled as, objective realities which transcend the subjective psyche, while functioning at the same time as the elements which compose that (apparent) psyche; these transpersonal feeling-tones are the reflection, on the affective level of the psychic plane, of the Names or Attributes of God. I would say—though God and the Sufis know best—that this is how feelings are experienced on the level of the spiritual Heart, which is not, as is often believed, the seat of subjective emotional reactions, but rather the site where objective Divine realities are witnessed. And the quintessence of these four elements, the mother of these transpersonal feeling-energies, is Love—the direct reflection, at the center of the psyche, of the objective Love of God. Again in Sufi terminology, I would tentatively identify this level of objective Love with the Spirit (*Ruh*), which is both Divine Love and the Universal Intellect, with absolutely no distinction between them.

When "negative" emotions are recognized as the veiled faces of Love, they are transmuted into avenues leading to Love's realization. Conscious *anger* is the defense of Love against all that would violate it. Conscious sadness—*dard* in Persian—is the longing for the (apparently) absent Beloved. Conscious *hurt* is the ability to welcome the "unfairness" of the Beloved, all the plotting, the teasing, and the slaps. And Conscious *fear* is the clear recognition, and full acceptance, that end of True Love is Death. Thus the four classic elements of *romantic* love, spiritually transmuted, stand as the four pillars of the throne of Divine Love.

When this is recognized, the second two of Schuon's stations of wisdom have been accomplished: the peace of intimacy with Divine Beauty, and the fervor which, by means of the attraction of manifest Beauty—Paradise—hurls one toward union with the Invisible Beauty—*Layla*, the Divine Essence. According to the *hadith*, "God is beautiful, and loves beauty." That "God is beautiful" is the archetype of peace; that He "loves beauty" is the archetype of fervor. God's nature is Beauty, and whatever is beautiful is intrinsically lovable; this is why the Sufis most often call Him "the Beloved" and not "the Lover." Peace and Beauty are intrinsically of God; fervent love of Beauty is intrinsically of man. Yet God also "loves Beauty"; this Love is His act of Self-witnessing. And in the identical way, God loves man. In the Qur'an (20:39-40) God says to Moses, *And I loaded on thee love from me, and to be formed in My sight.* Moses, here, stands for the Human Form, the *insan al-kamil*, which is formed and created, as Love, by God's act of witnessing His own Essence. *God loves man because God's rapture before His own Beauty is the essence of man.*

This rapture of Divine Self-regard is the first archetype and final end of all human emotion. Therefore, as human emotion is alchemized, the obstacles become the Path. In the words of al-Hallaj, "The gnostic's ladder is his *nafs*. His essence is the gateway to Union with God's Essence." (Nurbakhsh, 1992, p. 47)

Metaphysically, the truth that "the obstacles are the Path" is based on the nature of God as both transcendent and immanent: in the words of the Qur'an, *all is perishing except His Face*, and yet *wherever you turn, there is the face of God.* These are the last two of Schuon's six stations of wisdom: *all is perishing* posits discrimination between the Real and the unreal; *wherever you turn* posits identification and union with the Real. Given that God is transcendent and unknowable, He is realized only by *fana*—by the letting go of the perishing, contingent self and the world it perceives, till nothing but Allah remains. Yet the other side of *fana* is *baqa*. The duality of subject-and-object, based on our false sense of self-existence, is annihilated in *fana*—but in *baqa*, it "returns"—in appears in the realm of form, though understood to be unreal in the realm of essence. Where once it was a veil over Reality, it is now a manifestation of Reality. What were once the obstacles to the realization of the Divine are revealed as aspects of the Divine—and since this revelation, because it is objectively true whether or not we ever experience it, is virtual from the very beginning, the obstacles can indeed become the Path.

But the principle that "the obstacles become the Path" must not be confused, as it too often is, with the antinomian tendency which preaches that it is only through sin that one can become holy, since God is beyond good and evil, that the way to avoid existential anxiety and painful self-division is to make common cause with the commanding *nafs*, and obey its every whim. The divinely-revealed *shari'ah* of Islam stands as a solid bulwark against that particular form of self-oppression. The practice of taking the obstacles as the Path is not a way of shirking the greater *jihad* against the *nafs-al-ammara*, but is in fact the very center of this *jihad* at its point of greatest intensity—comparable, in terms of the lesser *jihad*, to hand-to-hand combat.

Hard, painful emotions are a lot closer to True Love than is the intoxication of the self-satisfied *nafs*, no matter how deft it has become at reflecting metaphysical realities in order to avoid being transformed by them. To face such feelings directly is to practice spiritual poverty, *fakr*, in its most concrete form. When intolerable feelings arise, and the power to avoid them is nowhere to be seen, then God is our only refuge. In the words of Dr. Nurbakhsh, "One who possesses such spiritual poverty is referred to as 'an impoverished one' *(fakir)*. Spiritual poverty is a state born of a sense of need, giving rise to the search for a remedy" (Nurbakhsh, 1979, p.14).

One consequence of such spiritual poverty is that we will not make the mistake of thinking that we can fight the *nafs* with our own self-will; not only is our willfulness too weak a weapon to overcome the enemy, it is in fact an aspect of that same enemy. This is what Jesus was alluding to when, in reply to those who accused him of casting out devils by the Devil's own power, he answered that the Devil would never consent to perform an exorcism because "a house divided against itself cannot stand." Our responsibility is to be present to the Presence of God, and let That One take the field against the rebellious *nafs* on His Own initiative, no matter how much suffering this might entail. This is the meaning of the Qur'anic verse, *You did not slay them, but God slew them; and when thou threwest, it was not thyself that threw, but God threw* (8:15), alluding to the moment, at the battle of Badr, when the prophet Muhammad (peace and blessings be upon him) threw a handful of pebbles at the enemy, after which the tide of battle turned. The same idea is expressed in a poem of Maghrebi:

No one can journey toward God on his own feet;
To arrive at God's district, one must go with God's feet.
[Nurbakhsh, 1996, p.34]

The essence of spiritual combat is succinctly expressed in the 41st chapter of the Book of Job, verses 1–10, King James Version:

Canst thou draw out Leviathan with a hook? Or his tongue with a cord which thou lettest down?

Canst thou put a hook into his nose? Or bore his jaw through with a thorn?

Will he make many supplications unto thee? Will he speak soft words to thee?

Will he make a covenant with thee? Wilt thou take him for a servant forever?

Wilt thou play with him as with a bird? Or with thou bind him for thy maidens?

Shall the companions make a banquet of him? Shall they part him among the merchants?

Canst thou fill his skull with barbed irons? Or his head with fish spears?

Lay thine hand upon him, remember the battle, do no more.

Behold, the hope of him is in vain: shall not one be cast down,
  even at the sight of him?
None is so fierce that dare stir *him* up: who then is able to
  stand before *Me*?

Leviathan, the sea-monster, is obviously the *nafs al-ammara*. God
here is denying, or actually satirizing, the foolish and arrogant idea
that the instinctual powers of the psyche are ours to use however we
will, that we can control them with ease because they are "who we
really are." To "play with him as with a bird" is to believe that we can
control our own thoughts simply by deciding to, while to "bind him
for thy maidens" to "make a banquet of him" and to "part him
among the merchants" refer to the equally foolish belief that lust,
gluttony and greed can be controlled in the same way. "None is so
fierce that dare stir *him* up: who then is able to stand before *Me*?"
means that God alone has the power to subdue Leviathan. Our sole
duty in the war between God and the great sea-monster is to "lay
thine hand upon him"—that is, not to repress or deny the *nafs al-
ammara* but simply to stay "in touch" with it, while in every other
sense *getting out of the way* so that God Himself can subdue it. To
"remember the battle" is to remember that only God fights this battle and only He can win it; it is also and equally to understand that
the remembrance of God *is* the battle, and that constancy in this
remembrance is entirely our own responsibility. The power to subdue and pacify the *nafs* is God's alone; our part is simply to *be the
channel* by which the power of God can come to grips with it. Thus
the ultimate weapon in spiritual combat is, precisely, the act of
attention, which in spiritual terms, as an established level of being,
is none other than *al-Qalb*, the spiritual Heart.

The relationship between "self-power" and "other-power" on the
field of spiritual combat is concisely rendered in these terms by
Frithjof Schuon, in the last paragraph of *Stations of Wisdom*:

All great spiritual experiences agree in this: that there is no common measure between the means put into operation and the
result. 'With men this is impossible, but with God all things are
possible,' says the Gospel. In fact, what separates man from divine
Reality is the slightest of barriers: God is infinitely close to man,

but man is infinitely far from God. This barrier, for man, is a mountain; man must stand in front of a mountain which he must remove with his own hands. He digs away the earth, but in vain, the mountain remains; man however goes on digging, in the name of God. And the mountain vanishes. It was never there [Schuon, 1961, p. 157].

REFERENCES

Feng, Gia Fu and English, Jane (1972), *Tao Te Ching,* NY: Vintage Books.

Ibn al-'Arabi (1980), *The Bezels of Wisdom*, New York: Paulist Press. Translated by R. W. J. Austin. From the chapter "The Wisdom of Expiration in the Word of Seth."

Kelley, C. F. (1977), *Meister Eckhart on Divine Knowledge*, New Haven: Yale University Press.

Lings, Martin (1987), *The Eleventh Hour: The Spiritual Crisis of the Modern World in the Light of Tradition and Prophesy,* Cambridge: Quinta Essentia.

Nasr, Seyyed Hossein (1978), *An Introduction to Islamic Cosmological Doctrines*, Boulder: Shambhala.

Nurbakhsh, Javad (1978), *In the Tavern of Ruin: Seven Essays on Sufism*, NY: Khaniqahi-Nimatullahi Publications.

———. (1979) *In the Paradise of the Sufis,* New York: Khaniqahi-Nimatullahi Publications.

———. (1981), *Sufism: Meaning, Knowledge and Unity,* NY: Khaniqahi-Nimatullahi Publications.

———. (1985) *Sufism III,* London: Khaniqahi-Nimatullahi Publications.

———. (1992), *The Psychology of Sufism,* London, NY: Khaniqahi-Nimatullahi Publications.

———. (1996), *Discourses on the Sufi Path,* London, NY: Khaniqahi-Nimatullahi Publications.

Schuon, Frithjof (1954), *Spiritual Perspectives and Human Facts.* London: Faber & Faber.

———. (1961), *Stations of Wisdom,* Bedfont: Perennial Books.

———. (1986), *Survey of Metaphysics and Esoterism,* Bloomington: World Wisdom Books.

———. (1991), *Roots of the Human Condition,* Bloomington: World Wisdom Books.

3

MORALITY AND GNOSIS

The letter killeth; the Spirit giveth life

INTRODUCTION

In modern psychology, the concept of "behavior" has replaced the concept of morality, and behavior is viewed almost entirely in social terms. One's soul may be profoundly corrupt, or one may be suffering great torment—deserved or undeserved—but as long as one's behavior is acceptable to society, nothing is considered to be "wrong". Depression, for example, is looked at as pathological not so much because it is a source of suffering to those affected by it but because it prevents them from being "productive members of society". Where once we had "sinners" who offended God—or, as the Qur'an puts it, *wronged themselves*—now we have "sociopaths" who offend the collective, which has taken God's place. It goes without saying, however, that if the collective itself is corrupt, deluded and self-destructive, no amount of "conforming to it" or "pleasing it" will do us, or it, one bit of good.

Psychology since Freud has tended to see feelings of guilt not as an internal check against immoral actions, as a protection against kinds of behavior destructive to ourselves or others, but as a pathological condition based on introjected parental or societal norms; the ideal of *freedom from guilt* has thus replaced the ideal of *freedom from sin*, from various vices that would "naturally" make us feel guilty for our own good. And the collective consequence of this suppression of natural guilt is the creation of a society in which the ideal of successful self-indulgence, defined as "freedom", has replaced the ideal of political and social liberty, thus compromising that liberty both by diverting our attention from the sort of intelligent action necessary to maintain it, and generating forms of self-indulgence that are so excessive and destructive that they seem to justify the creation of a police state in a attempt to prevent them, an attempt that is usually unsuccessful. There is certainly such a thing as "toxic" guilt, the sort of guilt that makes us keep on committing the very acts we feel guilty for, as a hung-over alcoholic will take a morning drink to drown not just his throbbing headache but also his feelings of guilt for last night's excess. This is what guilt must finally become in the absence of *forgiveness*, in a world which has lost faith in any Authority with the actual power to forgive. If we lack this kind of faith we will turn for forgiveness to the collective instead, to the "viewing audience" of the Dr. Phil or the Oprah show, who are voyeuristically watching our tearful confession of our sins for mere distraction and entertainment—a habit which is itself a sin in many ways; the collective, the viewing audience, has not the power to forgive. Furthermore, if we have been subjected during our lives to a morality without forgiveness, a *compulsive* morality that is used entirely as a method of familial or social control, not as a way of teaching what is objectively good for us and helping us to distinguish that good from what is objectively bad for us, then we will have a hard time distinguishing such false toxic guilt from true *intelligent* guilt; we may in fact find ourselves ashamed of what is best in us, and proud of what is destroying us.

This is why effective psychotherapy must never be divorced from true morality, just as morality must never be divorced from an understanding of the true goal of human life, which in "exoteric" terms is the salvation of our souls, and in "esoteric" terms, Liberation from the world of becoming; perfect total Enlightenment; Union with God. It is only in the service of these goals, and with the help of the grace emanating from them—considering them to be not only states that we might someday attain for ourselves but as realities which already exist, realities which call us to realize them—that we will understand what it means to become true human beings, and the precise steps are necessary to reach that state of "ideal normalcy". In the following essay we will consider what morality might look like from the standpoint of this ultimate purpose.

I

In some self-styled "esoteric" circles, it is common to hear phrases like: "The sage is beyond good and evil." Often this is taken to mean that, by virtue of his wisdom and/or spiritual power, he has earned the privilege of doing anything he wants. Morality is for the unenlightened; the Sufi shaykh or powerful shaman or "Crazy Wisdom Guru", in St. Paul's words, is no longer "under the curse of the law." This *antinomian* tendency may have been given a new lease on life in the west by people like Friederich Nietzsche or Aleister Crowley, but in reality it is ancient; when the idea that sufficient magical potency gave one the *power* to break taboo with impunity was replaced by the idea that spiritual exaltation gave one the *right* to break sacred law, antinomianism was born. Certain heterodox Gnostic sects within both Judaism and Christianity have been antinomians, believing that esoteric knowledge absolves the elect from conventional morality; the famous Sufi Mansur al-Hallaj *apparently* violated the Muslim *shari'ah* by such statements as "I am the Truth" (i.e., "I am God") and was executed for them; and Jesus himself outraged the sensibilities of the Jews of his time by shocking acts such as driving the money-changers out of the Temple, and by declarations like "before Abraham came to be, I am"—the last two words being the English translation of the first part of the Name of God in Hebrew, *Yah*.

It should be fairly obvious that the antinomianism of the magician Aleister Crowley is poles apart from the apparent antinomianism of Jesus and Paul, and in no way to be compared with the ecstatic excesses of al-Hallaj. Among Crowley's dicta were: "Do what thou wilt shall be the whole of the Law" and "Love is the law, love under will." His error, (intrinsic to the sin of lust, among many others) was to believe that love can be ruled by self-will. Paul's teaching, on the other hand, and Christ's, is that the only way to overcome self-will is to place it under the rule of love. According to Crowley, to be beyond good and evil is to reserve the "right" to break any law. According to Paul, only someone ruled by love can perfectly fulfill the law, and thus escape its curse.

But if the sage or saint or master or avatar is indeed "beyond good and evil," what does this mean? Nowadays, whether or not we admit it or are fully conscious of it, this phrase usually suggests to us a *right to sin*, a license to do evil. What else could it mean to no longer be bound by the law, except that we now possess both the power and the opportunity—and implicitly, also the desire—to violate the law to our heart's content? In line with this usually unstated belief, and to Satan's great delight, the notions of *enlightened sage* and *sociopath* have begun to become confused in the collective mind, a confusion that seems to be validated anew whenever a religious figure is convicted of a crime, or a criminal madman invokes a "spiritual" mission or the commandments of a divine "voice" or to justify his bestial acts.

To be beyond good and evil, however, to be no longer under the curse of the law, is not simply a license to kill. Rather, it is to be bound by essentially gnostic norms rather than behavioral ones.

According to the well-known Sufi proverb, "what is paradise to the believer is only a prison to the gnostic." This is not, however, because the gnostic is free of all constraints to his self-will, but because he is bound by a higher and more rigorous law than any that can be expressed in terms of explicit behavioral rules. The more rigorous the law we obey—if that law is truly an expression of God's Reality, and of His sovereign will through which that Reality is made manifest—the greater is the degree of freedom conferred by that very obedience. The believer is commanded to avoid, repent of, and make restitution for *sins of action*; the gnostic must do the same in relation to *sins of attention*. When Jesus said, "whoever looks at a woman with lust has already committed adultery with her in his heart," he was giving a concrete and easily understandable example a sin of attention, and thereby positing a higher, gnostic morality that transcends behavioral rules. To transcend the morality of action, however, is not to overturn that morality; as Jesus said, "I come not to destroy the law but to fulfill it." Nonetheless, those who are bound to a higher law than the external and behavioral will often appear to those whose level of understanding stops at outer, visible actions to be violating the sacred norms of religion; so Jesus appeared to the Scribes and the Pharisees when he performed miracles of healing on the Sabbath. In the Qur'an, in the *surah* of The

Cave, the story is told of an encounter between Moses and a mysterious servant of God whose acts are shocking and incomprehensi-
ble, a figure the Sufis identify with their hidden and immortal
patron, Khidr. Moses asks this person to be his guide, but the sage
predicts that the prophet will not be able to abide his actions. But
Moses insists, and so the sage takes him on. In their travels the pair
come to the seashore, where the mysterious guide vandalizes a fishing boat; Moses objects. Next they encounter an apparently harm-
less young man, whom the sage immediately kills. Moses objects
again. Finally they come to a town where they are spurned and
denied hospitality, and the sage responds by repairing one of the
walls within that town. Moses objects a third time, and the sage tells
him that they must now part company; but before they do, he
explains the purpose behind his apparently aimless and destructive
acts. The fishing boat was vandalized to make it of no interest to a
piratical king who was in the habit of stealing all the boats he
encountered. The young man was killed in order to stop him from
harming his parents, and so that God could give them a new son,
pious and dutiful. And the wall was repaired so as to prevent a great
treasure buried beneath it from being stolen before it came into the
hands of two orphans, its rightful owners. Thus the actions of this
mysterious master whom Moses could not abide are a shown as
examples not of an antinomian amorality, but of a *gnostic morality*.
They were based on *knowledge*; anyone who knew what he knew,
God willing and permitting, would presumably have acted as he did.
Clearly he did not act in obedience to his passions, or according to
false or incomplete views of the situations he encountered; he acted
on the basis of a higher Knowledge that was also a higher Mercy.

The major behavioral vices—anger, greed, lust etc.—remain vices
in terms of gnostic morality because attachment to such desires
destroys unity of attention. We are commanded to remember God, to
love the Lord our God with all our heart, soul, mind and strength,
to "pray without ceasing." We are called upon to make the living
presence of God a constant reality to us, and to see all Being as a
Unity in light of it. But if our attention is abducted by anger, geed
and lust, whether or not we express these inner vices of attention in
terms of outward sins of action, then we have violated that Divine

command. Such vices are universally recognized as evil because their outward expression so obviously has a destructive effect on human society. But there are other sins of attention which destroy our sense of God's presence and our vision of the Unity of Being just as effectively as anger, greed and lust—and many of them, because their destructive effects on human society are not so obvious, are not even recognized as sins. Among these sins of attention are *fear* and *sadness*, *dullness* and *moroseness* (when we indulge in them as methods of denying and fleeing from the Truth and Love of God), as well as *cynicism*, self-indulgent *fantasies* of all types, *levity*, *giddiness* and *scatteredness*. All of these fracture the Unity of Being just as effectively as attachment to thoughts of lust or anger. And if we will take a moment to consider their ultimate effects, we may realize that they are just as destructive to human society in the long run as what are usually considered to be the major sins. When we consider that a large percentage of our children, due to diagnoses of Attention Deficit Disorder and similar "syndromes", must be drugged in order to keep them in school, the dire effects of mental scatteredness should become immediately apparent. To process too much information (as we are increasingly being forced to do) is just as much a mental or emotional disease, just as much a sin of attention, as drinking too much alcohol or eating too much food.

Certain uses of the mind may even have positive effects on society—or at least effects that initially seem positive—and still be sins of attention. A scientist or political activist who one-pointedly, but also obsessively and narrow-mindedly, pursues the solution to a scientific or social problem, may do much good. But he or she is also creating imbalances in his or her psyche, imbalances whose effects on society at large must eventually come due. Even the philosophical or contemplative pursuit of spiritual Truth may, under certain circumstances, become a sin of attention. In the words of Frithjof Schuon, "mental passion pursuing intellectual intuition is like a wind that blows out the light of a candle."

So we can see that gnostic morality, far from representing a relaxation of moral strictures earned by the great sage as a reward for his spiritual attainments, is actually a subtler, more rigorous and more all-embracing burden of moral duty than any mere behavioral moralist could ever imagine. It is a burden so great that, in the final analysis, only God can bear it.

II

To get a clearer idea of what sins of attention actually are, and how they relate to sins of behavior, let us consider them in terms of what, in the western church, have come to be called the Seven Deadly Sins: pride, avarice, lust, envy, gluttony, anger and sloth.

Pride is the luciferian counterfeit of union with God, Liberation, Enlightenment. To be proud of oneself, for whatever reason and in whatever context, is to claim to be God in one's separate selfhood, whether or not one is conscious of making this claim. The one united with God is not, however, united with Him in the sense of two real entities which have now become one, but rather is liberated from the belief in himself as an entity who intrinsically possesses Being, in the full knowledge that the only One to Whom Being can be attributed is God. Thus the true opposite of pride is not humility, but self-respect. To respect ourselves is to respect the God within us, Who witnesses us as we are—and the only way to perfect this witnessing is to realize the Witness as the Self, and the witnessed as nothing in itself other than this very Self, Who is God as "I", not myself as "me." Pride is the origin of all the other sins, because without self-worship, the worship of anything other than God is impossible. In terms of behavior, pride licenses us to commit every other offense; in terms of attention, the essential act of pride is to place our attention on our own existence apart from God—that being the sin of Lucifer, the root of all the others. Pride, as self-worship, is the basis of all idolatry; whatever idol we may serve, whatever object we may worship in place of God, that thing only becomes an idol by *identification*, by our own act of associating it with our ego: every idol is a mask of "me". And here the self-contradiction hidden within the sin of pride becomes apparent: to worship oneself as God is to worship *another*—but God can never be "another" to Himself, because God is One.

Avarice is the compulsion to solidify one's separation from God by identifying with one's possessions, to so completely surround and entrench and fortify oneself with material and psychological goods that one begins to unconsciously believe that one will never die, never be forced to let go of anything one has ever identified with. In behavioral terms it encompasses all forms of greed. In terms of attention, it is the compulsion to studiously avoid any true knowledge of oneself by treating oneself as a possession, an object; as such it is the satanic counterfeit of *jñana*, or contemplative objectivity. Instead of knowing oneself as objective to the Absolute Witness within us, the *atman*, the Eye of the Heart, we treat ourselves as quasi-material objects held fast by a reclusive miser who never sees or understands himself, only his precious gold. Avarice is the luciferian counterfeit of God's will and power to preserve the existence of His creation.

Lust is the act of denying the personhood of another (or oneself) for purposes of pleasure. As avarice transforms one into a soulless object, so lust transforms the other. Lust is a denial of the love of God. God loves us because He is totally aware of us, or rather aware of us in our totality. He sees us as He made us, in terms of our original and perfect conception, not as the partial and divided things we have made of ourselves (though He is certainly not unaware of these distortions). According to the *hadith* of Muhammad, peace and blessings be upon him, "Pray to God as if you saw Him, because even if you don't see him, He sees you." God can see us but we cannot see Him, at least in His totality; the sin of lust, however, falsely inverts this relationship. The lustful one either treats his "beloved" as if he or she were not a conscious perceiver at all, only a kind of sex toy, or acts as if she (the object) had only an imperfect knowledge of him (the subject), while the subject's knowledge of her (the object) is perfect, resulting in a craving on the part of the object of lust for fuller knowledge of the lustful one—a knowledge that is forever denied her, producing in her a longing that the lustful one takes as a form of worship. In other words, the lustful one, in claiming to be the Knower but not the known, puts himself in the place of God. Alternatively, as we approach the "masochistic" end of the spectrum, the one ridden by lust may desire to be encompassed by the greater reality and consciousness of his or her object, thus falsely worshipping the other instead of God. But in both cases, the reality of full, sincere and conscious human relationship is contradicted by the denial of the reality of either the other or oneself. As a sin-of-attention, therefore, lust involves an imbalance in attention between subject and object, a partial unconsciousness of one side or the other of the subject/object dichotomy, thus making their ultimate re-union, and thus the transcendence of the pairs-of-opposites, impossible. This sort of imbalance-of-attention is analyzed in another way by Martin Buber, in *I and Thou*, as either a flight from the subjective self into the outer world, or a flight from the outer world into the subjective self—two forms of alienation that make any encounter between a genuine "I" and an authentic "Thou" impossible. Lust is the luciferian counterfeit of God's love for and delight in His creation, which He knows as of one Essence with Himself.

Though *envy* can take the form, on the behavioral level, of the intent to commit theft, it is perhaps the most mental of the seven deadly sins; it can be defined as the obsessive sense that what belongs to another should really belong to oneself (envy proper), or that what was once one's own, or is some way *intrinsically* one's own, now unfairly belongs to another (jealousy). In terms of the sin of lust, the need for union coupled with the impossibility of it necessarily results in sexual envy. But we may also be envious of the material, the psychological, even the spiritual possessions of another; in spiritual terms, to pry into the secrets of God instead of waiting on God's good pleasure to reveal or conceal them, especially when we feel that God has unfairly gifted another with the knowledge we crave, is also a form of envy. The other six deadly sins are usually defined in terms of sinful acts; only envy is more or less clearly defined as a sin of attention, which is sinful even if it never leads to theft, or adultery, or detraction, or spying, or malicious gossip. Envy is mental avarice, an avarice which blots the desiring self out in the face of the desired object; it might be defined as self-loathing objectified. The good we enviously desire is an idol to us, since we worship it with our attention; but we also despise that object (as we despise ourselves in desiring it), since we see it as having no intrinsic value in the hands of another. Its only "value" comes from its perpetually incomplete identification with our own unsatisfied, greedy little selves—and this (paradoxically) indicates that the opposite evaluation is also at work, the feeling that the desired object (another person's spouse, for example) only has value because it is possessed by another; as soon as it passes into our own hands it falls under the power of our self-loathing, and turns to ashes. As a sin of attention on the psychic level, envy often includes a "paranoid" tendency to obsessively analyze another's motives while remaining blind to one's own; we spy upon and plot against the object of our envy, while falsely seeing him or her as plotting against us. On the spiritual level, the sin of attention inherent in envy is the tendency to ignore both one's own intrinsic poverty and God's essential generosity, or to transform the knowledge of one's poverty into a false sense of grievance, and God's generosity into a false sense that He, or rather the world we worship in His place, is stingy and possessive; ultimately the envious one will see anyone's good fortune as his or her own loss. If we were to place our full attention upon God we would understand both His generosity and our poverty, and know our poverty as our greatest conceivable good fortune in the face of His generosity. Envy, in the sense that it claims the right to know every secret, is the luciferian counterfeit of God's omniscience.

Gluttony is the futile attempt to widen the area of one's own selfhood by devouring the world. Where avarice wants to possess and hold on, gluttony wants to incorporate. Gluttony is imperialistic, like a young king ruling an expansionist state; avarice is like an old king who wants to hold on to what he has already acquired, and to acquire more only to maintain his position, not to build it. Gluttony resembles an inverted generosity. Instead of giving out of our abundance, recognizing it ultimately as God's, we revel in it, and end by robbing God of what He would have given freely, taking Him for granted instead of accepting His generosity with humility and gratitude. Gluttony is complacency, as in the phrase "comfort food"; as a sin of attention, it is based on a denial of our intrinsic need, as creatures, for God's abundance, as well as on an unconscious *identification with God*, the One Reality Who is the nourishment of all, and to Whom all is nourishment. It is also a false identification of the world with God and His generosity; to the gluttonous individual, whether he be a glutton for food or a glutton for attention, "the

world is his oyster." Gluttony is the luciferian and *inverted* counterfeit of God's creative power.

To fall into the sin of *anger* is to claim the divine right to determine what has the right to exist and what does not. As pride is a
luciferian counterfeit of the Absolute, so anger is a counterfeit of
God's omnipotence, which has absolute rights over all things, and
both the right and the power to annihilate anything that believes it
can oppose the Divine Will. As a sin of attention, anger manifests as
an obsession with the existence of something, whether thing, person
or situation, that it feels has no right to exist. Anger demands that
any obstacle to the triumph of its will be annihilated *right now*; the
self-contradiction inherent in this sin is that by its obsessive attention it is continually giving existence (as obstacle, not as essence), to
the very thing that it wills not to exist; this is the frustration inherent
in rage. In its most intense form, anger counterfeits the Divine
Transcendence, in the face of which nothing "other" than God has
the right to exist.

The darkest of all sins is *sloth*. Pride is an attempt to overcome the
subject/object split by seeing oneself as Absolute and Infinite; avarice is the attempt to overcome it by identifying oneself with and
possessing the world; lust is the attempt to bridge the gap by possessing or being possessed by a desired object; envy is the attempt to
overcome the subject-object split by identifying oneself with the
possessions of another and losing oneself within that identification;
gluttony is the attempt to overcome it by incorporating the world so
as to transform the world into the self; anger is the attempt to overcome it by ruthlessly destroying all things that seem to come
between the self and its world, one by one. But *sloth* is the attempt to
overcome the subject-object split by sinking below it; it is an act of
inverted Transcendence. Sloth is a seamless union of complacency
and despair: complacency, because it is an acting-out of the proposition "nothing need be done"; despair, because hidden beneath
"nothing need be done" is the opposite proposition, namely "nothing *can* be done." Avarice wishes to possess matter; gluttony wishes
to incorporate matter; sloth wishes to *become* matter. If I am matter
then I am safe, because matter/energy can never be created or
destroyed, only changed in form. If I am matter then I am immortal,

because matter is dead, and what is already dead can never die. As a sin of attention, sloth is based on a total and willful ignorance of spiritual reality (resulting in an ignorance of psychological and material realities as well), an ignorance that involves both the repression of the subject, since if there is no Spirit there is no consciousness of self, and the repression of the object, since if there is no consciousness in the subject, then no object appears. The other six deadly sins are based on partiality and perversion of attention; sloth is the complacent, despairing, and ultimately futile attempt to destroy attention entirely. As such it is the luciferian counterfeit of the Cloud of Unknowing, the unknowable Essence of God.

The seven deadly sins, conceived of as sins of attention, can only be definitively overcome by gnosis, by the clear and objective understanding of the true nature of things. Behavioral morality serves this gnosis by restraining the passional actions that obscure it. Nevertheless, such morality can only be perfected by the full realization of gnosis itself, both because of the gnostic understanding that the ultimate motivations behind the passions are none other than erroneous beliefs about the nature of things, and because only in the established vision of plenary Truth can the struggling partiality of an existence defined primarily in terms of the apparently independent actions of its various creatures be transcended, and ultimately laid to rest.

III

In the myth of the Fall from the book of Genesis, to eat of the Tree of the Knowledge of Good and Evil is to fall from the level of a unified, *cardiac* consciousness that sees Truth directly, to that of a divided, *cerebral* consciousness based on discursive reasoning. Once sin divides our vision of reality in two, it becomes our duty to choose the better half; the fall into sin is also necessarily the fall into morality. And yet the effects of the Fall cannot ultimately be redressed unless we transcend the world of morality and return to Unity—a transcendence which, however, cannot be accomplished except through morality itself, at least initially: to choose the better half of a dichotomy is to choose what, in the world of oppositions and divisions, is nonetheless closer to Unity. Yet where *any* level of choice is still in force, the "choiceless awareness" of metaphysical Unity cannot be attained; and the only way beyond the partiality of choice is perfect *islam*, perfect submission to the Will of God. Morality is necessarily involved with choice, therefore it behooves us to choose wisely. Gnosis, however, is not choice but Vision; to witness Truth is to realize Unity, a Unity that embraces all conceivable dichotomies but is not determined by them. The relationship between morality and gnosis is expressed in the Qur'anic story related above, where Moses symbolizes law and morality, and Khidr, gnosis. It is true that Khidr vastly transcends Moses' conception of things; it is also true that if you want to meet Khidr, first you have to be Moses.

Among the dichotomies encompassed by the Unity of God is the one called "good versus evil." This, however, does not mean that God is somehow half good and half evil—as Carl Jung, for one, speculated in his *Answer to Job*. For the inconceivable reality of God to appear in relative, dimensional existence, dichotomies are necessary, given that polarity is the principle of all manifestation; without some kind of "figure/ground" relationship, nothing at all would appear. And there is nothing that can highlight the immense and intrinsic goodness of God like the dark appearance of evil. To be "beyond good and evil", therefore, is not to be half good and half evil, or to enter some nihilistic twilight zone where the appearance of good or evil is a matter of indifference. It is, rather, to realize the Sovereign Good. Partial good is always opposed to evil, and therefore involved with it, but no shadow of evil remains within the Absolute Good, because the Absolute has no opposite. The only way to be done with evil is to be done with the opposition of good *versus* evil, along with all the other pairs-of-opposites. Morality is the *Torah* of the Tree of the Knowledge of Good and Evil; gnosis of Absolute Reality is the *Torah* of the Tree of Life.

4

DOVES AND SERPENTS

On the Virtues and Drawbacks of Seeing Only the Good

As should be fairly obvious, an obsession with evil is detrimental to the spiritual life, and to life in general. It can result in fear, grief, anger, suspicion, and despair, as well as deluded and destructive attempts at flight and/or retaliation. But at what point does the entirely healthy practice of not letting one's mind dwell upon evil become a denial of the Truth, and consequently a denial of God? God is the Sovereign Good, but He is also the One Who sends both good and evil, the Principle behind *all* phenomena, not just those we judge as "positive". He is beautiful, but also majestic; He is merciful, but also just and rigorous. His Mercy takes precedence over his Wrath, but does not abolish it; rather, His Justice and His Wrath are ultimately the servants of His Mercy.

It is in seeing God Himself as He really is that we become able to see only the Good, and are justified in doing so, given that God is the Only Reality, the only One who possesses Being intrinsically, not as given, or borrowed, or stolen, from some other source. And the effort to see the good in all situations is a true approach to this realization. Unless we are fully-realized saints, however, life will inevitably present us with circumstances that are not only painful, but those which, on one level—an inescapable level, at least initially— we are both justified and required to judge as *evil*. How can we admit the existence of evil on the relative plane without losing sight of the Sovereign Good on the plane of the Absolute? How can we learn to *take refuge in the Lord of Daybreak from the evil of that which He created*?

Whoever denies the relative reality of evil in the name of the Sovereign Good cannot be said to have perfect faith in that Good, since to deny the existence of evils that are staring us in the face is to imply that if we were to admit their existence we would lose our faith in God, either judging Him to be in some way evil in Himself, or as unable, at least as far as we are concerned, to ameliorate or abolish the evils which beset us. Thus, paradoxically, a denial of evil is equally a denial of the reality and power of the Good.

Evil, as a privation of being—a privation that, if taken as a positive principle in itself, must ultimately be judged to be non-existent—is fundamentally absurd. And to grant reality to the absurd is to become deluded, and draw a veil over the face of the Absolute. In Dante's *Inferno*, Virgil places his hands over Dante's eyes at one point so that he will not see the evil of the Hell he is passing through; Jennifer Doane Upton, in *Dark Way to Paradise*, comments as follows: "That Virgil places his own hands over Dante's eyes symbolizes the 'Divine ignorance' spoken of by Scotus Eriugena; illusion must be understood, insofar as the absurdity of evil allows; nonetheless the Divine 'ignorance' of illusion is in reality the highest Wisdom."

Evil, as the "principle" of absurdity and privation, is inseparable from delusion, just as the rebellion of the will known as "sin" is inseparable from a darkening of the individual intellect; it is impossible to rebel against God without first believing that such rebellion is possible, which—given that God is Omnipotent, All-Merciful, and All-Just, and that nothing happens outside His sovereign Will—is in itself a delusion: a delusion whose consequences are unfortunately all too real. Therefore the station of "seeing only the good" cannot be attained without overcoming delusion, which for its own part cannot be accomplished without the realization that we, or some among those around us, or the society we inhabit, are in fact deluded. And both the real presence of delusion, as well as the fundamental non-existence of it, can only be seen by virtue of the Truth. The light shines in the darkness, and the darkness comprehends It not—but It most certainly comprehends the darkness—comprehends it as absurd, and as non-existent. Thus we may confidently assert that each concrete step we take toward the Sovereign Good will uncover another layer of delusion, and dispel it. And if this process is not in evidence, if the scales are not continually falling from our eyes, then we can be equally sure that our "progress" on the spiritual Path is largely fantastic and delusory. The closer we get to being able, without delusion, to see only the Good, the deeper our insight will be into the evils of society and the hidden agendas of the evil men and women who seek to pervert it, undermine it, dominate it or destroy it, as well as into the fundamentally deluded condition of these people, and the essential unreality of the evil they worship. This World is a system of collective egotism, to which our individual ego grants us membership. Insofar as we are in This World, we cannot see it. Insofar as we break with our ego, we break with This World. The more completely we break with This World, the more clearly we can see that World—and see *through* it as well, all the way through to the Face of God, the Absolute Reality, the Sovereign Good.

One approach to seeing only the Good as a method of realizing the Sovereign Good is to attribute all evil only to oneself; as Lao Tzu put it, "All things are clear; I alone am clouded". This method is fraught with dangers, however, among them being the danger of blaming ourselves for the actions of others in such a way that we come to believe that only *we* are real and the others unreal, thus increasing our egotism by the negative route of self-hatred rather than by the positive one of self-aggrandizement. This method can be powerfully effective only if we are truly at the station where all that exists are God and the ego, Truth and illusion; at this point we can legitimately assert that all Good and all Reality are from God alone, while all evil and all illusion are only from the ego, and that when this fundamentally illusory ego is dispelled, only the Sovereign Good remains. But insofar as we see ourselves as existing in relation to other selves, all inhabiting a collective "self" known as society, to attribute all evil only to ourselves serves delusion, not reality, and consequently pays court to evil. If we blame our limited and contingent selves for actions that are really performed by other limited and contingent selves, we lie to ourselves and thereby wrong ourselves. And those who falsely blame themselves may also get into the habit of unjustly blaming others, of "blaming the victim", and thus giving aid and comfort to the oppressor. The reverse may also be true; as William Blake remarked, "if you love your enemies, you may end up hating your friends". Sometimes evil will try to provoke our pity, using the argument that to practice evil is even harder upon the evil one than it is upon his victims. We can avoid such "sympathy for the Devil" by realizing, as Jennifer Doane Upton puts it, that "to pity the damned is merely a way of hiding from the deeper aspects of love; [righteous] anger, for all its problems, is closer to true love than this kind of cloying pity". Our love for evil men and women, given that we cannot know for certain the destiny of another soul, must remain provisional: ever ready to forgive in the face of repentance, never willing to extend love to evil itself, in a misguidedly idealistic attempt to love those who are totally dominated by it.

There is a basic difference between the evils that come to meet us on our path through life and in the course of the Spiritual Path (if we are truly walking this Path, these two will be one), and those evils we seek out on our own initiative, through either concupiscence, curiosity or false idealism. God will support us in our battle with the first, but will not automatically bail us out—in the absence of true repentance—if we foolishly involve ourselves with the second. The difficulty lies in being able to tell the difference. If we know our true path in life, then "the evil of the day is sufficient thereto" because we are able to recognize it as the Will of God—as the darker, and thus the deeper, face of His Mercy. If we do not know our true path, then we will inhabit a world where the evils of life, either deliberately sought out or helplessly encountered, will form a terrible and mean-ingless landscape of darkness and oppression, where the absurdity of evil will appear as the absurdity of existence itself, and God as a childish fantasy upon which it would be foolish to rely. To submit to the Will of God is the royal road to the conquest of evil and the real-ization of the Sovereign Good; to submit to some conjectural "will of the situation", as well as to the subjective fantasies into which we always flee in order to hide from this fatal illusion, is to embrace nihilism and despair.

But in a world like ours, the question arises: what evil in the world around us is *not* ultimately a part of our own path through life? We increasingly live in "one world" where the decisions and agendas of the ruling elites, or social or ecological breakdown or war in any part of the world, immediately affect all of us. In order to get a clear idea of the true nature of the evils that already beset us, or may in the near future, it seems that we must investigate the entire system of the world both in terms of general trends and, insofar as is possible, specific details. In view of the fact that such information is apparently necessary for the maintenance of simple realism and objectivity, how can we keep our balance and avoid obsession and despair? How can we retain our objectivity, in terms our reaction to events and circumstances, our vision of the metaphysical order, and insight the state of our own soul? How can we see the hand of God in all things, and recognize all events as ultimately nothing other than the manifestation in space and time of the Absolute Reality and the Sovereign Good?

Firstly, we must love Justice, and understand that Justice and Omnipotence are ultimately inseparable. In the words of Jennifer Doane Upton, "To cry out against Fortune while demanding Justice is a contradiction; in doing so, one turns away from God's Will and toward self-will...." If we understand that all events are authored by God, we will know them either as expressions of Mercy, or as manifestations of a Justice that ultimately serves Mercy. Those who love Justice will hate the injustice of the oppressor, but will not be led thereby into the belief that God is an oppressor as well. Injustice is concocted by man; only Justice emanates from God. And, as should be obvious, the best way to love Justice is to do it.

Secondly, we must realize that even though we only encounter those evils which are "destined" for us according to the principle, as expressed by Heraclitus, that "character is fate"—evils which, if met in the course of a life dedicated to God, will purify us and free us, while if encountered as expressions of a life dedicated to the passions will only bind and corrupt us—any evil which occupies the level of being upon which our consciousness resides goes to condition our character, and is thus a part of our fate; as the popular song expresses it, "what you see is what you get". This does not mean that we should work to deny the existence of evils that are obviously a part of the world we live in, but rather that we should aspire to rise, by God's grace and our willing cooperation, into higher worlds of consciousness where such evils do not exist, or where they are recognized as direct, albeit rigorous, manifestations of the Sovereign Good. And in order to purify our vision so that it may gain us entry to these higher worlds, there is nothing like Awe before the terrible Majesty of God. In the words of Hazrat 'Ali, "If you are able, increase your fear of Allah while at the same time having a good opinion of Him; the best of actions is to achieve a balance between fear and hope."

Lastly, we should understand that many of the evils resident on the level of being we occupy affect us unconsciously; This World is not only a set of circumstances we encounter, but a set of uncon- scious influences that occupy our souls and determine, insofar as we are unaware of them, both the quality of our consciousness and the nature of our actions. Therefore every evil we analyze and expose in the *zahir*, the outer world of circumstances, immediately (or eventu- ally) loses its influence upon the *batin*, the inner world of the soul. Insofar as we want to live in a "fool's paradise", a fantasy-world that, with the help of the system of collective egotism and illusion known as This World, we have created in a self-defeating attempt to protect ourselves from that very World, these revelations of the existence of evil, its nature, its agenda and its effects, will produce suffering; insofar as we are fully dedicated to the Truth and have conformed our lives to the Truth, they will produce only joy—a rare thing, for who among us can confidently claim that he loves Truth in its every manifestation and under all circumstances? The suffering produced by the vision of evil encountered by those whose lives are in service to the Truth but not yet perfectly conformed to It will have a strengthening and purifying effect which will ultimately flower, God willing, into vision of the Sovereign Good. Those who flee from this suffering, however, will experience the opposite effect: corruption of the will, poisoning of the affections, and darkening of the mind; and this is simple justice. Nor is the joy which follows upon submission to God's will, in the consciousness that ultimately only He is the performer of all actions (including our own), a selfish or self- enclosed joy: rather, it is the root and power of compassion. Only those immersed in the Divine Bliss can have perfect compassion for the suffering of those not so immersed—a compassion by which the pain of the suffering ones is fully experienced with no denial, no recoil, but one which remains at the same time, in its intrinsic nature, beyond suffering entirely. Pity for the suffering ones only increases their pain; a cold indifference in the face of their suffering, masquerading as *apatheia* or spiritual impassivity, increases it as well. Only a compassion that fully "feels with" the pain of the sufferer, but at the same time is totally beyond it and unaffected by it, has the power to alleviate that suffering, because it neither remains aloof from the other (false impassivity) nor identifies with the other (pity). True compassion is of God—which is why, like God, it must be both immanent and transcendent.

In the vision of the Sovereign Good we recognize that even the most abysmal spiritual power of evil, even Satan himself, has no power over God or apart from God; as Frithjof Schuon reminds us, the Devil is man's enemy, not God's. If we rebel against God or are seduced by the ego and the passions, then it is only right according to God's Justice that we fall under Adversary's power. And if the world rebels against God, it immediately turns (whether or not it is aware of this) to worship the Prince of This World, and earns the consequences. This too is just. The "one thing needful" here is to avoid idolatry, to guard ourselves against worshipping something other than God, something with no intrinsic reality—a thing whose worship nonetheless has terrible consequences. Devotion to governments, spiritual and political leaders, heroes, celebrities, races, classes, even true and God-given religions *outside* the Will of God turns them all into idols. All we need do is remember: *la ilaha illa 'Llah*, there is no god but God. The suffering we experience in the course of remembering this One Truth is purgatorial, not infernal. It is the suffering of purification, the suffering produced by the overturning of the idols in the Kaaba of the Heart. It is all hope, since its end is total submission to Allah; it is all love since its end is the embrace of the Beloved. Infernal suffering, however, is all despair; it leads only to numbness, frozenness, petrification, like those souls frozen in the ice in the Lake of Cocytus in the Ninth Circle of Dante's Hell. The whole idea is to locate and suffer the appropriate suffering, find and carry on the appropriate fight. As Hazrat 'Ali said, "Paradise is beneath the shadow of the swords". Satan is nothing but God's misguidance to those who choose to be misguided, God's punishment visited upon those who choose to rebel. If, by His Mercy, we come to see the Adversary as he really is, then he becomes a great teacher. The Qur'an teaches that Harut and Marut, angels sent by God to test man who taught magic to the human race at Babylon, first said, *we are only a temptation, so disbelieve not.* But many don't want to hear this; to them, a temptation is not a warning but either an unavoidable curse or a license to transgress. Fascinated with evil, they identify with it either through pride or through fear; these are the ones who will have to learn the hard way—if indeed they ever do. Instead of identifying with evil on the basis of ego, the true way is to impassively witness it with the Eye of the Heart— which is none other than the Eye of God within us, Who shows us His *signs on the horizons and in our souls* and is *Witness over all things*—and so break that identification. Evil is based upon illusion, and illusion comes about only through ego-identification with things, persons, situations or inner psychic states, and is dispelled only by the annihilation of the illusory separative ego through which all identification takes place.

Investigating the actions of evil men and institutions is not a denial of God's Mercy, but a meditation upon His Justice. It only leads to despair for those who believe that this world is all there is and who forget that life is short. The more clearly we understand evil, the freer we are from its effects. What was hiding inside our heart as a poisonous half-conscious fear is now revealed as an Act of God against those who have denied Him, as a manifestation of His awesome Majesty—a Majesty that is so Terrible and at the same time so Beautiful. If those evil men were to accept this Majesty as just punishment then it would be all Mercy, because His Mercy takes precedence over His Wrath.

So why do the innocent suffer? They suffer so that they may become *perfectly* innocent, and thereby enter Paradise—even in this life.

5

CAN JUNG BE SAVED?

A Sufic Re-Envisioning of the Jungian Archetypes

Carl Jung was an important figure to many of my generation, especially the poets. In the poetry scene of '70s San Francisco, he almost held the position of Chief Hierophant, guide to all the mysteries of the Unconscious. In the '70s, the counterculture, and increasingly the culture of the U.S. as a whole, was living through an Age of Mythopoesis. Jung and his followers were being read; Joseph Campbell (who ended up as "mythic adviser" to George Lucas for his *Star Wars* movies) was becoming known; and poet Robert Bly and others were laboring to bring the mysteries of Jungian psychology and mythopoetic literature to the masses. At the same time, Jung was exerting a powerful and destructive influence upon the Catholic Church which—having been all but abolished in its traditional form by the Second Vatican Council—was groping for some way to relate to its own rich mythopoetic heritage, so much so that Jungian psychology almost replaced the Church Fathers as the golden key to scriptural exegesis for Novus Ordo Catholics. This was also the Age of the Goddess, when western civilization, in the process of its self-deconstruction, was processing great waves of "matriarchal" material liberated from its repressed collective memory. While the Leftist/ Feminists were pressing for women's rights, weakening the family and destroying any viable social role that a man *as man*, or woman *as woman*, could base his or her life upon (this being an expression of the anti-sexual Puritanism that hid under the so-called "sexual revolution"), the tender-minded among us, both men and women, were deliquescing in the murky "feminine" waters of the Collective Unconscious. And it is certainly true that Jung's greatest followers of the second and third generations were mostly women: Esther Harding; Marion Woodman; Marie-Louise von Franz.

The best critique of Jung from a Traditionalist/Perennialist perspective is to be found in the essay "Modern Psychology" by Titus Burckhardt, which appears, among other places, in the anthology *Every Branch in Me: Essays on the Meaning of Man*, edited by Barry McDonald for World Wisdom Books. Jung seems to have a more metaphysical approach to the psyche than Freud, but this is not really the case. He "officially" denied the existence, or at least the psychological relevance, of the Transcendent (though it appears that he believed in God), and defined his "collective unconscious" as intrinsically incapable of being perceived as it is, being detectable only by the reactions it provokes; he saw it as based on residues of ancestral experience reaching back even to the animal level, residues which are presently mediated by the structure of the brain as it has evolved over the aeons. Thus Jung effectively deified the sub-human, by misrepresenting the psychic reflections of the Archetypes of the Intelligible Plane he encountered in his own psychic experience and that of his patients as the upsurgings of various primitive emotional/cognitive reactions. Consequently his goal of "individuation" simply mimics, and may in many cases block and subvert, the traditional goal of self-actualization, seeing that there can be no self-actualization without self-transcendence, no ordering of the psychic subjectivity except in reference to, and by the power of, a Spiritual objectivity that transcends it, witnesses it, and by the Grace of which it may be instructed, saved and healed.

What interests me about Jung is not his theoretical structure, which is both erroneous and subversive, but the various psychological and psychic phenomena he encountered in his researches. "Archetypes" such as the Ego, the Persona, the Shadow, the Anima, the Animus and the Self seem to me to be true psychic traces or reflections of metaphysical principles—or of the egoic subversion of these principles—which might be capable of providing both valid intimations of celestial realities and various perspectives on the "fall" of the human psyche into egotism and identification with the material world. The canny "hands-on" expertise that Jung showed in his dealing with these manifestations, when it was not vitiated by his "Jungianism", undoubtedly gave him the ability to act as a true psychopomp from time to time, at least on certain levels. (The same can certainly be said of his disciple Marie-Louise von Franz.) But he was in no way a spiritual master, and his strictly psychic approach to the psyche may have effectively blocked the further spiritual development even of those he was able to help. Suffice it to say that Jungianism is filled with errors and dangers, and consequently can be of no real help on the spiritual Path—until, that is, it is definitively criticized according to sound metaphysical principles so as to reject whatever is clearly erroneous and recast the rest according to the traditional norms of the Path of self-transcendence—a process I have begun, in a small way, below.

What did I learn from the Jungians? I learned that dreams are of great import, that they are a language of symbols, and that I knew how to read that language; I learned that psychological understanding is a necessary element of the spiritual Path, and that such understanding can throw a valuable light on life as a whole; I learned that psychic experience provides insight into dimensions of reality that are often neglected but that nonetheless impinge upon all of us; and I learned (though this lesson derived as much if not more from the writings of Ananda Coomaraswamy and René Guénon as it did from the Jungians and various writers influenced by them, such as Joseph Campbell) that mythopoesis—poetry, folklore, fairy tales, folk songs, scripture, myth per se, as well as most or all of the premodern arts taken in their symbolic or "didactic" aspect—concealed and revealed profound mysteries, so much so that it was correct to say that myths were often simply metaphysics told as symbolic narrative, while much of metaphysics was nothing less (as with Plato) than the discursive exegesis of myth. All these lessons suffered, however, from lack of a traditional, objective context that could unpack their riches and protect those studying them (including myself) from the intellectual errors and psychic glamours that unprepared excursions into the underworld of the "collective unconscious"— often aided, in my generation, by psychedelic drugs—inevitably carried in their train. I ultimately found that context, thank God, in the writers of the Traditionalist/Perennialist School and the lore and practice of Sufism. When Huston Smith first showed me Guénon's

Symbols of Sacred Science, I said to myself: "This is what I was looking for in Robert Graves' *The White Goddess* but never found".

The Primacy of the Unconscious

The idea that the entire phenomenology of the psyche arises from a substratum known as the Unconscious (personal or collective), which for Jung sometimes nearly takes the place of Divine Providence, inverts the true hierarchy of things; and since it posits unconsciousness as the source of consciousness, the only way consciousness can return to its archetype is not for it to illuminate the Unconscious, but for it to become unconscious itself. This is certainly not the outcome posited or desired by Jung, but insofar as the Unconscious is seen as paramount, the work of attaining greater consciousness, which is the stated goal of Jungian "depth psychology", is compromised.

Limitations of the Idea of a "Collective Unconscious"

The idea that all psychic experience ultimately arises from a Collective Unconsciousness puts mass subjectivity (which certainly does exist and is most often entirely unconscious) in the place of the objectivity of the metaphysical order. This mass subjectivity "stands in" for such objectivity, since it can be seen as relatively objective vis-à-vis the personal unconscious. But since the doctrine of the Collective Unconscious does not envision any level of consciousness or being that transcends subjectivity, collective or individual, it ultimately offers no way out of the prison of the self-referential Ego. Jung himself expressed the irony of this state of affairs when he said, "The object of psychology is the psychic; unfortunately, it is also its subject".

Denial of the Transcendent

The failure to posit any level of being or consciousness transcending the psychic ultimately results in the denial of God, or the relativization of God as merely one more "dominant" or "archetype" within the field of the subjective psyche, personal or collective. Thus Jungianism, for all its apparently metaphysical or at least mythopoetic quality, ultimately ends in simple atheism, just as Freud's psychology did. God is not a Supreme Being but merely a universal story—and you can't pray to, or beg mercy from, a story, universal or otherwise. This is not to say, however, that depth psychology may not sometimes uncover potent traces of the reality and action of God in the human psyche, simply that Jung's theories as to the nature of the Unconscious work against the correct understanding of Who God is and what He requires of us.

Psychic Archetypes

Jungianism misinterprets the Platonic Ideas or Archetypes as psychic rather than intelligible realities, whereas the phenomena Jung called "the Archetypes" are actually the *reflections* of the "permanent archetypes" (Ibn al-'Arabi's *ayan al-thabita*) in the shifting waters of the psyche, collective or individual. Jung saw them as arising from an instinctive substratum, not as descending from a higher, celestial world that is relatively eternal in relation to the dimensions of nature, history, society, and human life on earth. Consequently our interactions with these Archetypes, if based on Jung's conception of them, will tend to lead downward in the direction of psychic dissolution, not upward in the direction of psychic integration and self-transcendence. I am not saying that our confrontation with these archetypal reflections in dreams or in what Jung calls "active imagination" will always serve chaos, given that they actually are psychic reflections of higher, more integrated realities, simply that Jung's interpretation of them tends to stand in the way of their optimum influence and use.

The psyche is inherently multiple; the Spirit is One. For this reason, the interpretation of the archetypes in strictly psychic terms will militate against psychic unification, positing the psyche as inherently "polytheisic" in the horizontal dimension rather than as host to a vertical hierarchy of increasing depth as we move from Ego to Shadow to Syzygy to Self—a hierarchy which is the reflection (inverted as reflections are) of the Ontological Hierarchy itself: the higher the plane of Being, the more deeply the psyche must be plumbed in order to find it.

This tendency to "psychic polytheism" becomes explicit in the work of Jungian revisionist James Hillman. Hillman is essentially a brilliant nihilist, a true Loki-trickster, whose so-called "Neo-Platonism" only hides his lack of any sense of either pneumatic anthropology or metaphysical cosmology, of the traditional hierarchy of the microcosm (the human form) and macrocosm (the universe). If he understood that the Unity of the Spiritual or Pneumatic plane is higher than, and encompasses, the multiplicity of the psychic plane, just as the psychic plane is higher than, and encompasses, the material world, he wouldn't have had to posit his notion of "polytheistic psychology"—the idea, destructive to any form of psychic *integration*, that because the psyche presents us with a multiple face (we don't dream the same dreams every night, do we?), it must therefore be based upon multiple *principles*. This is a denial of the hierarchy Jung himself established between Shadow psychology, Syzygy psychology and Self psychology, the idea that hidden under the Shadow are the Animus and the Anima, which are more complete and more integrated, while beneath the Syzygy of Animus and Anima lies the principle of ultimate integration, the Self. The essentially post-modern idea of a psyche of multiple dominants with no hierarchical relation between them—that is, a psyche with no *center*—led him to the depressing postulate that we are all suffering from multiple personality disorder, since this is our intrinsic nature, and so rather than asking to be cured of psychic dissociation we'd better hurry up and get used to it. If he had taken the time or had the inclination to study metaphysics in any depth, he would have encountered the concept of what the Sufis call *wahadiyya* (Unicity), and what Frithjof Schuon named *maya-in-divinis*: not the many standing as opposed to the One, or as a sort of refutation of it, but the many in the eternal embrace of the One. Lacking the knowledge of such a concept, all he could do—in line with his postmodern ideology— was characterize all aspiration to Unity as a doomed obsession hatched by the Ego in order to deny, dominate and falsely regiment the spontaneous and sprightly denizens of the psyche; as the mantra of every good postmodernist goes, "unity is hegemony; integration is imperialism." In other words, in denying the supremacy of the Self, he mistakenly identified the Ego *as* the Self, thus presenting something that was really a rebellion against the Principle of Integration, the Spiritual Center of the Psyche, the Spirit of God, as a rebellion against the *Ego*, *princeps huius mundi*, the Prince of This World. (Antichrist, I dare say, will do the same thing. As we can clearly see from the history of the 20th century, there is no better way to gain followers for the war to establish universal tyranny than to present yourself as the Great Liberator.)

Psychology Replaces Theology

Jung was unfortunately quite suspicious of theology in any form, largely because he saw his father, a Lutheran minister, as someone suffering from an unsuccessful spiritual life due to a shallow mental approach to Christianity that blocked his access to the *existential* dimension of his religion, giving him no way of accessing, or dealing with, actual spiritual states or the transformations of the psyche they may produce. Jung was consequently led to deny the whole dimension of Revelation, as well as the function of the rational mind in interpreting this Revelation, as in the case of Scholastic Philosophy. This led to serious theological errors on his part. For example, because he had no adequate doctrine of *theodicy* (the explanation of the existence of evil given that God is both all-good and all-powerful), he had to posit God as in some sense half good and half evil—and who would willingly place his trust in such an ambiguous deity?

Wholeness vs. Perfection

Jung's suspicion of theology due to the manifest failure of his father's spiritual life led to a further suspicion of the whole idea of "perfection", which Christ commanded his followers to realize when he said, "be ye perfect, even as my Heavenly Father is perfect". Judging from his father's example, Jung saw the struggle for perfection as an ill-considered aspiration to a sort of false moral elevation that tended to narrow the base of the psyche and produce the kind of disequilibrium that could result in psychic collapse. Over-compensating for this perceived one-sidedness, he posited "wholeness" as *opposed* to perfection, recommending not only awareness of, but the incorporation of, virtually *all* psychic tendencies—except perhaps the most obviously pathological—thus separating psychic integration from the entire notion of moral purification and awareness of higher realities. The fact is, however, that perfection and wholeness are two names for the same thing. *Vertical* psychic hierarchicalization that does not produce a broad enough base of character and self-knowledge cannot establish any stable degree of spiritual elevation; likewise, any *horizontal* "wholeness" that effectively represses the aspiration to spiritual elevation has cut itself off from the very influences that can order and purify the psyche. The center of the mandala of the integrated psyche is a projection upon the horizontal plane of the *peak* of the psyche where it touches the Spirit; if there is no peak, there can be no center.

HIS POSITIVE CONTRIBUTIONS

Jung's strong points, where he did much valuable work, include his use of mythopoesis to interpret dreams and his parallel use of dream analysis to deepen our understanding of mythopoesis; his psychic hierarchy of Ego, Shadow, Syzygy and Self; his definition of the extraverted vs. the introverted character; and his system of psychological types—the sensation, feeling, thinking and intuitive types respectively. (This *horizontal* typology has certain drawbacks, however, in that it tends to veil the *vertical* hierarchy of the psychic faculties, namely Intellection, thinking, will, and affections. Jung's "intuitive faculty" is a horizontal reflection of Intellection; his "sensation faculty" is a horizontal reflection of certain aspects of the will, since the will appears most concretely in terms of voluntary motion, and in most cases cannot be purified and developed without physical work.) And Jung's analysis of the phenomenology and dangers of collective egotism or herd psychology, one of the major barriers to individuation, is of the highest value: what we believe or are attracted to or are identified with is of no significance whatsoever, except in terms of this or that collective enthusiasm or disaster, if we never become ourselves.

Jung's researches into the cosmological science of alchemy were a bit more ambiguous. The material he presents in *Psychology and Alchemy* and *Alchemical Studies* is very interesting, and he does succeed in throwing some light on those aspects of alchemy which relate to psychotherapy. But his basic assumptions remained materialistic and anti-transcendent, consequently he was unable to present a complete picture of alchemy as comprising the "lesser mysteries", and as a preparatory course to the "greater mysteries" that constitute the spiritual Path *per se*, or at least the higher reaches of it. It was partly to redress these shortcomings that Titus Burckhardt wrote *Alchemy: Science of the Cosmos, Science of the Soul.* (For some ideas as to how alchemy should be viewed in light of the spiritual path, see the section *Dimensions of Alchemy* below.)

A METAPHYSICAL/SUFIC
RE-VISIONING OF THE JUNGIAN ARCHETYPES

If the Jungian Archetypes are indeed reflections of the metaphysical or intelligible Principles in the individual and collective psyche, what specific principles do they relate to? Was Jung's understanding of the significance of the Archetypes he encountered in his exploration of the psyche valid in any way? Or must we throw out virtually everything he said about them? I will attempt to answer this by re-envisioning the Jungian Archetypes according to the "pneumatic psychology" of classical Sufism, and the pneumatic anthropology upon which it is based, supplemented with concepts from Scholastic Philosophy and other sources.

The SELF is roughly equivalent to *al-Qalb*, in Sufi pneumatic anthropology, the Spiritual Heart. The Heart is the center of the psyche (*al-nafs*, the soul), the point where it is intersected by the ray of *al-Ruh*, the Spirit, the equivalent of the Greek *Nous*, the indwelling Divine Intellect, also known as the Eye of the Heart. (Jung, of course, posited no Spirit higher than the psyche; nonetheless I believe that *al-Qalb* was the reality he called "the Self" without fully understanding its nature.) According to Sufi doctrine, the Heart may be "occupied" either by the *nafs* or by *al-Ruh*, but not by both at once. In other words, as soon as the psyche falls under the power of egotism, and consequently considers itself to be virtually self-created, it turns away from the Transcendent dimension; the Heart, the center of the psyche, becomes opaque to the light of the Spirit, and thus ceases to be—except in virtual terms—a Heart at all. In this condition the psyche effectively has no center, and is therefore subject to psychic dissociation and fragmentation. But to the degree that egotism is overcome, the psyche regains its true center. The Heart opens to the light of the Spirit, and progressively conveys it, over the course of the spiritual Path, to the psyche or *nafs* as a whole, ultimately transforming it from the *nafs al-ammara* into the *nafs al-mut-ma'inna*, the "soul at peace". [NOTE: Jung's Self Archetype is not quite the same thing as the Self or *atman* of the Vedanta. The *atman* is the Absolute Reality appearing within the human microcosm, where it takes the form of the Absolute Witness of both the psyche and the world. Jung's Self Archetype, on the other hand—as well as *al-Qalb* of the Sufis—are more like a reflection of the *atman* within the psyche. Jung's Self is *al-Qalb*, the Heart, while the *atman*—identifiable in Sufi terms with *al-Ruh* (the Spirit) or *al-Sirr* (the Secret) depending upon which authority one consults—is the Eye of the Heart.]

It is important to understand that the symbols of the Self that Jung identified in the dreams and spontaneous fantasies of his patients are psychic representations of *al-Qalb*; they are not the Heart or the Self per se. The Mandala, for example, is a symbol of the psyche ordered and constellated in relation to the Heart or Self as its spiritual center. The appearance of such symbols, however, does not mean that the level of the Heart has been effectively realized, simply that such realization is being "proposed". An understanding that the Mandala, or the Philosopher's Stone, or the Jewel, of the Sun, or the Child, or the Sacred Marriage, or the Wise Old Man are symbols of the Self does not effect the realization of the Self. As Jung himself discovered, psychotic patients whose psyches are in complete disarray may still have visions or dreams of such symbols. It is only when one is initiated into a traditional spiritual Path and dedicated to pursuing it to its end that such images may become more-or less reliable signposts—though the possibility of demonic delusion and counterfeit should never be discounted. In the last analysis, it is the spiritual Master who will be able to provide reliable interpretations of such visionary symbols, unless one has truly reached a certain degree of mastership oneself in this regard.

The "vestibule" to the Self archetype is what Jung called the SYZYGY: the union of opposites, the Sacred Marriage. The Self expresses itself as a polarity of opposites, while the Sacred Marriage, the union of these opposites (which also posits the transcendence of them) actualizes the Self. Here is where the archetypes known as the ANIMA and the ANIMUS make their appearance, the Anima according to Jung being the feminine soul of a man, the Animus the masculine soul or *spirit* of a woman.

Jung departs here from the traditional Scholastic meaning of the terms Anima and Animus. According to Scholastic Philosophy, the Anima is the soul or psyche as a whole, the seat of *ratio* (the rational faculty) and the affections, along with the other faculties of the soul, while Animus is synonymous with *Intellectus—al-Ruh—Pneuma—Nous*—the Eye of the Heart: the faculty that sees Truth directly just as the eye sees light. And so is it right to imply, with Jung, that the soul of a man is the soul per se, while the "soul" of a woman is actually the Spirit? It is not. Every human person possesses, virtually if not actually, both an Animus, an indwelling ray of the Spirit, and an Anima, a soul, a psyche—on pain of being less than human. So what was Jung seeing, if anything, when he discerned a feminine quality in a man's interiority, a masculine one in the interiority of a woman—a truth also alluded to in The Holy Qur'an when it says, *They* [wives] *are raiment for you and ye* [husbands] *are raiment for them* [Q. 2:187]?

It is true that a man, when archetypally considered as a member of the active sex, will tend to see his soul as a separate figure, and the Spirit as standing behind him as it were, as the informing principle of his own actions, insofar as he is faithfully submitted to it. (See *Alchemy as Spiritual Psychotherapy* in *Dimensions of Alchemy*, below.) The Spirit or Necessary Being, gazing through the eyes of the masculine psyche, beholds the entirety of Possible Being as its *Shakti*, in the person of Holy Wisdom. God beholds all the possibilities inherent in Him reflected in Torah (in Hebrew terms), or in *al-Umm al-Kitab*, the Mother of the Book (in Islamic terms), the Celestial Qur'an of which the written Qur'an is only a fragment, and which contains the eternal prototypes of all things. And insofar as a man stands in the archetype of his masculinity, he can participate up to a point in this mode of perception.

A woman on the other hand, insofar as she participates in the archetype of her femininity, which is spiritual receptivity, will witness the Spirit as standing before her and entering her; if she fully realizes herself according to her archetypal femininity, she will manifest in her own person the qualities of the psyche in the mode of the soul-at-peace. On the other hand, it is also true to say that "all human beings are feminine before God". If a man is incapable of receiving the Spirit in feminine mode, he will be equally unable to act on the basis of the commands of the Spirit in masculine mode. Likewise if a woman cannot realize the Spirit, in masculine mode, as standing behind her or looking out from within her, she will not have the capacity to be receptive to that Spirit conceived of as standing before her. Only if we know the Spirit, the *imago dei*, as already dwelling within us, can we open to receive It; only if we know ourselves as possessing no intrinsic being of our own except as we are receptive to the Spirit's gift to us of its own Being will we be able to actively see with Its Eye and vigorously act according to Its commands. So the strict schematic idea that a woman's interiority is masculine and a man's interiority feminine needs to be balanced by the opposite polarity of psycho-spiritual modes, thus making four in all: not a Syzygy but a Mandala.

The Syzygy, the union of masculine and feminine, the Sacred Marriage, represents the union of the Spirit and the psyche, the full conformation of the contingent psyche to the Absolute Spirit, the *salvation of the soul* precisely. One traditional symbol of this union, sometimes used in alchemy, is "the Sun in the Moon-cradle", a flaming sun-disk riding in a downward-curving crescent Moon as if in a boat. When the soul is pacified in submission to God it becomes receptive to the light of the Spirit, just as the Moon is receptive to the light of the Sun. In Sufi terminology, this is the *nafs al-mutma'inna* in union with *al-Ruh,* which together constitute the spiritual Heart, *al-Qalb.* It is true that the *nafs* in the sense of the self-involved, self-willed psyche, the *nafs al-ammara,* cannot share with the Spirit the center of the psyche, the station of *al-Qalb*; but some Sufis maintain that when it is transformed into the *nafs al-mutma'inna*, the soul-at-peace, it is virtually identical with *al-Qalb*.

In metaphysical terms, the Self is the psychic reflection of Necessary Being, the Animus the active expression of the Self in the psyche, and the Anima the receptive expression of the Self, the psychic reflection of Possible Being.

When dealing with the Jungian archetypes known as the EGO, the PERSONA and the SHADOW, we enter the realm of the fallen psyche, the *nafs al-ammara* (the "soul commanding to evil") and the *nafs al-lawwama* (the "accusing soul" or troubled conscience). The Ego is a necessary aspect of any psyche that is "normal" in terms of This World; a psyche that never develops an Ego is either psychotic or mentally retarded. However, This World, defined as the Collective Ego, is not normal in itself; it is essentially sub-human, the product of the Fall of the Human Form from its own proper nature as God created it—which is why the task of realizing our full humanity, of becoming in Sufi terms *al-Insan al-Kamil* or the Perfect Man, necessitates an internal break with This World. In terms of "worldly normalcy" an Ego is necessary; in terms of "spiritual normalcy" it is both our greatest enemy and something that intrinsically does not exist, any more than This World itself really exists apart from God. But no-one who has not reached a degree of worldly normalcy can attain spiritual normalcy; to attempt to do so is to court madness. There is a certain class of spiritual devotees known in Sufism as the *masts*, the drunken ones. These are people who have gained or been granted access to the Spiritual realm without first having stabilized their psyches in the worldly realm, or whose Egos have been shattered by a premature contact with the Spirit. In Jungian terms (which, however, are not entirely accurate in this context) they are similar in some ways to those who have encountered the archetypes Collective Unconscious without sufficient ego-strength to relate to them through conscious polarity, but have simply been unconsciously possessed by them, leading to Ego-*inflation* and a subsequent titanic fall, rather than to the kind of progressive widening and "limbering up" of the field of the Ego (neither a contractive hardening nor a dissociative fragmentation) that may ultimately give access to the realm of the Self. More accurately, however, the *masts* are those whose souls have been fragmented and shattered by their encounter with the Divine, which condition allows them to act as channels for Divine or angelic influences and messages, but certainly not as spiritual guides. To encounter them briefly and unexpectedly according to God's command may be beneficial to us, but to consort with them on a regular basis is detrimental. (In my experience, the hippie counterculture certainly produced a big crop of *masts*!)

So a degree of Ego-strength is needed at the beginning of the Path. A weak Ego cannot actively submit to God and its own annihilation, while a strong Ego may if God so wills. But in itself, the Ego, weak or strong, is a veil over the face of God, a dark cloud of self-involvement obscuring Divine realities. And once the Ego is established, it is inseparable from the PERSONA and the SHADOW.

In Jungian terms, the Ego is our image of ourselves, the Persona, the image we present to others, and the Shadow, whatever aspects of our psyche are excluded from consciousness by the Ego, including our Persona insofar as it is unconscious, as well as the Syzygy and the Self insofar as they are hidden behind the Ego's veil. The polarization between conscious Ego and unconscious Persona defines the vice of "foolishness"; the polarization between conscious Ego and conscious Persona where they are deliberately placed at odds defines both the vice of "hypocrisy" and the virtue of "discretion"; the polarization between the conscious Ego and the conscious Persona where they are deliberately brought into line with each other defines the virtue of "sincerity". Dr. Javad Nurbakhsh, in his *Sufism V*, defines the virtue of *veracity*, the root archetype of sincerity, in these terms: "Veracity is being truthful with God and the creation, both outwardly and inwardly, and being what one shows oneself to be".

The Ego develops by a simultaneous process of "projection" and "introjection". What is actually within the soul is falsely seen as in the outer world or *as* that world; and whatever aspects of the outer world receive these projected psychic contents are simultaneously introjected—swallowed by the psyche. The psyche is dissipated in the world, in worldliness; at the same time it is *possessed* by the world, controlled by it from within. In metaphysical/cosmological terms, the primal process of projection actually *creates* the world, the outer material universe—not in the same sense that God creates, however, seeing that man is not really a "co-creator", but a "sub-creator" who effects a "stepping down" of God's creation to a lower and more circumscribed level. In the words of William Blake from *Jerusalem*, "Man anciently contain'd in his mighty limbs all things in Heaven & Earth ... but now the Starry Heavens are fled from the mighty limbs of Albion" (Albion being the "Ancient Man" or Primordial Humanity, the equivalent of the Adam Kadmon of the Kabbalah); when Blake writes, "My Spectre before me night and day/ Like a wild beast guards my way;/My Emanation far within/Weeps incessantly for my sin", he is describing this fallen condition. The Spectre represents the projected psychic contents; the Emanation symbolizes the introjected world. In the unfallen soul, the Heart remains the conscious center of the psyche, and from that vantage point witnesses the world as the true outer manifestation of the all the Heart contains, the ensemble of the signs of God; this is the condition alluded to by the Holy Qur'an (41:53), when it says: *We will show them Our signs on the horizons and in themselves, till it is clear to them that it is the truth. Suffice it not as to thy Lord, that he is witness over everything?* But when the Heart is occupied by the *nafs al-ammara*, it loses its position at the center of the psyche and is consequently projected. It assumes the guise of a Spectre, an Ego. At the same time, the world ceases to be the radiant Self-expression of the Heart—the true Emanation or Shakti of the Divine Witness, the *atman* within us—and is transformed into a mass of alienated and repressed psychic contents, an "Unconscious". And as the individual Ego "creates" the individual Unconscious, and prevents it from entering consciousness by "guarding" it like a "wild beast", so the collective Ego creates and enforces the Collective Unconscious, which is the psychic aspect of *al-Dunya* or "the Darkness of This World". (Q. 41:53, by the way, reveals the true nature of the phenomenon that Jung named *synchronicity*, which is not based—as he and physicist Wolfgang Pauli speculated—on some mysterious affinity between mind and matter that might be explained by the "non-locality" principle of sub-atomic particles, but which simply reflects the truth that only God is the Real; consequently the world of subject-object polarities that both veils and reveals Him, that He both pervades and transcends, is ultimately unreal. To the degree that we believe it is real, however, an act of God that is one in essence will falsely appear—refracted through the prism of the Ego—as divided into "inner" and "outer" events. If we were totally free of the power of the Ego, *all* events would appear as synchronicities.)

The Ego, then, is the principle that splits subject from object, Witness from Witnessed, Shiva from Shakti, self from world. And just as it alienates the psyche from the world which is its outer reflection, so it introduces division and fragmentation into the psyche itself, and consequently into the psyche's perception of the world. The Ego presents itself to us as the principle of self-actualization, as the great Promethean unifying principle that promises to overcome the chaos of self-division and the alienation between world and psyche, if we only have the courage to "take ourselves in hand". But this is a complete delusion—a lie, in effect—which is why Satan, the archetypal principle of the Ego, is called "the Father of Lies". It is the generation of the Ego that itself introduces chaos into the psyche and its vision of the cosmos; when the Ego is dissolved at the dawning of the Spirit (*not* as it may be disordered and dissolved through corruption by the passions and the forces of the lower psyche), the psyche is spontaneously re-ordered and unified—the state symbolized by the Mandala, and named by the followers of Ibn al-'Arabi "the Transcendent Unity of Being". Here we can see how the alchemical idea of *psychosynthesis*, the unification of the soul, the forging of the Philosopher's Stone, and the mystical idea of the spiritual transcendence of the Ego, are really two sides of the same coin.

When the Ego comes to dominate the psyche through the primal separation between, and mutual alienation of, subject and object, it introduces a further split into the subjective psyche itself, that between the Ego/Persona complex and the Shadow. Since the Ego is the principle of partiality rather than wholeness, it cannot bring all of the psyche under its conscious dominion; consequently those psychic contents it cannot integrate into its narrow authoritarian system will fall into the Unconscious and come to constitute the Shadow. Since the Shadow is a legitimate part of the whole psyche, it continually attempts to reassert itself, much like the Freudian Id. But unless the psyche is consciously reoriented to the Spirit or the

Heart or the Self Archetype—which is where its lost wholeness still exists, virtually intact—these incursions of the Shadow will only further disorder the Ego/Persona complex, thus leading to "mental illness" and "social maladjustment". It is certainly true, as Jung maintained, that the quest for psychic wholeness or "individuation" must begin with an exploration of the Shadow. We must remember, however, that this quest can only succeed under the guidance of the Spirit, which means that any "individuation", if it hopes to remain stable, can only be the fruit of self-transcendence. If undertaken without spiritual guidance and aid it will result only in further psychic fragmentation and the progressive possession of the psyche by infra-psychic forces.

The final fruit of the fragmentation introduced into the psyche by the Ego, the final stage of the Ego/Shadow split, is the split of the Ego itself into the Ego per se, the self-image, and the Persona, the image we present (most often unconsciously) to the world. And here is where the ironic nature of psychic fragmentation becomes most apparent. If we are extraverts, we will attempt to present our self-image as our true self and impose it upon others, unconscious of the fact that we are thereby revealing a Persona that is most often at odds with our self-image, if not actively opposed to it. Likewise if we are introverts, we will commune internally with our own self-image, completely unconscious of the Persona we present to others; an introverted person who is simply shy for example (remembering that introversion and shyness are not the same thing; plenty of introverts are entirely content to be more-or-less alone in social contexts), will often appear to others as conceited and aloof. Thus we may define our egotistical self-love as projected on other people as "extraverted narcissism", and such self-love when indulged in within the confines of the Ego itself as "introverted narcissism". In both cases, our ability to relate to others is destroyed. No love worthy of the name, and no *self-respect* worthy of the name, can survive in a regime of self-love, whether it takes an introverted or an extraverted form. This destruction of our ability to relate to our fellow human beings, which effectively transforms them for us into objects that we see as either supporting or threatening our self-image, represents the penultimate phase of the fall of the human soul into the hell of the Ego. After this there remains nothing but true psychic dissolution: psychosis itself.

And so the initiation into the "lesser mysteries", the quest for psychic reintegration, begins with an exploration of the Shadow. But the fact is that only the Spirit can throw light on the Shadow, and so dispel it; only the Spirit can reveal to us the secrets of the *nafs*. If we attempt to explore the Shadow on the basis of the Ego and *as* the Ego, we will inevitably go astray; since the Shadow is made up of whatever is excluded by the Ego, how can the Ego explore it? When the Ego turns its narrow beam upon one aspect of the unconscious psyche it necessarily leaves all the other aspects in darkness, resulting in a condition of fascination and delusion. And the Spirit can only throw light on the unconscious psyche in any stable way when we have declared our allegiance to the Spirit and fulfilled the moral and ritual conditions that such allegiance demands. Leaving aside certain rare exceptions, this can take place only in the context of a traditional spiritual Way: paths that have never been tread before, paths without landmarks and signposts, tend to move in vicious circles, or else go nowhere.

In terms of the spiritual Path the psyche or soul is redeemed from chaos, self-division and alienation from the outer world first by actualizing the virtue of *veracity*, which heals the split between Ego, or self-image, and Persona; once we see how the image we present to others is different from the image we present to ourselves, the split between Ego and Persona is healed. Next, the Ego must agree to its own deconstruction by the power and guidance of the Spirit. In phenomenological terms this deconstruction will begin with the exploration of the Shadow, which will initially appear as the *nafs al-ammara*; this confrontation requires the development of the first of the three theological virtues, namely *faith*, the belief that the redeemed and re-ordered soul already virtually exists in "the mind of God" as "the presence of things hoped for, the evidence of things not seen"—and also of the second theological virtue, namely *hope*, the hope that this psychic redemption and healing might really be actualized in one's own life. This fundamental act of *islam*, this submission to What Is on the part of what is not, will begin the exploration and illumination of the Shadow, which will ultimately result,

God willing, in the appearance of the Syzygy, and finally the dawning of the Self, as true spiritual potentials which the Spirit Itself will give us the power to actualize. And once this actualization is completed, once the level of *al-Qalb*, the Heart, is reached, then the lesser or psychic mysteries, the return of the soul to its Paradisiacal or Adamic state, is finished, and the third theological virtue, the virtue of *love*, fully realized. After this the greater or Spiritual mysteries begin, which culminate, speaking in Sufi terminology, in *fana*—annihilation of ourselves as separate entities—and *baqa*, the subsistence of ourselves as unique sets of qualities, eternally created by God, within the embrace of the Divine nature, eternally objectivized before the face of the Absolute Witness. As Frithjof Schuon teaches, the "passional" or *psychic* soul sees itself as "I" and God as "He", while the Intellective or *pneumatic* soul sees itself as "he" and God as "I". This objectivization before the Witness, based on the annihilation of all the self-referential habits that constitute the Ego, is the essence of subsistence within God, and constitutes "eternal life": the transcendence of the soul in Spiritual terms results in the "individuation" of the soul in psychic terms. This is the station that Schuon identifies with the eschatological doctrine, expressed in the Holy Qur'an, which he calls "the Mystery of the Two Paradises": the Paradise of eternal Form, and the Paradise of the Formless.

The lesser mysteries are horizontal; the task here is to find and attain the Heart, the Center; in terms of Dante's *Divine Comedy*, they constitute the *Purgatorio*. The Spiritual mysteries, on the other hand, are vertical, comprising ascent from the Center to the celestial worlds, and ultimately to the Absolute itself; in terms of the *Divine Comedy*, they comprise the *Paradiso*. When the Prophet Muhammad, peace and blessings be upon him, made his "night journey" from Mecca to Jerusalem, to the Temple Mount, this represented his completion of the lesser mysteries; when he ascended from there to the celestial worlds in his *miraj*, this represented—and also really enacted—his completion of the greater mysteries.

This, then, is how the Jungian Archetypes might be defined, how they might actually appear and function, in terms of the spiritual Path in its Sufi rendition.

6

DIMENSIONS OF ALCHEMY

GENERAL INTRODUCTION

Alchemy is the art of attaining and perfecting the complete human form. None of us are born entirely human; of all God's creatures, the human being is the only one required to *become* itself through conscious labor, a labor that can only succeed by the power of Divine Grace and according to a knowledge of the eternal human Design to which we must conform ourselves if we are to become real human beings, not merely virtual ones. Alchemy is thus, in traditional terms, the "royal art", the central method of forging a psycho-physical entity capable of walking the Spiritual Path to its end.

Carl Jung suspected this, which is why he based his "archetypal psychology" largely upon his researches into the alchemical tradition. He failed to understand, however, that an art such as alchemy cannot be learned (though it can certainly be learned *from*) in the absence of initiation under a duly-empowered teacher operating within an intact esoteric lineage, nor did he understand that alchemy is an art whose true form and requirements cannot appear unless it is seen in the context of the objective metaphysical order, which in turn cannot be *effectively* discerned (in our time at least) outside the bounds of a legitimate spiritual dispensation granted by Divine Revelation.

The reader should note that in my description of the respective natures of the alchemical principles known as Sulfur and Mercury I follow the lead of Titus Burckhardt in his book *Alchemy: Science of the Cosmos, Science of the Soul*, which presents attributions of these two principles which are *apparently* the inverse of those given by both Paracelsus and Shaivite alchemy. In the latter, for example, Sulfur is related to the feminine principle, while Mercury—known as "the sperm of Shiva"—is identified with the masculine principle. Ignorant as I am of the intricacies of both these systems, I cannot elucidate this divergence with any certainty. But I suspect that it has to do with the truth that a man's soul (Jung's *anima*) is feminine, while a woman's inner center (Jung's *animus*) is masculine, reminding one of the T'ai Chi or "Ying/Yang" symbol in Taoism, where a black dot appears within the red swirl (red signifying Yin), and a red dot within the black swirl (black signifying Yang). In Tibetan Tantric Yoga, for example, semen is called "moon-fluid", thus identifying it—quite counter-intuitively! with the feminine principle, at least as this principle is conceived of in most traditional symbol-systems, where the Sun is masculine and the Moon, feminine. Tibetan Tantra is the inverse of Hindu Tantra in that the Hindu system identifies the impassive Witness with the masculine principle—*Shiva*—and the dynamic manifesting-and-reintegrating force with the feminine principle—*Shakti*, while the Tibetan system identifies intrinsic Wisdom—*prajña*—with the feminine principle, and the active Means leading to Enlightenment—*upaya*—with the masculine principle. *Prajña* is of the nature of Space, and therefore motionless, while *upaya* is the principle of Time, therefore dynamic. Suffice it to say that the polarity of masculine and feminine, spirit and psyche, Sulfur and Mercury can play out in a variety of ways, depending upon the tradition we are considering and the perspective we adopt. (It is a principle of esoteric mathematics that every duality takes two forms, every trinity, three forms, every quaternity, four forms, etc., depending upon which point in the duality, trinity or quaternity in question is posited as representing Source.) Suffice it to say that the art of Alchemy is in service to the "cosmological vision" whose archetype is the Immanence of God: neither a polarity manifesting as contradiction and conflict, nor a Unity that transcends polarity entirely, but Unity *within* polarity, and polarity within Unity.

I: NATURE, ART AND ALCHEMY:
AN ISLAMIC PERSPECTIVE

Introduction

One of the limitations of contemporary psychology is that it tries to gain insight into, balance, and stabilize the individual psyche while ignoring the fact that there is no psyche without a world—a world that, on the outer level, is "nature" and "society", and on the inner one, the psychic plane, and beyond that, the metaphysical order. Present day psychology deals with interpersonal relations and family dynamics up to a point, but does not see them as true objective factors, only as examples of a sort of shared subjective dream. And ever since Carl Jung developed his theory of Archetypes, and investigated the art of alchemy (with some interesting results) purely as a form of psychology, not as a cosmological science, if psychology touches upon the metaphysical order at all it tends to falsely view it as a Collective Unconscious whose Archetypes are not objective realities but merely dominant factors in the mass subjectivity of society and subhuman nature.

Both the outer world of the senses and the inner world of the eternal Principles are objective in relation to the individual psyche: relatively so, in the case of the sensual world, absolutely so in the case of the metaphysical order. Without a clear recognition of the objective matrix that embraces our psychic subjectivity there is no way out of this subjectivity; and few today realize that it is this very subjective self-entanglement—which in terms of spiritual psychology is called *egotism* or *ignorance*—that is at the origin of *every* obsession, every compulsion, every neurosis, every mental illness, except those obviously caused by an external factor such as physical trauma. In this essay I will attempt to present a picture of the objective matrix, both sensual and metaphysical, without which the spiritual development of the psyche cannot be actualized. It is certainly not necessary that the individual grasp the philosophical concepts involved for such development to take place; all that is required is that he or she understand that the visible world is as real as his or her inner subjective world, and that both worlds are created by a

God who transcends them, yet is everywhere within them. In the words of the Qur'an, 41:53, *We will show them Our signs on the horizons and in themselves, till it is clear to them that it is the truth. Suffice it not as to thy Lord, that he is witness over everything?* Alchemy is the art of perfecting the human form according to the design of, and within the context of, the objective metaphysical order, whose outer projection is the natural world. When the alchemical *magnum opus* is complete, man both transcends the natural order and epitomizes it, as well as taking his proper place within it.

The Human Form as Work of Art

The image of humanity as the destroyer of nature is so overwhelming in our time that we have forgotten the traditional doctrine that man is the perfecter, and also the perfection, of the natural order. A western Muslim equestrienne and scholar of horsemanship, particularly of the Arabian contribution to European horse-training, was once heard to say: "Whoever sees a finely-bred and well-trained Spanish horse next to a wild mustang, no matter how ignorant of horsebreeding he or she is, will recognize at a glance that the blood horse is the more beautiful of the two. Horsemanship is a spiritual art, because to train a horse correctly, so that animal and rider respond as one, is also to train one's *nafs* (one's lower soul, one's passions)—not by grossly dominating it, but by teaching it to follow, willingly, the human spirit that rules it." *And [it is He who creates] horses and mules and asses for you to ride, as well as for beauty; and He will yet create things of which you have no knowledge* (Q. 16:8). This passage may indicate, among other things, the transformation, through perfect submission to God, of the commanding self or headstrong ego into the self-at-peace, the psyche submitted to God. It may also refer to the body which will be ours after the Resurrection. The human-headed mule-like beast named *Buraq* which, according to legend, the Prophet rode on his *miraj*, is a symbol of the self-at-'peace.

This is alchemy: man is both the substance to be refined, and the crucible; God is both the Refiner, and the Fire.

Al-Ghazali classified alchemy as among the "intellectual sciences" that are permissible to Muslims, unlike such arts as magic and sorcery. We usually think of alchemy as an early precursor to chemistry, and that's certainly true as far as it goes. But there is more to this craft than simple chemistry. According to Seyyed Hossein Nasr (who, besides being a Sufi and a master of Islamic history and doctrine, earned a degree from the Massachusetts Institute of Technology), in his *Islamic Science: An Illustrated Study*,

> [A] few practicing alchemists were reported early in [the 20th] century in such areas as the Maghrib. But few realize that in those centers of the Islamic world where the traditional arts are still alive—in such cities as Yazd and Isfahan in Persia—alchemy still survives on a much larger scale than is outwardly suspected. Its dispensations . . . make the continuity of such arts as the weaving of traditional cloth possible.
>
> A few real masters of the art survive along with many amateurish aspirants. The masters are well-hidden and usually veil their activity by some kind of outward occupation such as shopkeeping or the practice of medicine. Yet they are not wholly inaccessible to those who really seek them. To meet with one of these masters is to be faced with the blinding evidence that alchemy is not simply a proto-chemistry, for in their presence one feels not as if one were in the presence of an ordinary chemistry teacher but as if one were bathing in the sun on a cool autumn day. They exhibit a spiritual presence, intelligence and inner discipline which proves that they are concerned above and beyond all charcoal-burning with the transformation of the base metal of the soul and the unveiling of the gold or the sun which shines at the center of man's being, were he only to lift the veil which eclipses it before the outer eye. (pp. 204–205)

In the history of Islam, alchemy has always been related to the traditional crafts, to medicine, and to art. As to the question of whether base metal can really be transmuted into gold, on rare occasions, by alchemists in their workshops, it was always debated and has not yet been settled. What we can be sure of is that the symbols and metaphors of alchemy relate directly to the purification and integration of the human soul—which means that in one of its aspects, alchemy is a form of traditional psychotherapy. In this special psychotherapy, however, unlike the modern brand, we do not "adjust" to society or our natural passions, but to our *fitra*, the eternal form of Humanity in the mind of God.

The spiritual secret of any traditional craft is: as nature is shaped and refined, so is human nature. As every traditional craft is also an art, so every art is also a craft; it is an alchemy which works to synthesize beauty and use, just as they are synthesized in virgin nature, or in the normal human body, and thereby purge the soul of the grossness or capriciousness that could conceive of an ugly usefulness, or a useless beauty. That so much of what modern society produces in the name of usefulness is so ugly, and that so much it produces in the name of beauty is actually useless—as well as being, in many cases, far from beautiful—shows how far society has departed from the sound spiritual principles upon which Islam is based.

The Great Work

A key concept in alchemy, which is derived from Aristotle, is the polarity between *matter* and *form*. Form is the true essence or spirit of something; matter (in the traditional, not the modern sense), is the formless, receptive field where that form manifests. Like a mirror, it has no form of its own, but impartially reflects any form that comes near it. In the case of a lion made of gold, the *lion* is the form and the *gold* is the matter.

The idea, in alchemy, is to bring the two together, so that form is actualized and matter spiritualized. An automobile is more organized and useful than a collection of automobile parts; a house is more complete, more fully realized, than a pile of bricks. When a field is ploughed and sown and fertilized, when iron is extracted from ore and transformed into steel by the addition of carbon, a kind of alchemy is being done. Alchemy works with nature to transform nature, to bring it to a higher level of organization, closer to form, closer to spirit.

All of us have ideas or plans or aspirations which are not yet realized. We also have capacities and resources which have not yet been put to use. To realize an idea is to embody a *form*; to put one's resources (which are related to *matter*) into the service of a form or an idea is to wake them up, to bring them out of chaos, to raise them to a higher level. Whether you are making a copper pot or writing a computer program or starting a business or developing your character, you will always need both a *plan* to follow and the *resources* to finish the work. The more completely you can bring these two together, in both the spiritual and practical parts of your life, the closer you will come to deserving the name of "human being." And besides the plan and the resources, one more thing is needed: the wisdom, the skill and the character-strength to unite them. In alchemical terminology, which uses the properties of certain metals and chemicals to symbolize the basic elements needed to complete any kind of work, three basic elements are required: Sulfur, Mercury and Salt. The *plan* of the work (the *archetypal or spiritual design*) corresponds to Sulfur, the *resources* (which include the necessary *psychic energy*) to Mercury, and the requisite *skill*, which can only be developed in relation to a tradition which incarnates it (these together constituting the *vessel* or *body* in the widest sense of that term) to Salt.

Perhaps the central concept in Islamic philosophy is the polarity between essence (*mahiyya*) and being (*wujud*), which is something like the polarity between form and matter, but on a higher level. Almost every major Muslim philosopher—al-Farabi, Ibn Sina, Mulla Sadra—has dealt in one way or another with the question of essence and being. According to traditional Islamic philosophy, for example, essence and being are only partially united in the forms of the world; in God are they perfectly united. In the single case of God, Who is the Unique (*al-Wahid*), *what* He is (His essence) is identical with *the fact that* He is (His being). *Essence*, as the higher octave of form, relates to *Sulfur*; *Being*, as the higher octave of matter, relates to *Mercury*; *Salt* is the power that unites Sulfur and Mercury, essence and being, as well as the vessel or matrix in which they unite. This union of essence and being takes place not only within the psycho-physical entity, but also in terms of that entity's vision of the world around it; each of these two unions helps to accomplish and complete the other. [NOTE: *Mahiyya* is essence in the sense of "whatness" or quiddity; the unknowable Absolute Essence of God, however, is not *mahiyya* but *al-Dhat*, which, since it is realized via the union and transcendence of opposites, takes as Its outer sign not Sulfur, but Salt.]

The Alchemy of Perception

Being is the "isness" of things; essence is the "whatness" of things. That a rock *is* is its being; that a rock is a rock, and nothing else, is its essence. Now this way of thinking will sound to many people like a meaningless mental exercise. After all, since no thing exists that has being without essence (since it wouldn't be anything) or essence without being (since it wouldn't be), and given that being and essence can only be separated within the mind, then why separate them? Why, except to create an empty illusion?

The answer to this question, or one answer, is—in the words of William Blake—"to cleanse the doors of perception." If you drive by an oak tree that you've whizzed past a thousand times before, you will tend not to really see it; you will take it for granted. But if one day you were to see an oak tree, normal in every way except that it was hanging in mid-air, it would rivet your attention. You would see it in dazzling clarity and incandescent detail. The "real" tree was of no particular interest to you, but this "unreal" tree, this *apparitional* one—how vivid it is; how *real*.

The alchemy of essence and being is to separate them within the mind, and then reunite them on a higher level. This separation and reunion is what all true art does, to break us free from our stale habits of perception. In a classical Persian miniature, the images of the rocks, the trees, the birds, the human figures take place in a magical world of their own, in what is called the *alam al-mithal*, the Imaginal Plane where eternal truths appear as living beings, as they often do in dreams. The great Persian painter creates this impression simply by removing the literal being of his subject, and leaving only the essence. What was once given existence by air and water and wood and stone is now embodied in the existence paint and panel. His painting is obviously not a reproduction of nature, like a painting by a "realistic" or "naturalistic" artist; the perspective is collapsed, for one thing, so that everything appears as if woven into a carpet or painted on a screen. It is made like this deliberately so that it will appear as an apparition, an image, not an imitation or counterfeit of the "real thing", which Islam forbids as a form of idolatry. This is how it reveals the essence of its subject, so that, when we find ourselves walking through a land of rocks and trees, the trees filled with singing birds, and happen to recall the image of a Persian miniature, the imaginary landscape and the "real" one may suddenly merge in our consciousness. When this happens, the landscape suddenly becomes transparent—not to sunlight or human vision, but to *meaning*. The world appears not as a set of material objects and forces, but as a pattern composed of the living signs of God's presence: *Wherever you turn, there is the face of God.*

If we always think we know *what* things are, we may forget to realize *that* they are. Our world will become matter-of-fact, boring, literal—opaque to the Light of God. This is a state of mind the alchemists symbolized as *lead,* where being and essence, or Source (God) and His manifestation (nature) are chaotically mixed or crushed together. In the art of alchemy, these two must first be separated, and then reunited on a higher level, so that essence *reveals* being instead of hiding it; this is what is meant by the alchemical recipe *solve et coagula,* "dissolve, then coagulate". This higher union of being and essence produces the condition that the alchemists call *gold*; when we see nature as composed of nothing but the signs of God, we live in a *golden world.* To stop viewing the world as a materialistic machine and start seeing it as a carpet woven with the mysterious signs of God is to transmute lead into gold.

This is the alchemy which all true art serves. As the human substance is purified through the remembrance of God, nature becomes a vision of the signs of God. And as our vision of nature is refined through art, the human substance is refined as well, so that it can more perfectly reflect its Divine Source. The world around us is transformed into the Walled Garden of the Mysteries, the image of Paradise.

II: MORTIFICATION, DEPRESSION,
AND THE DARK NIGHT OF THE SOUL

The science and art of alchemy teaches that a properly human soul cannot be forged without the breakdown of the *subhuman* soul of the "natural man"—in Sufi terms the *nafs al-ammara*—without the loosening of its grip upon the human faculties so that they may be conformed, not to the subconscious passions, but to the conscious Spirit; in this it is analogous, though on a more circumscribed and essentially psycho-physical level, to the Sufi doctrine of *fana* (ego-annihilation) and *baqa* (subsistence in God). If the crop of integral humanity is to sown, cultivated and harvested, the ground of the soul must first be cleared, plowed and harrowed; its resistance to spiritual fertility must be broken up.

The three basic phases of the alchemical Great Work are *melanosis* ("blackening", spiritual mortification, symbolized by the metal lead), *leucosis* ("whitening", spiritual receptivity, symbolized by silver), and *iosis* ("reddening", spiritual realization, symbolized by gold); in terms of the classical stages of the mystical way, these correspond to Purgation, Illumination and Union. Nothing can be accomplished on the Spiritual Path without mortification of the ego; those "spiritualities" which give access to apparently exalted psychic states without affecting, or even calling for, a death to the old self are delusive, possibly even Satanic: twice born needs once dead.

Sometimes this mortification, this *melanosis* may be deliberately produced through asceticism and self-mortification (though in the absence of Grace such asceticism is usually nothing but spiritual egotism, an exercise in self-will); at other times it is directly *infused* by Providence. The hardships and tragedies of life—in the presence of a true spiritual doctrine, the Grace of God, and the requisite skill—can be turned to the purpose of spiritual purification; this is deepest and most radical method of transmuting personal tragedy into great good fortune. But at other times a darkness will come over the soul for no apparent reason. God simply decides to withdraw His support and favor from the soul sunk in the world of material nature ruled by the passions, so as to call it to something higher. The Prophet Elijah flees into the wilderness to escape the tyrannical and idolatrous King Ahab (the ego), where he is fed by ravens (the dark wisdom of God); Job, due to Satan's wager with Yah-weh, loses all he has—wealth, health and family—undergoes a true *metanoia*, meets God face-to-face, and is ultimately given a new life much greater his former one because it is now enriched by Wisdom. And there is also some truth in the notion that the vulgarity, chaos and terror of modern life may in themselves act as a kind of mortification—if, that is, we avoid the temptation of escaping from them by adopting the very toxic passions and distractions they offers us, and so seeing them for what they really are.

The human psyche is not designed to be self-sufficient; it is designed to reflect, and conform itself to, the light of the Spirit. If it does not consciously conform itself to the Spirit's call, it will be taken by matter, by a cold materialism, a leaden heaviness that crushes out all hope. And we will usually not be willing to sacrifice our attachment to the psychic level until such leadenness threatens to turn our soul into a sepulchre filled with death and corruption.

The psyche doesn't "want" us to be aware of this heaviness and paralysis, however, even if we are already immersed in it; that's why it secretes various delusive glamours so as to hide from us our real condition, and why the *collective* psyche (with the help of the social engineers) creates its fantastic "entertainment culture" filled with "weapons of mass distraction". Psychic glamour is not always entirely delusive, however; it sometimes partakes of *vidya-maya* ("wisdom-appearance") as well as *avidya-maya* ("ignorance-appearance")—by which I mean that physical and social realities, as well as Spiritual ones, sometimes initially appear to us in dramatized symbolic form on the stage of the psyche; if this were not so, we could derive no psychological or metaphysical insight from dreams. But just as the alcoholic only increases his dryness by drinking, so the one who holds on to the psyche and the glamour of the psyche for longer than the appointed time will encounter only lead, and leaden ashes.

According to a proverb of the alchemists, quoted here in William Blake's rendition of it, "all that can be destroyed must be destroyed!". Psychic glamour is a kind of hemorrhage, like that produced by alcohol or cocaine or psychedelic drugs. We feel that we are in the midst of all the richness of life, then wake up to find ourselves lying in a pool of our own blood. This sort of hemorrhage, if we survive it, may (God willing) act to burn out and exhaust our attachment to psychic glamour. If so, it will be succeeded by true mortification, true *melanosis*, in which we will doubtless lose our life, but lose it for His sake. (A strictly accurate cinematic representation of the stage of *melanosis*—as well as *leucosis* and perhaps the beginning of *iosis*— may be found in Robert Duvall's motion picture, *Tender Mercies*.)

One of the first steps in the alchemical process, then, is to burn everything that is combustible, to reduce everything we can— everything that is cut off from the eternal Principles, that is involved with the ego, and therefore intrinsically mortal—to ashes and cin- ders; in the famous words of poet and priest John Donne, "Death, thou shalt die!" The fire is the fire of the Spirit, and the ashes—the substance that has been stripped of all that is time-bound, contin- gent and perishable—are the *prima materia*, which on one level is nothing less than the passive pole of the Divine Nature, the imper- ishable Substance of God which is eternally formed and imprinted by the eternal Act of God. (The uncovering of the Divine Substance is *leucosis*; the formation and imprinting of that Substance by the Divine Act, *iosis*.) We are born with millions of inherited psychic tendencies, only a few of which can be brought into the magnetic field of the Spirit by conscious effort. The rest, the ones that are cen- trifugal rather than centripetal, that want to dissipate themselves in flight from God instead of returning to their Origin, must be burned in the fire of their own passions (which is the secret and darker face of the Spirit) until all is reduced to ashes.

The time of ashes is the time of the mortification of self-will, the stage that San Juan de la Cruz called "the dark night of the soul". It may seem in some ways like a clinical depression, or even by accom- panied by such a depression, but the two are not really the same. In a depression we hate ourselves, fight against ourselves; we can't pre- vent our unresolved psychic conflicts from burdening and embitter- ing us. The dark night of the soul, on the other hand, happens only to those who are on a serious spiritual Path. The spiritual consola- tion, the sweetness and light of the earlier stages of the Path simply disappear. None of our prayers or meditation practices "work" any more, and we are left face-to-face with a great void. Secondarily speaking, we may become depressed upon encountering this void, but that's not quite the same thing. A clinical depression takes place entirely within the body and the psyche. In some ways it may be even more physical than psychic, since vegetative depression (when it does not primarily spring from some organic disease), though it may be accompanied by feelings of sorrow (or anger, or fear) is not in itself an emotion, but rather—like panic—a psycho-physical strategy for avoiding emotion. (Traditional Chinese medicine sees both depression and anger as related to the liver, which would seem to confirm Freud's intuition that depression is introverted anger, anger turned against the self; this would also explain why herbs such as St. John's wort, and possibly milk thistle, are effective against depression, since they detoxify the liver. And a particular *qigong* exercise, where the right hand sweeps over the heart and liver, is prescribed for depression.) The dark night of the soul, on the other hand, is the time when the light of the Spirit is withdrawn from the psyche, in order to lead us on from psyche to Spirit.

And yet the two are related. In the dark night, we have completely lost the power to direct our own spiritual life. In a depression we are threatened with the loss of the ability to lead our own lives in the direction we want them to go, but are still fighting (often on a deeply unconscious level) to get that ability back, otherwise we wouldn't be depressed; the anger that usually underlies depression is an expression of this frustrated effort, which is based on a lack of true submission to God. If we have sincerely been trying to lead our daily lives as a spiritual path, however, a depression may present us with an opportunity to enter that very dark night: if God takes our coat, we can decide to stop struggling to get it back, and give Him our shirt as well.

According to traditional pneumatic anthropology, the soul is composed primarily of intellect and will ("intellect" here referring to *ratio* or *dianoia*, the rational faculty, not to *Nous* or *Intellectus*— the ability to perceive Truth directly just as the eye perceives light— which is a faculty of the Spirit), and the root of the spiritual life is the mortification of the will. (According to this particular perspective, the affections are considered to be an aspect or "disposition" of the will.) Before such mortification takes place, before we learn how to say "not my will but Thine be done", our intellect will be *natural*, purely psychic, based solely on the abilities we were born with and our acquired skills, impressions and knowledge. Indulgence in psychic glamour is merely one manifestation of this natural intellect. But when we submit our will to God's will, the intellect changes. Our glib brilliance may be mortified; we may feel as if we are becoming old, dull and stupid. Thought, feeling, intuition, sensation, imagination, memory—all the faculties of the soul are darkened. And what emerges from this darkness is no longer the being that used to be called "me". If there is light, it is no longer our light. If there is love and knowledge, it is no longer our love and knowledge; rather (as the Sufis say), God loves God, and God knows God, in us; our only responsibility is to get out of the Way. *Ratio/dianoia* has given way to *Nous/ Intellectus*.

Neither mercury, nor copper, nor iron, nor tin, nor even silver— metals that stand for various psychic powers and dispositions—can function as the root of the alchemical *metanoia*. Only if we are first reduced to lead, through *melanosis*, through radical mortification, can our soul be transmuted (via the receptive silver of *leucosis*) into the alchemical Gold.

III: ALCHEMY AS SPIRITUAL PSYCHOTHERAPY WITH AN EXEGESIS OF THE EASTERN ORTHODOX ICON OF ST. GEORGE

In the healthy soul, as we have seen, the affections are in harmony with the will, the will with the rational mind, and all three with the transcendent Intellect. It is also necessary for us, however, to have a clear image of the condition of the sick or fallen soul, as well as the method by which this soul can be healed. This image and method can be found in the science of alchemy.

In the alchemical art, the goal is to forge "the Philosopher's Stone" or "the alchemical gold," through a marriage of Sulfur and Mercury in the context of Salt, which acts as a catalyst. As we have already seen, the main stages of the Work are *melanosis*, "blackening"; *leucosis*, "whitening"; and *iosis*, "reddening." Blackening is radical humility

and self-mortification, symbolized by the metal lead. Whitening is
virginal receptivity to the light of the Spirit, symbolized by silver.
Reddening signalizes the completion of the Work, the attainment of
the Philosopher's Stone whereby the body is spiritualized and the
Spirit embodied. It represents the establishment of permanent psychic stability under the rule of the Spirit; it is symbolized by gold.

According to Titus Burckhardt, in his *Alchemy: Science of the Cosmos, Science of the Soul* and the chapter "Insight into Alchemy" in
his *Mirror of the Intellect: Essays on Traditional Science & Sacred Art*,
Sulfur is the Spirit, Mercury the soul, and Salt the body. However, it
is more strictly accurate to call Sulfur "Spirit as reflected in the soul,"
since alchemy, as one of the lesser mysteries, is properly a psychic
art. And the elusive quality of Mercury, as well as the acrid, volatile
and inflammatory quality of Sulfur, also make them apt symbols of
the various powers of the soul *in their fallen condition*. If Sulfur and
Mercury were not fallen in some sense, and therefore estranged,
their union would not represent the purification and re-ordering of
the soul.

Specifically, unredeemed Sulfur symbolizes *rationality in bondage
to the will*, and unredeemed Mercury *will in bondage to the affections*.
When the rational mind is bound to the will, it becomes "sulphur-
ous": dry, explosive, volatile, self-willed, and filled with fixed ideas.
It believes not what the transcendent Intellect reveals as true, but
what it arbitrarily decides to believe. Likewise when will is bound to
the affections, it becomes "mercurial": manipulative and capricious,
seductive and yet "playing hard to get." It does not do what the rational mind demonstrates it ought to do, but only what it wants to do
at the moment. Thus fallen Sulfur is in some ways like the character
of an immature man,[†] fallen Mercury like that of a childish woman.
If the healthy or "edified" soul (edified in the sense of "built up," as
in our word "edifice") is hierarchicalized with the rational mind at
the highest level, as interpreter of the Intellect, the will at the mid-

† This description of unredeemed Sulfur applies to the character of certain contemporary Muslim men, those who might be called "infantile authoritarian misog-
ynists". If a Muslim man aspires, in line with his tradition, to be the true spiritual
authority and center of his family, he must first learn to submit to Allah Himself not
to this or that idolatrous, modern, so-called "Muslim" ideology. And if he wishes to

level, as servant of the Intellect, and the affections at the lowest level, as receptive mirror of the Intellect. In the fallen soul (as we have already seen above) this hierarchy is inverted: the affections rule the will; the will rules the rational mind; the Intellect is veiled.

The alchemical cure for the "sickness" of Sulfur and Mercury, the power which brings them together, is, in the terminology of Sufism, *taslim*: submission to God. *Taslim* is Salt, the simplest and most basic truth of things, as when we call someone "the salt of the earth." Salt is the matrix, the alchemical vessel, the *context* which allows Sulfur and Mercury to marry. And although Salt is usually identified as the principle of the body, it is, mysteriously, also a symbol of the Divine Essence, since submission to God puts us in direct touch with the Absolute Itself, on a level deeper than even pure Intellection can unveil. As the marriage of Spirit and soul takes place within the context of the body, so the union of Truth and Love subsists within the context of the Essence. What is highest is best symbolized by what is lowest; the relative stability of the material world more perfectly reflects the Absolute than do the shifting images of the psyche—even though, ontologically speaking, the psyche is closer to it. This is why the alchemists teach that the first prerequisite for the alchemical *magnum opus* is the heaviest and most material of the metals known to classical antiquity—lead. In Islamic terms, the union of Spirit and soul in humanity, reflecting the unity of Truth and Love in the Divine Essence, is related to the doctrine of *al-Insan al-Kamil*; the Perfect or Universal Man. In Christian terms, it has to do with the mystery of the Incarnation. [NOTE: The identification of Salt as submission-to-God with the Divine Essence is largely my own. The only traditional source I can cite to support it is from *The Psychology of Sufism* by Dr. Javad Nurbakhsh, p. 66, where salt is listed among the symbols of the "*nafs*-at-peace", the human soul submitted to

---

stand as the spiritual center in relation to his woman, he can only gain this right and this power by contemplating her as the site-of-manifestation of all the signs of Allah; in the words of Ibn al-'Arabi, "if you have [truly] seen a beautiful woman, you have seen God." Men of Islam! If you cannot sincerely say, in the words of our Prophet, "three things have been made delightful to me: women, perfume and prayer", then emulate him until you can, and do not blame your own spiritual shortcomings on your wives and daughters.

God, and where one of the symbolic meanings of salt in dreams and visions is given as "submissiveness", the implication being that all things, whether or not they submit to God willingly, are already submitted to God *in essence*, because God *is* their essence.]

On the psychic level, where the metaphors of alchemy apply, knowledge of God, love of God, and the will to follow God's Will as we understand it are all necessarily imperfect, since they are mediated by the limited human subject. Submission alone is virtually perfect, since in reality nothing happens outside God's Will; consequently all things, whether or not they *have* submitted, in essence *are* submitted. When the will submits to God, the rational mind, freed from the will's domination, becomes objective and impartial— obedient to the Intellect—while the will itself, since it is now submissive to a higher Principle, is freed from the domination of the affections, which in turn submit to it. So the true hierarchy is reestablished in the soul. Here the initial need of the will, in obedience to the rational mind, to battle against the unruly emotions of the passional soul, which Sufis call the *nafs al-ammara*, "the commanding self," is replaced by a state in which emotions gladly submit to the will, lend to it the fullness of their power, and become to it the very Mirror of Allah. (In Sufism, as we have seen above, the human soul goes through several stages of alchemical transformation in the course of the spiritual Path. It begins as "the commanding *nafs*" or passional soul, is transformed through spiritual struggle into "the accusing *nafs*"—the remorseful conscience—and ends by becoming "the *nafs*-at-peace", the purified soul obedient to God's will.)

The story of this "war against the soul" and the alchemical transmutation it produces is told—in the language of mythopoetic symbolism—in one version of the Eastern Orthodox Christian icon of St. George (who, interestingly, is identified by Sufis with the "immortal prophet" Khidr or Khezr, the Green One, their hidden patron). St. George, mounted on a horse, with an angel above him holding a crown over the saint's head, impales a dragon with his lance, the opposite end of which points upward toward the angel, whose face is like a miniature prototype of the saint's. Behind the angel, beyond the butt of the lance, shining from the upper left corner of the icon, is a quarter-sunburst. The dragon seems to be lying on a body, not of ice, but of solid glassy-green water. In the background is a tower where, from the battlements, a king, a queen and a prince are watching the contest. In front of the tower stands a princess—who, like Andromeda or Psyche, has presumably been given to the dragon to devour, but is now freed from his power. She holds in her hand a crimson cord, which is tied around the dragon's neck.†

According to Titus Burckhardt in *Alchemy: Science of the Cosmos, Science of the Soul*, Mercury appears in two modes: dissolved/dissolving and coagulated/coagulating. In the negative or fallen (i.e., ego-bound) sense, dissolving Mercury is emotional capriciousness, seduction and dissipation, while coagulating Mercury is self-involvement and sullen resistance to the Spirit. In the positive or redeemed sense, dissolving Mercury is the power that breaks up hardened egotism, and coagulating Mercury the spiritual simplicity

---

† The crimson cord is associated with two prostitutes in the Old Testament. The first was Tamar, daughter-in-law of Judah, who disguised herself as a harlot after her husband died and lured Judah to sleep with her, becoming pregnant by him, because he had broken his promise to give her another one of his sons for a husband; when her son Zarah was born, the nurse tied a red cord around his hand [Genesis 38:6-30]. The second was Rahab, who hid the spies of Joshua at her house in Jericho before the Children of Israel laid siege to that city, and hung a red cord from her window during the siege as a sign for the victorious Israelites to spare her life [Joshua 2:1–22; 6:22–25]. To this day in Israel a red cord is wrapped around the tombstone of Rachel, then cut into lengths and distributed as a protective charm, called Rachel's Bracelet, to be wrapped seven times around the wrist. The word *Rachel* means "sheep" or "lamb" and is said to indicate humility and submission; Rachel is also associated with motherhood and fertility in Judaism. According to the Kabbalists, Rachel's Bracelet symbolizes the struggle against the passional soul, the *nefesh*, a Hebrew word strictly synonymous with the Arabic *nafs*; this is undoubtedly also the significance of the red cord by which the Princess leads the dragon in the icon of St. George, who is associated in the Near East with Elijah as well as Khidr. And Tamar, strangely enough, is considered by Eastern Orthodox Christians to be a prefiguration of the Blessed Virgin, the Theotokos ("mother of God"). Without victory over the passions there is no spiritual fertility; for God to be born in our hearts, the dragon of the *nafs al-ammara*, the *"soul commanding (to evil)"* must first be slain, then conquered, then pacified, then put to work. But once this is accomplished, the soul will appear transformed into the Virginal Maiden, the one who says "be it done unto me according to Thy Word". The maiden-soul, obedient to the Spirit of God, may now be taught, guided, and brought to final maturation as the Bride who is Wisdom, the *nafs al-mutma'inna*, the "soul at peace".

and sobriety that leads to emotional stabilization and maturity. Sulfur likewise appears in two modes: volatilized/volatilizing and fixed/fixing. In the fallen sense, volatile Sulfur is the psychic scatteredness that grows out of ego-identification with the Infinite, the belief that one is everything and the impulse to think or do everything, while fixed Sulfur is an authoritarian hardness, hard on other people and on itself as well, based on an ego-identification with the Absolute, that wants to reach stability and integrity by turning everything to stone. In the redeemed sense, volatile Sulfur is the power to open the affections (and those aspects of the will that have become mercurial) to the light of the Spirit by "melting" the coagulation of Mercury, while fixing Sulfur is the power to stabilize the affections (as well as the recalcitrant and coagulated aspects of the will) and render them submissive to the Spirit by fixing the dissolving tendency of Mercury. Thus the completion of the alchemical Magnum Opus, the forging of the Philosopher's Stone, may be depicted as a double marriage, like the one that concludes the most alchemical of the Arthurian romances, the *Parzival* of Wolfram von Eschenbach. (Carl Jung too saw the double marriage as a symbol of the establishment of the Mandala, the realization of the Self.) Fixing Sulfur espouses dissolving Mercury, thus producing psychic *stability* (in Sufi terms, *tamkin*); volatilizing Sulfur espouses coagulating Mercury, thus producing psychic *recollection* (in Sufi terms, *jam'*). If this double marriage goes wrong, however, dissolving Mercury will seduce volatilizing Sulfur, resulting in psychic dissociation and chaos, while coagulating Mercury will conclude an adulterous union with fixing Sulfur, resulting in total psychic petrification. And it is certainly true that chaos and petrification can co-exist within the same soul, such as that of the prurient puritan or the jaded libertine. (Hazarding a prophecy, I would predict that the soul of *al-Dajjal*, the Antichrist—the collective Ego it its terminal form—will be the "perfect" blend of these two apparently opposed but actually quite similar characters.)

In line with these doctrines, and with our general understanding of pneumatic anthropology and psychology, we can see the angel in the icon of St. George as the Divine Intellect or Spirit, and the sunburst above and behind it as the light of the Deity itself; the crown, as the rational mind in obedience to the Spirit; St. George, as the human will in obedience to the Spirit via the rational mind and thus as an aspect of the *nafs a-mut'minnah*; the horse, those relatively unconscious aspects of the personal will which have become submissive to the Divine Will and thus open to the Spiritual Intellect, which are consequently also aspects of the *nafs a-mut'minnah*; the dragon, the as-yet-unredeemed aspects of the *nafs* (the *nafs al-ammara*) as fallen Mercury, in the process of being fixed by St. George as redeemed Sulfur. That the dragon lies on a lake of solid (though not icy) water represents him as coagulating Mercury, which in its fallen aspect is lovelessness—the petrification of the affections—and in its redeemed aspect, emotional stability. The lance wielded by St. George is the *axis mundi*, which in terms of the soul represents the true hierarchy of the human faculties. This is the active, masculine aspect of the transmutation.

The feminine aspect—the goal of the transmutation already virtually present—is represented by the remaining figures. The princess is Mercury in its highest state, Mercury fixed as Silver, the redeemed human soul in which the three primal faculties of rationality, affect and will—the king, the queen and the prince—are in perfect balance on the psychic plane. This is the feminine, *horizontal* complement to their *vertical* hierarchicalization in which the masculine principle takes precedence. The tower is another representation of the soul, its vertical nature another symbol of the *axis mundi*, which the horizontal balance of the faculties can never replace, but must always complement. (In the Litany of Loretto the Virgin Mary is called "Tower of Ivory", an epithet taken from the Song of Solomon.) And the (same) dragon which the princess holds by a leash is the *nafs al-ammara* now considered as fallen Sulfur, in the process of being tamed and redeemed by Love, by dissolving Mercury, by the soul in its feminine essence. The very bond which began as a dominance of passion over Love, has now become—without the position of the two figures being changed in any way—a sovereignty of Love over passion. The icon graphically demonstrates how the dragon of the *nafs al-ammara* can be overcome and redeemed only by a combination of masculine severity and self-discipline and a feminine sympathy and empathy. If we only treat the *nafs al-ammara* with sympathy and understanding this will be nothing less than a "sympathy for the

Devil" which will allow the *nafs* to get away with murder. But if we only treat her like a dragon, with unbending severity, when will she ever become transformed into the soul-at-peace?

When the soul is submitted to God, Sulfur and Mercury unite. Sulfur, now redeemed, becomes the rational mind, governing the will as vice-regent of the Intellect; Mercury is now the affections as submissive to the will, and therefore ultimately obedient to the same Intellect. In active terms, the feminine or affective principle occupies the lowest rung of the hierarchy; in receptive terms, however, She is Silver, the pole of pure Substance, the perfect Mirror of the Divine Intellect, a receptive perfection which the masculine principle, in its twin modes of will and rationality, can never attain.

The union of the masculine and feminine principles within the soul is in one sense simultaneous, since it happens in a realm transcending linear time. In another sense, however, it is successive. According to this point of view, Mercury must first "solve" the willful prejudices and fixed ideas of Sulfur, melting the hardness of egotism and allowing all things to merge and flow, after which Sulfur can embrace and "fix" with its hierarchical lance the elusive capriciousness of Mercury, so that the chaotic impulses of the soul—the subconscious counterpart of hardened egotism—are ordered and harmonized. The same story is told in hexagrams 31 and 32 of the *I Ching*. In 31, "Wooing", the masculine principle places itself below the feminine; in 32, "Duration", the hexagram for marriage, it stands above the feminine. So even though the masculine principle is hierarchically exalted over the feminine, the primal impulse to the redemption of the human soul emanates from the feminine pole, from that "virginal" receptivity within us which says, in the words of the Virgin Mary, "let it be done unto me according to Thy word." This is why, in alchemy, the "hermetic art," Mercury is both the effective potency which makes the Great Work possible, and the psychopomp who guides the worker through the various stages of it—and why, in the icon of St. George, the queen on the tower stands *between* the king and the prince: affection, when purified, mediates between rationality (the king, the father) and will (the prince, the son), and reconciles them. And when affection is fully submitted to will, as will is to the rational mind, then, as the lowest principle, it regains its primordial power to reflect the highest principle, higher even than the rational mind: the transcendent Intellect itself, in which Love and Knowledge are one.

IV: THE ALCHEMY OF ROMANTIC LOVE

Alchemy, as the inner spiritual work that prepares the soul for union with God, is reflected in the world of human relations in terms of the Tantric polarity between man and woman—not simply on the level of primal sexual attraction, but in the fully personal realm of romantic love.

Integral to the alchemical Great Work is the union of Sulfur and Mercury, the masculine and feminine powers of the soul. Sulfur is the reflection of the active Spirit within the soul, and Mercury the potential receptivity of the soul to that Spirit. This synthesis produces the Androgyne, the restoration of the primordial Adam before Eve was separated. The polar union of masculine and feminine within the soul makes possible the spiritually fertile union of man and woman in the outer world—which means that the man or woman who has realized the Androgyne does not have what we usually think of as an "androgynous" personality—or a "macho" or superfeminine one either, for that matter—but rather an integrated masculine personality open to the feminine, or a complete feminine personality open to the masculine. In Jungian language, when the archetype of the Androgyne fails to be realized on its proper level— that of the inner "Syzygy", the vestibule of the Self archetype—it is displaced into the Ego and the Persona, where it produces a formless gender-ambiguity that is not essentially androgynous, but—to use Blake's terminology—"hermaphroditic". The Androgyne is the polar or tantric synthesis of masculine and feminine powers, positing the transcendence of these opposites on a higher, spiritual level; the Hermaphrodite is a chaotic crushing together of masculine and feminine, ultimately leading to a spiritual state that is lower than sexual polarity, not higher. According to the Qur'an, *surah* 2:187, where the law allowing if not encouraging intercourse between husband and wife on the nights of the Ramadan fast is laid down, *They* [the wives] *are raiment for you and ye* [the husbands] *are raiment for them*, which is another way of saying that the inner essence of the man is feminine, and of the woman, masculine—a traditional source, albeit veiled and allusive, for what we know from Carl Jung as "anima/animus" psychology. And the fact that this polar sexual quaternity is placed in the context of the "night" and prohibited during the "day" shows that it is properly an inner alchemical reality, not an outer psycho-social one.

The inner alchemical work prepares the soul for the romantic encounter, just as true love between a man and a woman, itself a mode of alchemy, empowers and deepens the inner transmutation. This quaternity of inner synthesis coupled without outer relatedness was consciously practiced in some alchemical schools, which held that the transmutation of "base metal" (the chaotic, hermaphroditic amalgam of Spirit-potential and soul-potential) into "gold" (the androgynous union of Spirit and soul, *forma* and *materia*, leading to the spiritualization of the body and the embodiment of the Spirit) can only be accomplished through a collaboration between the alchemist and his *soror mystica*, his female assistant or "mystical sister". And the greatest literary expression of this "Christian Tantra" in which inner spiritual development and outer romance, combat and courtesy challenge, purify and complete each other, is Wolfram's *Parzival*. (*Parzival* is revealed as an alchemical romance by the fact that it pictures the Grail not as a cup but as a stone—clearly the Philosopher's Stone—and by an episode near the beginning in which a dwarf named Antenor is thrown into the fire. "Antenor" is a character from the *Iliad*, but this name also suggests "athenor", the alchemical vessel in which is synthesized the *homunculus*, a tiny man, partly through the application of fire.)

Romance, which could be defined as Eros alchemically transmuted into Amor, is mysteriously capable of being "passionate, not passional". In genuine romantic love the fire of emotional and sexual passion is contained, therefore alchemical, rather than dissipative or concupiscent. It burns away the dross of attachment and egotism and synthesizes the Holy Grail, the Philosopher's Stone, which is the power of Divine Grace working in the vessel of the spiritual Heart, and thereby transmuting and purifying the field of human relations.

V: THE ALCHEMY OF THE AFFECTIONS

Affectivity is like a fuel that can be burned to empower either the will or the intellect. (By "intellect" I am referring not to the Transcendent Intellect but to the individual intellect, that faculty of the psyche designed to mirror the Transcendent Intellect in human consciousness, and one that is certainly not limited to rationality alone.) Without emotion the will cannot *will* anything, only impotently wish; but if (at the other extreme) the will is overwhelmed by emotion and therefore passive to it, it is no longer *will*, merely impulse.

Affect is the potency of the will. Speaking in terms of the spiritual Path, without affect the will cannot make good on its intent to concentrate on God; this is why some Sufi orders will make use of poetry and the spiritual concert (*sama*) as well as meditation and *dhikr* (remembrance of God through continuous invocation of His Name). And affect is the potency of the individual intellect as well. If we want to know anything thoroughly—including God, insofar as He can be known (and He will always absolutely transcend whatever we know of Him, no matter how true it is)—we need to be *interested* in that thing. But if we fail to meet the mark in terms of either intent or insight, both will suffer. The highest function of affect, which appears most clearly in the context of the spiritual Path, is to provide energy to will and intellect equally, and thereby reconcile them.

Emotional coldness contracts the perceptions; emotional warmth expands them. *Excessive* warmth or ardor can of course disturb the intellect and unbalance the will, but insufficient warmth will darken the one and paralyze the other. A certain degree of *sang froid* can help pacify an impulsive will and introduce order into a chaotic mind, but too much "coolness" is as bad as too little; one of the worse errors in spiritual psychology is to simplistically identify frigidity with spiritual detachment. Be that as it may, those whose affections are either too fiery or too frozen will certainly be blind in the area of interpersonal relations, and will therefore become either the victims or the perpetrators of psychological manipulation and injustice. One whose feeling-nature is unsound will be incapable of that aspect of intelligence known as "consideration", which etymologically denotes either the ability to choose gestures and actions "with the stars"—that is, in line with the particular qualities of the time—or the related ability to see situations in their fullness, as whole "constellations" of related factors.

Too often we see our emotions as a kind of fate that befalls us, as things we could never imagine ourselves as taking responsibility for, which is why we imagine that totally indulging in them or totally repressing them are the only real alternatives. It is true that we usually cannot summon emotions at will, but once they appear we can certainly deal with them if we possess sufficient capacity and have developed sufficient skill. If we become capable of witnessing our emotions—of seeing them as objective factors rather than simply seeing things, persons and situations *through* them—then we can develop the skill to control them, balance them, and apply their powers. Thus the virtue of *apatheia* or spiritual impassivity is not simply an emotional coldness that refuses to be affected by anything, but a degree of realization of the Absolute Indwelling Witness or *atman*, the Eye of the Heart. In the face of this Witness we are fully objectified; we transcend all self-identification. As Frithjof Schuon teaches, to the one who has realized the *atman*, God is not "He" but "I" and the entire psychophysical being is not "me" but "he". The *gnostic*, the *jñani*, the *arif* who is objectified in this manner is not devoid of feelings; it's simply that his feelings do not become *emotions* in the sense that they impulsively *motivate* the will to do or choose this or that. They exist as objective factors on the plane of being proper to them; and since they are fully witnessed by the Eye of the Heart they are also fully *experienced*, in a way that the emotions of the self-identified "passional" man never can be: as long as our feelings dominate our will and consequently act as impulses rather than as specific ways of knowing, they veil the Witness, and in so doing veil themselves. The feelings of the self-identified individual demand that we pay attention to them, but they refuse to be *seen*. To the degree that they are seen, however, they become whole; to the degree that they become whole, they are pacified; to the degree that they are pacified, they exist as modes or manifestations of the *nafs a-mut'minnah*, the vestibule of the spiritual Heart.

VI: THE UNION OF LOVE AND KNOWLEDGE

If we are to diagnose and prescribe for the psyche, either individual or collective, in alchemical terms, we must remember that the "humors" are not two, but four. As we have already seen, the archetypes that produce them, Sulfur and Mercury, each manifest in two modes, making four in all. On a certain level, the alchemical Sulfur represents the Spirit, and the alchemical Mercury the psyche or soul. But on the psychic plane itself, which is where alchemical metaphors are most completely applicable, Sulfur and Mercury, at least in their initial state, represent fallen powers of the soul in need of redemption, each one possessing within it the principle of that redemption, but both of them requiring that this principle be awakened and actualized via the alchemical Work, as initiated and sustained by God's grace. As we have seen above, Sulfur in its fallen condition is "intellect in bondage to the will", while Mercury is "will in bondage to the affections". The "sulfurous" personality is intellectually self-willed; the "mercurial" one is capricious, incapable of any stable intent. And so unredeemed Sulfur corresponds to the undeveloped male personality, Mercury to the undeveloped female one: Mercury is a "tease"; Sulfur is a "punk".

The two modes of archetypal Sulfur are fixation and volatilization, and of Mercury, coagulation and dissolution. When the soul is in a state of equilibrium, which renders it "virginally" receptive to the Spirit, volatilizing Sulfur is married to coagulating Mercury, and fixing Sulfur to dissolving Mercury. In an imbalanced or fallen state, on the other hand, fixing Sulfur unites with coagulating Mercury, producing the "hardness of heart", while volatilizing Sulfur unites with dissolving Mercury, producing pulverization and dissolution. In psychological terms, the first condition corresponds to fanaticism or Puritanism, the second to relativism and libertinism, both moral and philosophical. And these two states will often coexist not only in the same soul, producing the dangerous instability of the fanatic and the jadedness and dryness of the debauchee, but also in the same group, the same institution, the same society, leading to social fragmentation and interpersonal conflict.

So while it is true to say that the hardness of the ego needs to be liquefied, it is equally true that the chaos of the affections needs to be stabilized. In terms of the alchemical regime, if Sulfur is to fix capricious Mercury so that the soul can more fully reflect the principial domain, Mercury must first "solve" the incomplete and imbalanced fixations of Sulfur, its willful attachments and fixed ideas. And if Mercury is to temper and "incarnate" the mental volatility of Sulfur, Sulfur must first give Mercury a fixed an incandescent point toward which to flow. In other words, if the rational mind is to tame the affections, the affections must first moisten and vivify the mind. And if the affections are to help thought become fully three-dimensional and effective in actual life, thought must first show them a truth outside themselves to which they can become devoted, otherwise they will freeze into a state of sullen self-involvement. Furthermore, every stage of the inner alchemical regime is also a step in the development and purification of interpersonal relations. Alchemy is the courtesy of the psyche's relationship to the Spirit; courtesy is the alchemy of the relationship between one human being and another. And the essential scripture, in the West, of this twofold course is, as we have already pointed out, Wolfram's *Parzival*.

In one sense, Mercury, the feminine pole, can be seen as the psychic reflection of the Divine Love, and Sulfur, the masculine pole, of the Divine Intellect. But if we push this correspondence too far (as some of the Jungians have done), then what becomes of love *between* the sexes? If love is woman's work, and thought the province of men, then where can the sexes meet? At this point we need to remember that the magnetic pole of all psychic and spiritual development is the Divine Essence, in which intellect and love are one. In light of this we can see that love is not served only by the dissolution of hardened egotism but also by the intimation of transcendent Truth, by the disciplining of the emotions, and by the grounding and embodiment of the thoughts (although, from a wider perspective, all four of these developments can be seen as aspects of the conquest of egotism). A person imprisoned in a willful and petrified mindset cannot love— but neither can someone who has no sense of any truth outside himself, nor one whose emotions are chaotic, nor one who is possessed by abstract thoughts he is unable to realize. So the full service of Love entails the completion of the entire alchemical regime, the *magnum opus.* And what truly serves love equally serves knowledge, while what wounds love also darkens the intellect. If we have never learned to love others by knowing them, and know them through loving them, then we will not succeed in the Divine realm after having failed in the human one [cf. 1 John 4:20], since we ultimately know others with God's Knowing, and love them with His Love.

VII: THE PRACTICE OF SALT
—for John Eberly

> You are the salt of the earth –
> but if the salt loses its saltiness,
> what can it be salted with?
> *Matt.* 5:13

Sulfur is form, impulse. Mercury is material to be formed, and also the fuel or energy of impulse. Salt is the body, the matrix—the *athanor*, the *thalamos* ("wedding chamber")—the vessel in which they unite.

When we are internally divided, at war with ourselves, our Sulfur and Mercury are at odds. The impulse to impose form becomes either tyrannical and violent, or flaky and flighty; the potential to receive form becomes either elusive and "mercurial," or else sullen, in-turned and withdrawn; it either flees form or refuses to receive it. Consequently we are in a state of willfulness and moodiness, mania and depression—either that or petrification and flightiness, sulkiness and chaos. The more sulky or capricious Mercury becomes, the more violent becomes Sulfur's impulse to move it, its obsession to impose fixed form upon it—which, when it fails (as it must), turns into an explosive, dissipated impulse to totally express all possible forms. And the violence and inflexibility of Sulfur only makes Mercury that much more mercurial, that much more deeply wounded and congealed. In the words of William Blake:

> My Spectre around me night & day
> Like a Wild beast guards my way
> My Emanation far within
> Weeps incessantly for my Sin

King and Queen, Sulfur and Mercury go to war with each other when there is not enough Salt in the mix. Salt is the body, but it is also the character. It is wisdom, lore, informing context, character-strength. It is flexibility, reliability, humility—even humor, and certainly courtesy. But it is also more than that. It is *tradition*, an integrated vessel composed of doctrinal and ritual forms; it is also *attention*, both as supported by those forms and as an act in itself. It transcends all polarities. It is their field, their context; it contains them; it is also beyond them. As the lowest is the signature of the highest, so Salt as "body" is the signature of the unknowable Divine Essence. In the words of Jesus, "none has seen the Father at any time," and "who has seen me has seen the Father."

Salt is that which witnesses the polarity of Sulfur and Mercury without becoming involved with it. The divided soul is always identifying itself with its willfulness or its passiveness, its violent obsessiveness or its desire to hide and sleep. Sometimes it identifies with Sulfur, sometimes with Mercury—and whenever it identifies with one of the pair consciously, it always identifies with the other unconsciously.

Salt, however, is beyond identification. In its higher sense, as the "body" of the marriage of Sulfur and Mercury, it is formless, substanceless, neither agent nor patient. It is pure Witness, the vessel and the seed of Gold. So the practice of Salt is: to witness Sulfur and Mercury—*forma* and *materia*, impulse and *potentia*, active will and stored-up power—without fleeing, and without interfering. The identification of consciousness with its active and passive modes is what hides them from each other, prevents them from relating fruitfully with each other, and sets them at war. Salt breaks this identification. When Salt is added, Sulfur and Mercury become mutually aware; they balance each other, embrace each other. (Mercuric sulfide or cinnabar, a compound of sulfur and mercury, is classed in chemistry as a salt.) There is no conscious attempt to force them together (that would be Sulfur alone), nor any more aimless drifting in the currents of identification and desire (that would be Mercury alone); there is only the conscious withdrawal of the unconscious ego-identification that has for so long held them apart. To sit still, to witness *intentionally*, and not to interfere—that takes real Salt.

7

THE SHADOWS OF GOD

A "Gnostic" Analysis of the System of Antichrist

[This essay is an expanded version of the chapter "The Shadows of God" from *The System of Antichrist: Truth and Falsehood in Post-modernism and the New Age*, Sophia Perennis, 2001. It departs from psychology per se into the fields of social analysis and eschatology; yet without some sense of *social* psychology, and specifically of the operation of the *unconscious social mores*, the psychology of the individual lacks sufficient context to be understood in any depth. Furthermore, the realms of individual and collective psychology are inseparable in our times from the great emotional and spiritual stresses and delusions now abroad, in both the socio-historical and the subtle dimensions, in these last days of the Kali-yuga, when a vast, perhaps incalculable era of historical and biological time is so obviously drawing to a close. If our individual egos are "taxed" to establish the collective ego known as This World, and if This World in turn "charters" the egos of its members so as to enforce in them the sort of consciousness it can manipulate and control, then no analysis of the psyche, individual or collective, can be complete without an analysis of This World in which we are immersed—until, by the Grace of God and constancy in our own struggle, we are liberated from it definitively.]

If Gods combine against Man Setting their Dominion above
The Human Form Divine. Thrown down from their high Station
In the Eternal heavens of the Human Imagination: buried
   beneath
In dark oblivion with incessant pangs ages on ages

In Enmity & war first weakened then in stern repentance
They must renew their brightness & their disorganized functions
Again reorganize till they assume the image of the human
Cooperating in the bliss of Man obeying his Will
Servants to the Infinite and Eternal of the Human form
                                     William Blake, from *The Four Zoas*

In the well-known words of St. Paul from the book of *Ephesians*,
"We wrestle not against flesh and blood but against principalities,
against powers, against the rulers of the darkness of this world,
against spiritual wickedness in high places." These principalities and
powers, in my opinion, can be legitimately seen as elements of the
developing system of Antichrist, a system which "constellates" only
at the end of the aeon, but which is virtually present all throughout
"fallen" human history, as when Paul speaks of "the god of this
world [who] hath blinded the eyes of them that believe not" (II Cor.
4:4). The "god of this world" is obviously Satan, but Satan in his
particular aspect as the patron of "worldliness," of the organized
social and mass psychological system created by the human ego in
rebellion against God. The Antichrist per se represents the establishment of this system in its terminal form for this aeon via the
breakthrough (in René Guénon's terms) of sub-human, "infra-psychic" forces into human history, just as Christ—and Muhammad,
and the Buddha, and the Avatars of Vishnu—represent the breakthrough of Divine Wisdom and Love.

For many of the early Christians, the Roman Empire represented,
for obvious reasons, the system of Antichrist. The Roman Emperor
was worshipped as a god at one time, at least in the provinces, and
the Number of the Beast, 666, is often solved as a numerological reference to the emperor Nero. The central grievance of the Jewish
Zealots, the anti-Roman guerrilla terrorists of Jesus' time, was that
to require that the Jews pay taxes to Rome was an act of emperor-
worship and thus a blasphemy against God, especially since the
Roman denarius in which the tax was to be paid bore an image of
the emperor, and so was technically an idol in the eyes of many Jews,
who, like the Muslims in later centuries, prohibited the making of
any image of Yahweh, and considered any deity who could be

visually represented as inherently false. That Jesus was on one level sympathetic to the Zealots, though he was certainly not a political revolutionary—any more than he was a collaborator with Rome—is shown by the fact that he criticized every known Jewish sect of his time—Pharisees, Sadducees, Scribes and Herodians—except the Zealots and the Essenes, and numbered one Simon the Zealot among his disciples, though we can't be sure whether "Zealot" refers to Simon's affiliation or only his character.

In the *Apocalypse*, the central symbol of the Antichrist is the Beast, who acts as an agent of the Dragon (Satan). Upon the Beast rides the Whore, whose name is Mystery, Babylon the Great. The seven heads of the Beast, which are seven kings, are also seven mountains upon which she sits, like the seven hills of Rome. And so, on one level, the Beast is the Roman Empire, compared by the writer of the book to the Babylonian captivity of the Jews. This identification of the Beast with Rome has led certain Protestant sects to see it as a symbol of the Roman Catholic Church—an attribution which would be partly justified only in the case of the complete apostasy of Catholicism, which has only been in force since the Second Vatican Council.

The Dragon of the *Apocalypse*, identified with Satan, represents a perverted *spiritual* order. Based on this Satanic order is the perverted *social* order of the Beast. And the Whore of Babylon, who rides the Beast—that is, who both guides it and is carried along by it—is the perverted *psychic* order of the latter days. The seven heads of the Beast, who are seven kings with whom Babylon consorts and seven mountains upon which she reigns, symbolize—among other things—the seven major faculties of the soul, which in antiquity were represented by the seven planets: the Moon, fertility and subconscious emotion; Mercury, thought, cunning and the ability to deal with information; Venus, love, sexuality and relatedness; the Sun, intellect, the spiritual center of the soul and source of its life; Mars, will and aggression; Jupiter, leadership ability and philosophical intelligence; Saturn, long-term planning ability, mystical knowledge and the wisdom of old age. If the Beast and the Whore "occupy" the seven provinces of the soul, this indicates that the regime of Antichrist has conquered and perverted all these aspects of human life, both socially and psychologically, a perversion which is represented in Catholic theology by the seven deadly sins. According to Martin Lings, in his article "The Seven Deadly Sins in the Light of the Symbolism of Number", "*superbia* (pride) is related to the Sun, *avaritia* (avarice) to Saturn, *luxuria* (lust) to Venus, *invidia* (envy) to Mercury, *gula* (gluttony) to Jupiter, *ira* (anger) to Mars, and *accidia* (sloth) to the Moon. The power of the Beast over the human soul is symbolized by the "mark of the Beast"—who in this case is actually, according to the *Apocalypse*, a second Beast, servant of the first, identified as the False Prophet—which is placed either upon the right hand or upon the forehead. The mark upon the right hand symbolizes power over the will, and that upon the forehead power over the intelligence: when the intelligence is darkened, the will is overpowered as well, since it must now follow error instead of Truth.

The regime of Antichrist, then, operates on three levels, which are the three ontological levels of the human being: the material level, including both the socio-historical realm and the human body; the psychic level, embracing both the conscious and the subconscious mind; and the spiritual level, which though it cannot ultimately be perverted, since it is Divine, can be obscured by the powers of darkness, and also *counterfeited,* according to the principle that "Satan is the ape of God."

The Beast, who is Antichrist, is thus the counterfeit of Christ, a perverse and distorted version of the image of God within us. Under his regime, all the powers and qualities of the human form, considered as God's central act of Self-revelation in this world ("who has seen me has seen the Father" said Jesus, speaking as the Divine Archetype of Humanity) are aped by demonic forces: wisdom, love, miracles of healing and control over natural forces, and even the resurrection of the body, all will be enacted in counterfeit, "so as to lead astray, if possible, even the elect."

Evangelical Christians tend to concentrate on predictions relating to how the system of Antichrist will appear in future history and society. This is a valid and important level upon which to view the matter, though we have to be careful not to interpret scripture too narrowly, since an event recounted in a densely-symbolic text like the *Apocalypse* may appear in history as several different events, or trends, happening at various times. My intent, however, is to concentrate more on the psychic and metaphysical aspects of "the darkness of this world," including that level of things where the unconscious mind interacts with society, the realm where the powers of darkness appear as *unconscious belief-systems and social mores.*

A spiritually degenerate society rules its members not only by police-state tactics, or by influencing them to consciously believe in false doctrines, but also by indoctrinating them to adopt certain beliefs *unconsciously,* beliefs which will have all the more power over them by this very unconsciousness, since they are never brought into the light of day where they can be critically evaluated. An evil society will inculcate these beliefs deliberately, through various sorts of propaganda, indoctrination and mind-control. On the other hand, the rulers of the society in question will, in some ways, be just as unconscious as the population they indoctrinate. While they may consciously lie to the people on questions of fact, nonetheless they take the *fundamental* beliefs they disseminate absolutely for granted, and are therefore unconscious of them. The deepest lies—the unconscious social mores and the false conceptions of God on which they are based—appear to our rulers simply as the nature of things. Because they believe in them implicitly, they never have to become aware of them *as beliefs.* If you want to delude others it is best to begin by deluding yourself; that way no one can question your "sincerity."

These beliefs act like possessing demons, controlling the psyche from within, and punishing any move of thought, feeling or intuition which is at odds with their view of reality, most often through feelings of shame, fear, uncontrollable anger, frigid pride, or deep depression, all of which will be temptations to the same fundamental sin, the sin of despair. (This is not to say that all such feelings are demonic attacks. There is also a healthy shame which protects us from shameful acts, a healthy fear which defends us from physical and spiritual danger, a healthy anger at evil or injustice, a healthy "pride" which takes the form of self-respect or veneration of the worthy, and a healthy sorrow which appears as compassion, or remorse.) Furthermore, what is an unconscious false belief on the psychological level *is precisely a devil* on the psychic or spiritual level.

In the parable of Jesus' exorcism of the lone demoniac, the demons which possess him give their name as "legion," which is an obvious reference not only to the Roman military occupation of Judea, but also to the possession of the Jewish soul, via "internalized oppression," by the unconscious social mores of the Roman imperium.

The devils who "administer" the false belief-systems in question are not to be compared with those who tempt us to personal self-indulgence, to lust, for example, or sloth, or anger. They are more on the order of fallen cherubim, great spiritual intelligences who have turned against God. They are demons of the intellect, not demons of the will. When St. Paul speaks of "principalities and powers" who are "the rulers of the darkness of this world," these are the beings he is referring to, the ones that the sectarian Gnostics of late antiquity named the "Archons".

On a certain level, these Archons constitute an articulate system of error, a direct counterfeit of the divine or celestial *pleroma* which appears in the *Apocalypse* as the Throne of the Lamb surrounded by the four Living Creatures, the seven Lamps, the twenty-four Elders, etc. The symbolic meaning of these figures may never be precisely known (though it clearly was at one time); it is enough to say, in this context, that they represent God's first, spiritual creation, prior to the material universe, though they are "prior" more in the spiritual than the temporal sense, since the first creation is eternal in relation to our temporal, material one, not simply "prior" to it in time.

After meditating for many years on these subjects, I believe I have gained a certain amount of insight into what C.S. Lewis jocularly named, in his *Screwtape Letters*, the "Lowerarchy"—the system of infernal domination of collective human society, not simply of individual human beings—and most particularly into the level represented by the number *four*, which would appear to be the Satanic counterfeit of the Four Living Creatures. I have been deeply influenced in these meditations by the "prophetic books" of William Blake, *The Four Zoas, Milton* and *Jerusalem*—themselves influenced by the Hebrew Kabbalah—where in obscure and flaming visionary language he analyses the Fall and Redemption of Man in terms of the fall of the four central faculties of the human soul, the Four Zoas or Living Creatures, and their redemption by Christ, who is the eternal spiritual Intellect. My intent here is certainly not to create an alternate theology, but merely to throw a poetic and metaphorical light on certain psychic consequences of the fall of man, which, according to traditional authorities, as well as to the fairly obvious meaning of the book of *Genesis*, includes both the perversion of the will and the darkening of the Intellect.

The fall of man, seen in intellectual terms, begins as a primal misunderstanding of the true nature of God. All else follows from this, since a failure to understand Who God really is distorts our picture of every other thing, person, situation or level of being. Where the intellect is darkened by spiritual ignorance, it can reveal to us only shadows of the Truth, false objects which the will is attracted to because of their partial resemblance to the Truth they hide, in the course of which it becomes weakened and distorted, till it can no longer will the Good—even if, by the Grace of God, the darkness of the Intellect were to be lifted for a moment, and that Good revealed.

A shadow requires three things: a source of light, an opaque object, and a field where the shadow falls. If the light is God, the opaque object, the ego, and the field where the shadow falls, the universe, then the shadows of the ego, projected by the Divine Light, are false beliefs, which appear to that ego not as its own shadows, nor even as beliefs, but as the literal nature of reality: the shadows of God.

The ego, by definition, does not know itself. It tries to convince us that we can become unique and original if we submit to its magic. It forgets that egotism actually stereotypes us, makes us drearily predictable, because human egos, at root, are much alike. Our deepest fears and desires, of which the ego is composed, are very few and very common.

God is the only Reality, the sole object, and subject, of all knowledge. But when primal fear and desire, which are the seed-form of the ego, separate subject from object, so that the perceiving subject is apparently no longer God—as in Reality it always is, since only God, in the last analysis, is Witness of His own manifestation—then limited and conditioned views of Reality are born, held within the minds of limited and conditioned sentient beings. From one point of view these limited notions, and the limited subjects who perceive them, are the creative manifestation of God in space and time; from another, they are God's shadows, His veils. When these shadows become thick, and their darkness intense, it appears as if God were absent from His creation. It is into these places and times of the apparent "death of God" that God sends the prophets, saviors and/ or avatars who found and renew the great wisdom traditions.

Looked at in one way, false beliefs are nothing but illusions; to take them too seriously is to grant them more reality than they deserve. But to the degree that false beliefs are actually believed, especially on the collective level, they produce real effects, not only on the psychic plane, but on the social, physiological and environmental ones as well. Illusion—whose moral name is evil—is essentially a privation, a lack. One can never make complete sense of it because, as a "hole" in reality rather than a reality in its own right, it is fundamentally absurd. However, a condition such as starvation is also a "mere" lack, a lack of food; but its consequences are far from illusory. In the same way, false beliefs, and the demonic powers who administrate them, have real effects, which we ignore at our peril. The "principalities and powers", then, can be considered as fundamental *misperceptions of the nature of God* by the deepest, most hidden layers of the human ego—which, from another perspective, is entirely composed of these misconceptions. In other words, they are *idols*, false gods like the Golden Calf destroyed by Moses, or the pagan idols swept out of the Kaaba by the Prophet Muhammad (peace and blessings be upon him).

Imagine with me the most fundamental and universal idols, or Archons, the primal shadows of God, as four: the idolatry of *Law*, the idolatry of *Fate*, the idolatry of *Chaos*, and the idolatry of *Self.* These are the primordial elementals of the human ego, the analysis of the darkened order of perception created by the fall of man, the "rulers of the darkness of this world." To the darkened perception of the self-worshipping ego they appear as powers in their own right, and also—since they are in perpetual conflict—as real alternatives. But in reality they are in perpetual *collusion* to prevent us from seeing any light of Truth beyond the tragic and ironic alternatives they propose. And far from being independent self-existing powers, they are nothing at root but the emblems of our fundamental recoil from the incandescent Glory of God, projected, like the shadows in Plato's cave, on the landscape of the psyche, and thence on nature and society. Yet from another perspective, they are, precisely, demons, spiritual powers in rebellion against God. We can solve this apparent paradox if we realize that it is only the ego's alienation from God which opens it to the influence of such demonic forces, who are in a similar state of alienation, and that the origin of such alienation in both cases is ignorance or delusion. The deluded ego worships itself instead of God—whether in arrogance or in despair—and the forms which this self-worship takes are the forms of demonic powers. Practically speaking, we must admit both that these powers are in deliberate, active opposition to God and the spiritual life, and that they themselves are deluded, even as they attempt, with infernal cunning, to delude us. In other words, their power is entirely negative, being based on ignorance alone, which is why they are called "powers of darkness". And though it will always be necessary, given our fallen condition, to struggle with them will-against-will, it is only the dispersal of the shadows of ignorance, in the light of the Divine Intellect, which finally breaks their power.

IDOLATRY OF LAW

God is a lawgiver. The Torah, the Laws of Manu, the Islamic *shari'ah* were given to humanity not as an arbitrary imposition of tyrannical rules, but as mercy—which is why ancient peoples looked on lawgiving kings and sages as among the supreme benefactors of the race. Given that humanity had fallen from Eden, from the direct perception of Divine Reality, law became a necessity. A sacred law is an expression of the true shape of the human culture, and ultimately the Human Form, to which that law applies. By the divine act of lawgiving, God creates a given culture in space and time: not through an arbitrary decree, but through His vision of that culture as an eternal facet of the Divine Humanity within His own nature. To command, "you shall not kill, you shall not steal, you shall not commit adultery, you shall not forget to acknowledge the Divine Source of your life" is like ordering us not to cut our arms off or put our eyes out. As a safeguard of our integral humanity, the sacred law is beholden to that humanity. It is cut to fit us; we are not, as in the myth of the bed of Procrustes, mutilated to fit it. As Jesus said, "the Sabbath was made for man, not man for the Sabbath." Revealed law is necessary because we find ourselves within time, and so need a vehicle whereby eternal principles can be applied to changing situations.

The very sacredness of revealed law, however, makes it vulnerable to the growth of idolatry. We forget that it was given to protect us, and begin to use it as a tool in the service of the collective ego, a weapon against the Image of God within us. God is Absolute, and the eternal principles are absolute relative to cosmic manifestation, but when our sense of absoluteness is displaced by being identified with contingent situations, idolatry is born. And the essence of the *idolatry of Law* is that we impose it blindly, mechanically, without regard for the actual shape of the situations it was created to regulate, or the true nature of the people it was written to protect. Every truly sacred law is not merely a set of duties and prohibitions, but an expression in the moral realm of eternal, metaphysical principles. "Keep holy the Lord's Day," for example, refers, on an esoteric level, to the Eternal Present as God's resting-place, and "Thou shalt not covet thy neighbor's wife" to what the Hindus call *swadharma*, one's unique spiritual duty and destiny—symbolized by a man's wife, the image of his soul—which cannot be exchanged, and which no other can fulfill: "Better one's own *dharma*, no matter how poorly performed, than the *dharma* of another, no matter how well." These eternal principles do not exist behind the letter of the law alone, but equally behind the face of the human situation the law must confront and regulate. But when this is forgotten, when law is applied *indiscriminately* rather than impartially, it is transformed into a bloody idol, demanding, like the pagan god Moloch in the Old Testament, the sacrifice of our children (esoterically speaking, our creativity) and, like the Aztec war-god Huitzilopochtli, our still-beating hearts (the Image of God within us). Prescribing the same remedy for all seems impartial, yet nothing is more destructive, precisely as if a physician were to prescribe penicillin or insulin to every patient indiscriminately, to avoid the work of diagnosis and the humbling realization that he or she does not already know the precise nature of the disease. As Blake said, "One law for the Lion and the Ox is oppression." When the certainty derived from an understanding of eternal principles is used as an excuse for failing to engage with real people and actual situations in the work of discernment, the *idolatry of Law* is in full force.

The false religion of Law is best represented by the legalism of the Abrahamic religions, when it expands beyond its legitimate bounds and denies Mercy. A great deal of Jesus' ministry was directed against this idolatry, represented in the Gospels by the Scribes and Pharisees. The idolatry of Law includes either the false doctrine that God's law is greater than God, that He is a slave to it rather than its Creator, or the allied error—held by the more extreme Asharites within Islam—that His Will is arbitrary, and thus takes precedence over even His Nature, as if God could will to be whatever He wants, even if it be something other than God. This second error, however, could better be described as a synthesis of the idolatry of Law and the idolatry of Selfhood (see below) since it sees God as a kind of rebel—a rebel against Himself. When this spirit of legalism is expressed socially, it becomes a tyrannical police state, most likely (at least in these days) protecting an economic monopoly which impoverishes the masses and excludes them from participation in the life of the nation and/or world, and which protects its own power through various forms of propaganda, mind-control and state terror. Expressed psychologically, it becomes the rigid, authoritarian character, filled with frigid pride, which represses and dominates its own thoughts, feelings, sensations and perceptions as brutally as any dictator dominates the unfortunate populace.

IDOLATRY OF FATE

God is the nature of things. A recognition of the nature of things, which the Chinese call Tao, the Hindus *rta*, and the ancient Egyptians *maat*, the manifestation of Necessary Being in the cosmic order, is the basis of contemplative spirituality. The way things naturally are, the realm of natural law, manifests as appropriateness, beauty and inevitability; through it we can contemplate the Names of God or Platonic Ideas, the eternal archetypes within the mind of God.

Contemplation is like space. Empty in itself, it shows us the pattern whereby things are related to one another outside time, *sub specie aeternitatis*. Law enters time, and so manifests as speech and spoken scripture; contemplation, being of the nature of space, is better symbolized by the Hindu mandala, the sacred calligraphy of the Qur'an, or the Eastern Orthodox icon. But when pure contemplation is darkened, when the primordial receptivity of the soul is lost, then *Fate* is born. We can no longer contemplate the eternal pattern of things; consequently the Always So is transformed into the fated, the hopelessly inevitable. The still surface of the lake of contemplation is disturbed by time—not the creative time of sacred law, but time as conditioned by the fear of what might happen in the future now that we can no longer see the shape of what always is. Under the regime of Fate, vertical causality—the sense that everything happens by virtue of God's eternal will for this particular moment—is veiled, and replaced by horizontal causality. Past causes are now seen as the origin of future events, but since the roots of the past are hidden, the shape of the future is hidden as well. Events are unpredictable because their causes are veiled in mystery; by the same token, they are inevitable.

The pre-Socratic philosopher Heraclitus said "character is fate," an oracular statement that can be taken in two different ways. In the words of the Prophet Muhammad (peace and blessings be upon him), "he who knows himself knows his Lord." This means that if one can see oneself with the perfect objectivity of the Divine Self or Witness within the human soul, one will know that little "me" out there as a projection into space and time of a specific archetype within the mind of God—and so fate holds no surprises. All happenings are seen as perfectly appropriate to the shape of the self to which they happen; God's will for a particular individual within a particular moment is indistinguishable from that person's will for himself in obedience to God, since the two are one. On the other hand, if character is unconscious—which it usually is, no matter how much psychological introspection we do or how much feedback we get from others, since we can only know who we really are in the objective light of God—then it is projected into the world of events as a mysterious fate which we can't escape, no matter what we do. The same things keep happening to us, over and over again, and all our attempts to escape them only seem to quicken the pace of their pursuit. The Greek tragedies, with their sense of the "fatal flaw," are the best illustrations we have in literature of this darker side of Heraclitus' saying.

These obsessively repetitive events continue to happen because of the kind of fundamental forgetfulness which the Greeks called *amnesia,* and the Muslims *ghaflah*—the forgetfulness of the Divine Witness within us, which leads to a general inability to pay attention, as well as to an ignorance of our essential character and real needs. We keep asking for certain things, forgetting that we've done so, and then reacting with shock when our unconscious wishes come true. If we were aware of the wishes hidden within us then we could distinguish between *essential* and *imposed* character, between the accidental wishes implanted in us by circumstances or other people's agendas, and the essential wishes that are inseparable from who we are in the mind of God. The first kind of wish can never really be fulfilled; the second kind is fulfilled already, in a higher world—a world which, paradoxically, can only be unveiled to us through our struggle to find and fulfill our true wishes in this imperfect world, where that fulfillment can never be complete—or, even if momentarily it seems complete, can never last.

Until we awaken from our amnesia, we are under the regime of Fate. Every time something "fatal" happens, we are appalled to realize that we haven't escaped the curse even yet. And as each twist of fate which has sprung at us out of the mysterious future passes into the hidden past, it adds to the store of apparent *karma* by which the mysterious past seems to be the origin of the hidden future. Just as our body can become addicted to certain drugs, our destiny can become addicted to certain events. If an eternal archetype or character in the mind of God is veiled by the darkening of the individual mind, or the mind of society as a whole, it becomes the center of a karmic cycle or "vicious circle," something which Blake called "the circle of destiny." When the Stoic philosophers tried to absolutize natural cycles in the doctrine of the "eternal return", which maintained that all events endlessly recur in exactly the same way to exactly the same people through vast and unending cycles of time, they were erecting the "circle of destiny" into an idol, like the Greek

Fates, or the Roman goddess Fortuna who used to be worshipped by spinning the familiar "wheel of fortune". In so doing they were reacting to an alienation from the sense of eternity which was prevalent in classical antiquity. St. Augustine, in *The City of God*, criticizes this doctrine, implying that the belief in a circle of destiny is actually based on a circular argument, since (I would add) if the premises upon which an argument is based are not seen as axiomatic, and thus eternal in relation to the motion of the argument, that motion becomes circular. Those who remember God in eternity know all events as eternally present. Those who forget God become like "moving white dots" (Blake) between a forgotten past dominated by regret and nostalgia, and a mysterious future ruled by hankering and fear. They live in a world where forgetfulness of the past is compulsory, and where all who forget the past are condemned to repeat it.

The false religion of Fate manifests either as a cult of the cycles of nature, as in the negative and mechanistic aspects of the Mesopotamian star-worship from which *astrology* is derived (which is not in all cases fatalistic, since it can sometimes approach a vision of the eternal archetypes) and the philosophy of the Stoics, or as the Calvinist denial of free will based on a false doctrine of predestination, which sees God's eternal will for the individual as something other than the sum total of the individual's own decisions, whereas in reality God's "foreknowledge" of our decisions does not cause them, but is simply His vision of them *sub specie aeternitatis*. Expressed in psychological and social terms, this Fate-worship becomes a largely-unconscious "zodiac" of *social typology*—of imposed rather than essential character—where the unconscious social mores determine the individual's fate via society's expectations for him, which progressively become his own expectations for himself. As the idolatry of Law is pride, so the idolatry of Fate is *fear*. [NOTE: The best literary analysis of the Regime of Fate is the story "The Lottery at Babylon" by Jorge Luis Borges, from his book *Labyrinths*.]

IDOLATRY OF CHAOS

God is infinite life. The vast profusion of the "ten-thousand things" eternally overflows into manifestation out of the Divine Infinity.

God sends sacred laws, but He is greater than they. He manifests as the cosmic order, but He is not limited by it. There are no barriers in God to the infinite radiation of His Being, and this is His perfect freedom, a freedom which does not begin to be exhausted by universe after universe, bursting with life.

But we cannot act as God does. We are contingent, He is Absolute. He is beyond form, while we are bound to the forms in which He has created us. He absolutely transcends us. But when we forget this, when His transcendence is veiled and we see only His immanence in the world visible to our senses, and then *identify* with it, we start to believe that the path to freedom lies through formlessness and dissipation. Since we've lost the vision of how form emanates from what is *above* form, we seek the divine Infinity in what is *below* form, in a Dionysian intoxication which ends as it did with King Pentheus in Euripides' *The Bacchae*. Pentheus, king of Thebes, despises the new cult of Dionysius (or Bacchus, god of wine, and perhaps also of the psychedelic mushroom *amanita muscaria*) which has invaded Greece, and been taken up by women—the *bacchantes*—who dance ecstatically, and tear living animals apart in their frenzy. Dionysius assumes the guise of a suspicious underworld type, is arrested and brought to the palace. There he offers to tell Pentheus where he can view the Bacchic revelers in their secret forest sanctuary. Pentheus, voyeuristically fascinated, takes him up on his offer, goes out to spy on the *bacchantes*, and is torn limb from limb by his own mother, Agave, who in her frenzy mistakes him for an animal. Euripides is saying here that to seek the divine life in what is below form, by idealizing and worshipping one's animal nature, is to be torn to pieces by our mother, who is material nature; *mater* = matter. This is the idolatry of *Chaos*.

The false religion of Chaos is the Dionysian, which includes various kinds of political, social and moral anarchism; those forms of false mysticism which identify God with formlessness instead of supraformal Essence, and higher consciousness, in a simple-minded way, with intoxication; and those forms of psychotherapy which make release from constriction, inhibition and character-armor the central factor. Those who, like Pentheus, are narrow-mindedly "civilized" rather than broadly cultured, will often seek this kind of release in a return to the simplicity of Nature, conceived of as a maternal paradise of safety, self-indulgence, ease and irresponsibility—forgetting that, for example, no African Bushman or Australian Aborigine could survive for a single day without a greater degree of endurance, courage, and vigilance than most city-dwellers will ever possess. If the dominant emotion of Fate is fear, the dominant emotion of Chaos is *shame.*

IDOLATRY OF SELFHOOD

God is the Absolute Subject, the *atman,* the transcendent and immanent Self, the *imago dei* within each of us. By virtue of this *atman,* we are, at the deepest level of our being, both unique and universal. The Self within us is pure, impersonal, universal Being, without attributes; according to some metaphysicians it is better described as Beyond Being, given that it can never be an object of consciousness subject to definition, since "the eye cannot see itself." But because God is unique as well as universal, this Self is also the principle of our unique human integrity, the way in which we are not simply humanity in the abstract, but actual human beings, commanded by God to be precisely ourselves, no greater, no less, and no other. And yet this uniqueness is also universal, since it is shared by all human beings, and in fact by all things. Self as the principle of uniqueness is not other than Self as the principle of pure Being, as when God, speaking to Moses in *Exodus,* names Himself as "I Am That I Am": My unique Essence is not other than My pure Being; it is My unique Essence to *be* pure Being. And what God can say of Himself, we can also say, certainly not of our limited human personalities, but of the God, the *atman,* within us. In St. Paul's words: "It is not I who live, but Christ lives in me."

But when uniqueness is separated from being, it loses its universality. This is what happens when we ascribe uniqueness to ourselves alone while denying it to others. This is the *idolatry of Self.* When we worship our own separate selfhood as if it were God, we start to believe that self-willed isolation is the road to integrity, and that, in Sartre's words, "hell is other people." Consequently we can only relate comfortably to others if we see them as subordinates—

that is, as lesser parts of ourselves. This is the irony of self-worship. Seeking unity and integrity through isolation and dominance, we gradually become filled with the ghosts of all the relationships we have denied and betrayed. Our quest for individuality ("undivided-ness") at all costs results only in fragmentation. We ourselves become "the lonely crowd".

The false religion of Selfhood is Prometheanism, which includes all forms of *hubris*: the solipsistic, New Age belief that "I create my own reality" (the truth being more on the order of "I create my own illusion"); the idea that spiritual development is a kind of exploit or heroic achievement to be gloried in; the sense that the individual can only gain integrity and significance by breaking the law and rebel-ling against the mores; and the driving will of Western, and by now global, society to conquer nature, deny God, and remold human life according to the most demented "idealism" imaginable, even at the risk of destroying both humanity and the earth. If Law is ruled by pride, Fate by fear, and Chaos by shame, Selfhood is ruled by *anger*.

These four idols—Law, Fate, Chaos and Selfhood—are an analysis of the fallen order of perception known in Christian theology as "this world." They do not operate in isolation. Tyrannical and mechanistic Law takes on the aspect of mysterious Fate. Ignorance of the law is no excuse, we are told, and yet who can ever know that law in its entirety? And Fate, in reality, is not the operation of being-in-itself, but of an established, though hidden, order of things, an artificial system, an idolatrous Law. Tyrannical Law imposed on the individual produces the self-willed rebel, and so Law reinforces Self-hood. Imposed on society or nature, it produces Chaos by violating natural, intrinsic order in the name of an artificial, contrived order. And both Rebellion and Chaos make necessary ever-more tyranni-cal, blind and mechanistic Law. In the name of the war on drugs, we destroy civil rights. In the name of wildlands management, we burn Yellowstone National Park. But the more blindly we try to impose order on nature and society, the more chaos and rebellion we create.

Fate imposed on the individual promotes Selfhood, since to be self-willed, and suffer the consequences, seems inevitable, while the only way of possessing individual integrity seems to be to submit to one's Fate: "a man's got to do what a man's got to do," even if—or *especially* if—the results are fatal. And there is no surer way to meet one's doom than to fight against Fate on the basis Self-will, since Fate is the secret principle of Self-will, and thus inseparable from it.

Fate imposed on society produces Chaos. If a whole generation of adolescents believe that they are fated to fail, drug-taking and dissipation seem the only way out, and society dissolves. So both the self-willed individual fated to die—like the Irish hero Cuchulainn who was chosen, empowered, exalted and ultimately doomed by the Goddess Morrigan—and the chaotic individual destined to degradation and madness, are servants of Fate. The chaotic individual is susceptible to shame in the face of those more fortunate individuals upon whom Fate seems to smile; and these fortunate sons and daughters must maintain their high position in the court of Fate by casting shame upon those who are vulnerable to it, in an attempt to avoid an adverse fate by forcing others to live it out. So while Law manifests in terms of explicit rules, Fate often wears the mask of unconscious social morality. If we are the "right kind of person," society welcomes us; if we are the "wrong kind," even though our actions are impeccable, we lose. And if we try to free ourselves from this enforced moral typology, the only alternatives seem to be to violently rebel, or else to embrace the very shame society imposes upon us, and overcome its stigma by reveling in it. But to revel in shame is only to descend into Chaos, while to rebel against Fate is to sacrifice oneself to it. Cuchulainn fought against the Goddess to whom he owed his prowess, and was destroyed: he rebelled against his fate, and therefore met it.

So we can see that both submission to and rebellion against these Archons only grants them a reality they do not in fact possess, thereby increasing their power. To submit to false Law is ultimately to be forced to commit the very crimes which that Law punishes, just as to worship a false moral uprightness is to place oneself under a false shame. In the words of Blake, "Prisons are built with stones of [false] Law/ Brothels with bricks of [false] Religion." And to rebel against Law is to finally *become* it, as in the well-known fate of the successful revolutionary who replaces one tyranny with another. Furthermore, to become Law is to ultimately fall under the power of Fate, as when the established system grows beyond the control of those administering it, and descends into Chaos. To submit to Chaos in a deluded search for peace, as in the case of alcoholism or drug addiction, is to fall under both the shame of Fate and the punishment of Law, and to expose oneself to the willful impulses of the separate fragments or "complexes" of one's soul, which are part of Selfhood, thus making that soul vulnerable as well to the violent and willful Selfhoods of others. A person who is violently out of control attracts the violence of other people; a woman who has been drugged is in danger of being raped. And when the soul makes this willfulness its own in hopes of defending itself, when it aggressively asserts itself in an attempt to overcome Chaos, or to defend itself against other people's aggression, Law is always there to pass sentence. Likewise those who rebel against the shame of Chaos by trying to be "the right kind of people" in the eyes of a degenerate society, who seek the moral blessing of the system of "this world" in an attempt to get Fate on their side, will find themselves shamefully compromised. Passing from Fate to Law, they will become agents of the very system of oppression they once sought to oppose, of that tyrannical establishment whose blind, mechanistic Law created Chaos in the first place.

It should be obvious, then, that "this world" provides no way out, because no single worldly idol can give us shelter from, or power against, the others. They are in collusion, and their function is to prevent us from glimpsing any Reality outside the hopeless terms they lay down.

But why are the primal idols four in number? Is this just a convenient way of looking at things, or is there a deeper structure underlying this fourness? In a way, both statements are true. The mysteries of the Divine Nature, Its relationship to Its creative manifestation, and Its distortion by the human ego, can never be perfectly defined or systematized, mathematically or otherwise. And yet, in the process of contemplating these mysteries, certain forms arise, which are more suggestive of the "deep things of God" than anything our material or psychic consciousness can perceive or create. From tradition to tradition, from moment to moment of spiritual insight, the forms which appear are always similar but never identical, thereby demonstrating both that God is perfectly concrete, infinitely real and absolutely unique, and that His ultimate Essence is totally beyond conception.

See it like this: The subject/object mode of perception in which we find ourselves immersed, where "I" am a human subject, and "that out there" a world, is a projection, on a lower level, of God's mirror-like Self-understanding within the depths of His own nature. Hidden within my perceiving human subjectivity is the Divine Subject, God as the eternal Witness of all the worlds. Hidden behind the "world out there" is the Divine Object, the face of God eternally present behind the forms and events of our lives. Thus the dyad "God and His Self-knowledge" is the archetype of the dyad "me and my world," making four in all.

When the Divine Subject is veiled, its Divine Object is transformed from a perfect reflection of that Witness into a mysterious world with a "will of its own"—the world of Fate. Simultaneously, the Subject becomes conditioned by its attempt to make sense of that mysterious world—in other words, to impose Law upon it from without, rather than seeing the harmonious pattern within it—and is finally obscured. All that remains of it is the idol of Selfhood, an ego-bound, self-identified human subjectivity, attempting to impose its own will upon a "world out there"—a world which, since the one perceiving it is conditioned and obscured by that fallen subjectivity, must appear as a meaningless Chaos, as in Heisenberg's view of random indeterminacy as the fundamental principle of the material world. In other words, as consciousness falls from the level of Divine Self-understanding to the level of human egotism, idols are generated, which fill the void left by the (apparent) withdrawal of the Presence of God.

From one point of view, these four idols are the satanic counterfeits—the ego-based distortions—of what in the Hebrew Kabbalah are called "the four worlds," which are related to the Four Living Creatures (Hebrew *hayoth*) that appear both in the vision of Ezekiel and the *Apocalypse* of St. John. From the standpoint of the four worlds, the descent from Divine Subject to human ego is not a "fall" but a progressive manifestation of God which never fundamentally departs from the Divine Nature. Leo Schaya, in *The Universal Meaning of the Kabbalah*, describes these worlds in the following terms, as

the "esoteric anatomy" of Man considered as "the image and like-
ness of God":

> The revelatory, creative and redemptive light of the divine Being
> is, so to speak, 'refracted' through the causal 'prism' of His
> aspects, the *Sefiroth*, into the indefinite multitude and variety of
> universal manifestation. The immense hierarchy of onto-cosmo-
> logical degrees, with all they contain, is established by this 'refrac-
> tion' of the divine light; these degrees are recapitulated in the four
> 'worlds' (*olamim*), namely *olam ha'atsiluth*, the transcendent
> 'world of emanation' which is that of the *Sefiroth*; *olam haberiyah*,
> the ideal or spiritual 'world of creation,' filled with the divine
> immanence (*shekhinah*) alone; *olam ha'yetsirah*, the subtle 'world
> of formation' inhabited by angels, genii and souls; and *olam
> ha'asiyah*, the sensory and corporeal 'world made of fact.' (p. 26)
> Man is the most perfect image of universal reality in the whole of
> creation; he is the 'incarnated' recapitulation of all the cosmic
> degrees and of their divine archetypes . . . he represents the most
> evident symbol of the ten *Sefiroth*, and his integral personality
> embraces all the worlds: his pure and uncreated being is identi-
> fied with the Sefirothic 'world of emanation' . . . his spirit, with
> the prototypical 'world of creation' . . . his soul with the subtle
> 'world of formation' . . . his body, with the sensory 'world of fact.'
> (p. 70)

The "world of emanation" is related to the Divine Subject; it is the
archetype of sacred law—the ten *Sefiroth* being the prototypes of the
Ten Commandments. The "world of creation" is related to the
Divine Object; it is the archetype of wisdom and contemplation.
The "world of formation" is related to the subtle form of the cosmos
as the object of the individual human subject; it is the archetype of
universal life-energy, of the perceived world considered as the
shakti, or radiant self-manifesting energy, of that subject, by virtue
of the Divine Subject hidden within it. The "world of fact" is related
to the uniqueness of the human person. It is the archetype of the
human subject itself, as represented by the human body, the most
concrete fact of our experience. The idolatry of Law is the counterfeit of the world of emanation; the idolatry of Fate, of the world of

creation; the idolatry of Chaos, of the world of formation; the idolatry of Selfhood, of the world of fact.

But what is the way out of the system of this fallen world? The true and sufficient answer to this question is: to plumb the depth and fulfill the conditions of any one of the great religions or wisdom traditions, which were sent by God to save us from our fallen, or forgetful, or ignorant human condition. And the specifically intellectual or *jñanic* answer—within the context of one of these traditions, sincerely embraced and fully lived—is: not to struggle with the shapes of idolatrous illusion, not to rebel against or seek power from the shadows of God, but simply to *see* them, and, thereby, to see through them. Behind Fate is pure contemplation, whose symbols include the Buddhist Prajñaparamita, the White Buffalo Cow Woman of the Lakota, and the Judeo-Christian Holy Wisdom. Behind Law is the prophetic function which Blake called the Imagination, by which eternal principles forever renew their covenant with the unique moments of our lives. Behind Chaos is *shakti*, the universal power of the Absolute, the "spirit of God" which "moved on the face of the waters," and which, in its redemptive mode, is the cosmic attraction which returns all things to their single transcendent Source. And behind Selfhood is the unseen Seer, the One Self of All within the human heart. As we awake to these four aspects of the Divine, these "four living creatures"—by God's grace, and by our own full and willing cooperation with it—the abstract separative ego is dissolved in the light of the One Reality.

These "Four Living Creatures", as we have seen, appear in various modes upon all three primary ontological levels of universal manifestation: the Spiritual (*nous; intellectus; pneuma; al-ruh*); the psychic (*psyche; al-nafs*, including but not limited to *dianoia/ratio*); and the material (*hyle*, including both *soma/corpus/al-jism* and *oecumene/mundus*). Just as the celestial archetypes, when reflected on the psychic level, become polarized into inner and outer aspects—individual psychology and collective psychology—so the same archetypes appear on the material level as polarized into the Macrocosm and the Macrocosm—the material universe and the human body. (The dimension of history and society is part of the material universe on one end of the spectrum, and of the collective human psyche on the other.) In terms of the Macrocosm, the Four Living Creatures are reflected as *matter* (epitomized by the human body in its natural environment, whose *archon* is Selfhood and whose *spiritual faculty* is the *Atman*), *energy* (the subtle substance of material manifestation, whose archon is Chaos and whose faculty is *Shakti* or universal vibration), *space* (the subtle context of material manifestation, whose archon is Fate and whose faculty is *Contemplation*), and *time* (the driving force of material manifestation, whose archon is Law and whose faculty is the *Prophetic Imagination,* the "Poetic Imagination" of William Blake). In terms of the Microcosm, the Four Living Creatures correspond to the four quarters of the human body: the Prophetic Imagination to the left cerebral hemisphere, related to speech; the Contemplative faulty to the right cerebral hemisphere which governs spacial perceptions and relations; *Shakti* to the left side of the human body ruled by the right brain; and the *Atman* to the right side of the human body ruled by the left brain, which corresponds to Ramana Maharshi's "heart on the right", the psychophysical seat of *jñana*.

But to return to our main subject: how does the system of idolatry represented by the four Archons, and the fallen world based upon it, relate to the Antichrist? If we take Antichrist to be an individual, we can see these four primal idols as a kind of analysis of his character. In other words, we can expect Antichrist, and the system he administers, to be simultaneously the most authoritarian, the most rebellious, the most chaotic, and the most fatalistic one imaginable. To the degree that Antichrist is the "ape of Christ," however, his character as the quintessence of idolatry will be hidden from the people. His fatalism will tend to appear to them as certainty and assurance, his chaos as freedom and spontaneity, his rebelliousness as courage and integrity, and his authoritarianism as the aura of divine right.

All four of these elements, in one degree or another, appear in the character of Adolf Hitler, who can certainly be described as a precursor to the Antichrist. His authoritarianism is obvious, since he created an iron police state over most of Europe. But he was also a rebel, a "socialist" revolutionary, who overturned the hereditary power of the German nobility and the land-owning *junkers*. His appeal to the generation of his time was a call to "rebellion" against real or imagined authority: the Versailles treaty, the Weimar Republic, the Jews. And yet his language, and ultimately his actions, were fatalistic. In *Mein Kampf* he appealed to such "gods" as "nature" and "destiny" to support the contention that his Reich was destined to last a thousand years (making it, incidentally, a satanic counterfeit of the Christian millennium). He placed great reliance on astrologers and other prognosticators. And late in the war, with Germany in full retreat, when he could have cut his losses both militarily and politically in many ways, he chose to look at Germany's defeat in fatalistic terms. Rather than recognizing it as a tragic but not terminal setback for the nation, he saw it as a Götterdämmerung, an inevitable and apocalyptic cataclysm. Far from trying to avoid this fate, he demonstrated the depth of his fate-worship by ultimately siding with it, and doing all he could to make it as destructive as possible. He ordered Germany's vital remaining food stores and industrial plants destroyed, and even flooded the Berlin underground, killing thousands of German citizens who had taken refuge there against the invading Red Army. And apart from the chaos created by his authoritarianism, rebelliousness and fatalism, he also incorporated chaotic self-indulgence into his party program, as in the "Strength through Joy" movement within the Hitler Youth, where sexual promiscuity was made nearly compulsory. Furthermore, his erratic decision-making late in the war, to take only one of many possible examples, demonstrated the fundamental chaos of his character.

But we don't always need to turn to Hitler to understand the system of the Antichrist, though he will always be a highly valuable case-in-point. What about present day global society? Dictatorial regimes, religious and ethnic terrorism, a multinational economic order which enriches the few and impoverishes the masses, international criminal cartels which massively profit from this state of affairs, widespread moral degeneracy which calls into being repressive moral codes and attitudes, the natural environment descending into chaos, threatening our food and oxygen supplies, spawning new diseases, various proposals to turn the human body, via genetic engineering, bionics, psychopharmacology and electronic mind-control, into a bio-technological robot in order to control this social and biological chaos, if not the ultimate fantasy of "up-loading"

human consciousness into sophisticated computers and so dispens-
ing with the body entirely—this is the state of the world we live in.
And so those who want to pinpoint the exact year and month the
Antichrist will appear may be missing the point: in a sense, he is
here already. And even if he is destined to appear at one point as a
single individual, as evangelical Christians, traditional Muslims,
and Traditionalist writers (notably René Guénon and Martin Lings)
all predict, nonetheless we cannot conveniently isolate him within
that individual form and that historical period. He is everywhere
and at all times in the fallen order of human history, because, in
essence, he is nothing but the human ego in rebellion against God.
He has been virtually present in the human soul, and its social
expression, ever since Adam and Eve ate the apple.

In the 60's it was generally true that those with a liberal or left-
wing background would tend to see political or economic tyranny
(Law) and repressive, compulsive morality (Fate) as the ultimate
evils, whereas people with a right-wing, conservative background
would be more likely to view as absolute the evils of violent revolution and/or criminal activity (Selfhood) and moral degeneracy
(Chaos). This assessment is still accurate to a great degree. However,
it has been equally true since at least the late '70s—if not the '30s—
that "politically correct" liberals will identify with certain established governmental policies which conservatives view as tyrannical.
And now that our civil rights have been trashed by a "war on terror"
imposed by an establishment based in part upon the least libertar-
ian aspects of leftist mores, the torch of popular resistance has been
passed to the non-establishment conservatives, who have adopted
some (though certainly not all) of the values held by the New Left of
the '60s. But in any case, *I cannot stress strongly enough* that these
partial views, true as they may be in their own sphere, are totally
insufficient to define the social manifestation of the spiritual evil we
are here calling the Antichrist. Infernal evil can use *any* set of social
mores and any political or economic system to build its power, since
one of its ploys is to set up insoluble conflicts based on falsely-
defined alternatives. In other words, it draws the sides wrong, so
that, for example, "liberals" who think that they believe in the sanc-
tity of life as an absolute, opposing all war and defending even the

worst mass murderer against the death penalty, will find themselves supporting doctor-assisted suicide, deaf to all stories of its abuse (as well as to the understanding that it is an abuse in itself), while "conservatives" who vociferously oppose the use of illegal drugs will take somebody like Ollie North as their hero, deaf to all evidence that he may have participated in cocaine smuggling to help fund the secret Contra war. And once the conflict of good against evil is falsely defined, then all the courage and idealism in the world only goes to strengthen the evil and erode the good. Infernal forces set right against left, Jews against Muslims, women against men in such a way that their respective positions become so narrowly conceived that damage is done and darkness spread no matter which side one takes—a situation which led W.B. Yeats, in his poem "The Second Coming", which prophesies the advent of the Antichrist, to describe the latter days as a time in which "the best lack all conviction, while the worst are filled with passionate intensity". This is not to say, of course, that some social systems are not better than others, and that we are not sometimes called upon to take sides in social conflicts. Not all perceived oppositions are demonic delusions; to believe so is a delusion in itself. But unless we have a broad enough view of the nature of collective evil—which is nothing but the outer expression of the power of the human ego, and the infernal forces which that ego invokes, to pervert and appropriate *anything it can imagine*— then we will never understand the system of the Antichrist, and may consequently find ourselves unintentionally paying tribute to it, even (or especially!) in the very act of opposing it. It is true that Jesus said, "I come not to bring peace but a sword"—but he also said "resist not evil"; and (quoting from the Psalms) "sit thou at my right hand, while I make thine enemies thy footstool."

According to the story told in Plato's *Republic* of the degeneration of human society over the course of the aeon, first comes "aristocracy," which is identifiable with theocracy; this is rule by the "best," the spiritual intellectuals, in Hindu terms the *Brahmin* caste. Next "timocracy" ("government by fear") appears, rule by those of warlike character, the king and his courtiers, the *Kshatriya* caste. Next comes "oligarchy," rule by an ill-defined class of powerful individuals—perhaps the rich merchant class, given that Plato's other name for oligarchy is "plutocracy". After oligarchy comes "democracy," rule by the people. And last comes "tyranny", rule by dictators and demagogues. Thus, according to this view, even though we may lament that we are no longer ruled by wise philosophers and noble kings (to the degree that we ever were)—remembering that the "throne" itself could be a good thing, in times when the institution was spiritually alive, even if a particular king abused his authority and so was justified in being deposed—the fact that we are now in the last days of democracy means that we must do our best hold the line here as long as possible, whatever democracy's shortcomings (the degradation of objective truth to majority opinion, the attempt to base morality on an "enlightened self-interest" which always seems to degenerate into the worship of the passions), since the only alternative, according to Plato, is tyranny. And when it finally arrives on a global scale, this tyranny—authoritarian, rebellious, chaotic and fatalistic—will be (and is; it is already in evidence) the socio-political expression (the Beast) of the mass cultural and psychic disposition of the end times (the Whore), which is in turn the reflection of a counterfeit, and thus satanic, spiritual order (the Dragon). Even now we can see it recapitulating, in inverted form, all the phases that went before it: a spurious populism, a global economic oligarchy, a global militarism, and a false, globalist, one-world religion, which will be the last to develop. This is one possible rendition, and I believe it is a useful one, of the system of Antichrist.

But we must be careful never to assume that whatever most repels us and seems most evil to us must be the regime of the Antichrist. In worldly terms—and "this world" has struck its roots deep in the souls of most of us—the Antichrist will look like a good proposition. He will attract us by making a perverted appeal to what is best in us. He will not only seize power; he will also appropriate values. In the Shi'ite Muslim account, the Mahdi—the Islamic "messiah," sometimes identified with Elijah, who will appear before the Second Coming of Jesus—will wear a yellow turban, and the servants of the Antichrist green ones. This is strange, since the color yellow in Islam usually symbolizes weakness, as in western folk-symbolism it stands for either cowardice or infectious disease (remembering that plague-ships used to fly yellow flags to warn others to steer clear).

But green is the color of Paradise—specifically, in some systems, of the Paradise of the perfection of the Divine Immanence, which comes after the blackness of the transcendent, unknowable Divine Essence, and thus represents the highest stage of realization. So in the regime of Antichrist, as René Guénon predicted in his prophetic masterpiece *The Reign of Quantity and the Signs of the Times*, the significance of spiritual symbolism itself will be inverted. As it says in II Cor. 11:14, "Satan himself is transformed into an angel of light."

The Antichrist, or the system which will function as his "mystical body", must emerge in the Latter Days, at the end of the Kali-Yuga, because the veils covering the radiance of the Divine Light have started to thin due to the coming dissolution of this world; consequently God will dawn upon all of us whether we like it or not. When the Presence of God presses in upon the human soul, due to the approach of either physical death or ego-death, the ego rises up against Him. Realizing that the full dawning of the Presence of God will mean its own annihilation, it throws up every passion, mental distraction, intellectual error and emotional obscuration in its arsenal in order to hide from the face of that radiant Divine Reality—and when it fails in this, as ultimately it must, its last ploy will be to deify itself; its final way of denying God will be to present itself *as* God. And it's no different when it comes to the human collective: In its fear of the coming end of this world—which swiftly-advancing environmental destruction and the ever-present threat of thermonuclear war confront us with daily in increasingly undeniable terms—the collective psyche of global society will give birth to the Antichrist, just as the psyche of the passion-bound individual will inevitably attempt to take refuge in the ego—ultimately the self-deified ego—when confronted with the fear of death. God is rapidly approaching, faster every day, which is only another way of saying that God's eternal Presence, here and everywhere, is becoming increasingly apparent. But the collective denial of that Presence on the part of our benighted and God-denying society is swiftly expanding too, as our increasingly widespread use of "weapons of mass distraction" makes all too apparent. God will come; Antichrist will hide Him and impersonate Him; and finally Jesus Christ—the eschatological Christ, the "rider on the white horse" who appears in both the *Book of Revelations* and the *Bhagavata Purana*, and who is equally the Messiah, Maitreya Buddha and the Kalki Avatara—will slay him. Truth invokes the lie, is obscured by it, and ultimately triumphs over it. In the words of the Noble Qur'an, *Truth has come, falsehood has vanished away; truly falsehood is ever destined to vanish.*

It is important for us to be able to see the shape and nature of Antichrist in the beliefs, actions and agendas of the collective human psyche and the global society which it projects. Without a psycho-social analysis of these dynamics based on sound spiritual principles—an analysis which is adequate to the extremely dark times in which we live—our beliefs, the quality of our consciousness, and ultimately our most crucial choices, will be dictated by that very darkness; this is why the Eastern Orthodox Christians pray that God will forgive them for sins *both conscious and unconscious.* But unless collective evil is progressively recognized as a projection of the ego—and, ultimately, as the projection of *my* ego—then it will defeat us. In the last analysis we cannot conquer and save this world, except in very limited and temporary terms, no matter how acute our analysis, how energetic our actions, and how great our sacrifice. God has not granted us this power, nor will He come to our aid if in our *hubris* we foolishly attempt to do His work for Him. But He will and has granted us the power to overcome our own egotism—if, that is, we have true faith in Him—and He is ready on a moment's notice to aid us in this struggle. The war against the Antichrist may begin as the "lesser jihad", the battle against outer conditions, but it can only end after it has been transformed into the "greater jihad", the battle against the Dragon Within. And when the sword of *askesis* and *gnosis* is drawn in *that* battle, it encounters no alien flesh, it meets no enemy—because only God is.

APPENDIX: A DISCLAIMER
AND A WARNING RE GNOSTICISM

Gnosticism, which is a major influence on the worldview presented in this essay, no longer exists as a viable spiritual way—if it ever did. At one time it might have been a true Path, or embraced one (and God knows best), but as a *literal* belief-system it is heterodox (i.e., simply wrong) according to both Christian orthodoxy and the Primordial Tradition, since it by and large sees the psychic and material universes as a veil over God (which they definitely are) but not also as a theophany of His Attributes (which they also most certainly are). At one time the evil Gnostic Demiurge who creates the cosmic prison, the fallen universe ruled by *heimarmene*—grim stellar fate—might have been correctly understood as the *ego*, the lower passional self that the Sufis call the *nafs al-ammara*, "the soul commanding to evil", and the constellations of the Archons as the Names or Attributes of this very ego. If so, then it is abundantly clear that such understanding was lost at some later time through a mythological *literalization* of what must once have been nothing other than allegorical "teaching stories" related to the etiology, nature, and ultimate defeat of this ego. Through this process of literalization, a profound analysis of the tyranny of illusion became a tyrannical illusion in itself.

We can see this same process of literalization and inversion in the history of Zoroastrianism. In the earliest Zoroastrian scriptures, the *Gathas* (reputedly composed by Zarathustra himself), the Adversary—who later became Angra Mainyu/Ahriman conceived of as "God's evil twin", a power equal and opposed to Ahura Mazda—is clearly presented as a *subordinate* power, and thus as a figure entirely amenable to being employed as an allegory of the ego. And Zoroastrianism, as Hans Jonas has shown, was—through Manichaeism—a major influence on the spectrum of religious mythologies later classified by scholars under the term "Gnosticism".

So Gnosticism is best characterized as a heretical and fallen worldview. Once its dangerous deficiencies as a positive vision of Reality are clearly understood, however, it may still be of great use as a metaphysical/mythopoetic analysis of the System of This World as a "prison of unreality", a worldview capable of "speaking to the condition" of those who feel themselves to be the inmates of that prison, who must daily suffer the blows of the *cosmic paranoia* so common in our times. To those wishing to understand the Gnostic tradition in this light, I heartily recommend *The Gnostic Religion* by Hans Jonas, and also the "Prophetic Books" of William Blake, notably his three major epics, *The Four Zoas*, *Milton* and *Jerusalem*. Jonas' work is a valuable approach to the exegesis of these Books (my other favorite being *Fearful Symmetry* by Northrop Frye). And just as Jonas can be of great help in throwing light on The Prophetic Books, so these Books may in turn serve to illuminate Gnosticism as Jonas presents it, and thereby work to redeem the true insights of the Gnostic worldview from the collective darkness into which it has fallen.

Elaine Pagels on the other hand, who is recognized as perhaps the "foremost authority" on Gnosticism today, and whose *The Gnostic Gospels* does provide some useful information on the Gnostic tradition, nonetheless adopts a superficial feminist view of that tradition, and has consequently, in actual effect, become one of the major agents of *anti-tradition* if not *counter-tradition* (to use the terminology of René Guénon from *The Reign of Quantity and the Signs of the Times*) working for the destruction of the Christian revelation. Those wishing to undertake a study of Pagels would, in my opinion, best serve the redemption of the positive aspects of Gnosticism by investigating exactly how *The Gnostic Gospels* is in itself a manifestation of archonic tyranny and delusion, in the face of which the Living God must become, to use a common Gnostic term, ever more an *Alien* God. The Christian Tradition, one of the providential bridges which He Himself has established as a path of return to Him, has now been largely deconstructed, in part through the infiltration of the Church by the very Gnosticism that, if torn from the grip of Antichrist and firmly subordinated to the orthodox revealed faiths, might yet be of great help in exposing the Beast and his agendas. Gnosticism is almost never understood, however, as a mythopoetic analysis of the prison of unreality in which we lie entombed, only as a heterodox and literalistic "alternative" to the orthodox Christian tradition; the Neo-Gnostic revival, through the activity of Elaine Pagels and others like her, is thus fast becoming a pillar of the New World Order, and of the religion of Antichrist of which that Order is the outer political and economic expression. There are many worldviews that may have a limited but real use on the critical plane—Marxism, for example—but which, when translated to the positive plane, when adopted as programs for social change or primary views of Reality, can give rise to nothing but a hell on earth, and the destruction of the human soul.

8

PSYCHOTHERAPY
AND EXORCISM

For Dr. Rama P. Coomaraswamy

The traditional doctrine that some physical and mental diseases are caused by demonic possession began to lose credibility as the germ theory of disease became established; as early modern psychotherapy documented various cases of "hysteria" that were amenable to treatment by psychoanalysis and/or hypnosis; and as medical science discovered physical causes for more and more conditions originally suggestive of possession, such as epilepsy or Tourette's Syndrome. And although popular culture and various religious institutions continue to accept the reality of demonic activity, the same certainly cannot be said for most of modern academia and the medical profession. Demonic possession, however, is a very real phenomenon, which various advances in medical and psychotherapeutic science may have more clearly isolated, but have certainly not disproved. (Traditional Catholicism, for example, has collected many well-documented cases of possession, which are accepted as real only after a rigorous evaluation, and has also developed clear criteria by which possession may be determined, and according to which it may be distinguished from simple mental illness.)

Mental illness of any kind is the result of injury to the individual soul or psyche. Such injury may be produced by destructive influences emanating from three discrete planes of being: the physical, the psychic, and the Spiritual. Damage to the psyche can be caused, on the physical level, by disease, trauma, toxicity and/or a genetic defect; on the psychic level, by psychological trauma, either accidental or deliberate, either painful or seductive; and on the Spiritual level, by sin. The fact that the psyche can be profoundly affected by physical causes has been experientially validated by anyone who has ever ingested a psychedelic drug—or simply gotten drunk—and psychosomatic medicine has demonstrated that psychological trauma can produce measurable physical effects, some temporary, some virtually permanent, including changes in the gross anatomy of the brain. The psychological and somatic affects of sin, however, are harder for us in these materialistic times to discern, or even to believe in.

Sin is a perversion of the will whereby the individual freely chooses to engage in physical or psychic actions that divert his or her inner Spiritual attention away from God and the metaphysical order. Such a choice is never made in the absence of influences and temptations, but it is always a *choice*, not (in the last analysis) a compulsion. In the case of vice, or habitual sin, such temporary diversions of attention progressively erect a more or less continuous barrier or veil between the psyche and the Spirit, a veil that further weakens the will and diverts it from its true aims, and which transforms the psyche's experience of the presence of the Spirit from one of bliss into one of pain. It is by virtue of this very pain, if faced faithfully and courageously, that the veils covering the Spirit are dissolved; this process is known as *purgation*, which may be defined as a cooperation between the activity of the Spirit from above—Grace—and the work of the soul on its own ground—repentance. And such purgation, since it threatens to deconstruct various psychic dispositions inimical to the Spirit in which demonic entities usually, if not always, continue to play some part, will often be an occasion for attack upon the soul by such entities. When they perceive that their hold upon that soul is challenged, they are quick to react via seduction and terror, as in the case of the Buddha's confrontation by "Mara the Tempter" under the Bodhi Tree during his struggle to attain Perfect Total Enlightenment.

And whatever their etiology, demonic or simply psychospiritual, if such veils are not removed and such dispositions deconstructed, if purgation does not take place, the psyche or soul remains cut off from the possibility of conscious and willing participation in the

Spirit, the source of its own life. The Spirit may continue to give life to the body on an unconscious level, but as for the soul or psyche, alienated (as Dante described it) from the "good of the Intellect", it remains as if dead. It is capable of responding only to physical influences from below; it can no longer receive Spiritual impulses from above; it is closed to Grace, cut off from both love and wisdom. And the general deadness of the psyche in a state of sin may also contribute, in some cases, to the development of physical disease: in such instances we may confidently assert that a more-or-less visible *psychosomatic* disease is actually caused by an invisible *pneumopsychic* disease, which is precisely what a state of sin is.

A psychic injury may cause a physical pathology, and vice versa; a Spiritual wound (a sin) will also injure the psyche, and sometimes the body as well. But a physical or psychic injury cannot in and of itself injure the Spirit, only tempt the psyche to sins against the Spirit which will, not literally injure it, but certainly veil it. Sometimes these temptations are so fierce as to appear for all intents and purposes as true compulsions, which is why we should be careful not to harshly judge those who sin so as to escape from great psychic pain, as in the case of the traumatized war veteran who turns to drugs or alcohol to anesthetize himself against agonizing memories. Nonetheless such actions, in the last analysis, remain sins, not inevitabilities; the will, though seriously compromised, is still essentially free. And to accept that this is the case, even in the presence of almost irresistible psychic forces, actually has a positive and merciful side to it, since it does not reduce the human soul to a psychic automaton, but continues to grant it the power—no matter how weakened and injured that power may be—to respond to Divine Grace; even the "healthy" will, in the Spiritual order, can do nothing without Grace.

Although sin is may be termed a Spiritual injury, we must remind ourselves that the Spirit itself cannot sin; it is the soul, the psyche, that *sins against* the Spirit. It is tempted to such transgressions by forces from within it, and also by other forces inhabiting the psychic environment surrounding it, some emanating from living human individuals ("bad companions"), others from actual demonic entities; just as the physical world is the objective environment of the body, so the psychic world is the objective environment of the soul.

It is precisely at this point that the question of demonic influences becomes relevant.

Demons are essentially psychic entities, conscious entities possessing both intelligence and will, and even a sort of subtle body. Their activity, however, may be termed "spiritual" in that it is their role and their intent to tempt us to sin so as to divert our attention from the plane of Spiritual realities, and ultimately from God. Other psychic forces may be destructive, but not consciously and deliberately so; among these may be classed the psychic residues of traumatic events, individual or collective; other psychic residues that adhere to objects or places of great power whose informing Spiritual archetype has departed from them, as in the case of sites once sacred to now-dead religions, including certain Egyptian tombs; and various psychic "sheaths" sloughed off in the death-process by human individuals who, while not necessarily actively evil, were at least far from psycho-spiritually integrated—the residues or entities that we commonly refer to as *ghosts*. And certainly not all psychic influences or entities are actively evil or passively toxic. Some psychic "substances"—and every emotion, positive or negative, appears on one level as a substance or quality inhabiting the objective psychic environment—are positive and beneficent. A house or natural feature or human individual may emanate a quality of peace or joy or intelligent clarity that is uplifting and healing to all within its radius of influence; the cosmological science of *feng shui* was developed to exploit and channel such positive forces. Other people and places may give off destructive influences, producing feelings of fear, hatred, oppression, agitation or darkening of the mind. And there are many conscious entities residing on the psychic plane who are certainly not to be described as evil; they may be *diamones* (in Muslim terms, *jinn*), but they are not demons. Some are actively beneficent, particularly the ones that traditional shamans ally with in order to practice certain forms of psycho-physical healing; others are mischievous—dangerous, though not actively evil; still others are simply playing their part in the subtle dimension of earthly manifestation by acting as channels between angelic intelligences and physical forms, particularly living forms; among these may be classed those *daimones* who protect, govern and oversee particular plant or animal species, specific bioregions, etc. Tribes, cities, nations and locales have their protecting *daimones* as well. Nonetheless, an excessive sensitivity on the part of an individual to the influence of such entities, even if they are basically beneficent, may have a disordering effect on his or her psychophysical system, and thereby open the door to later incursions by other entities or qualities that are far from beneficial, and sometimes even demonic. Nor should all *daimones* related to geographic regions or human groups be classed as helpful or neutral; some may actually be demons. Could a subtle entity presiding over a city like Las Vegas, for example, or a group like the Mafia, be considered in any way beneficent?

To coin a phrase, "the Devil is an opportunistic infection". Whenever our "psychic immune system" becomes weakened, due to physical, psychic, or spiritual trauma, it becomes vulnerable to demonic incursions—either *obsession*, in which the person is tormented by demons but not dominated by them, or *possession*, in which the individual's will is in fact dominated by them. The influence of obsession, and more particularly possession, will in some cases extend to the body as well, producing such well-documented manifestations as spontaneous physical wounds, levitations, preternatural physical strength etc., phenomena which most often appear during the process of exorcism.

The point-of-entry for demonic possession is neither the body nor the Spirit, but the psyche; it is specifically the *soul* which is possessed. And since possession can result from—although it is certainly not to be identified with—forms of psychic damage that arise from physical or psychological causes as well as the specific sort of damage that stems from sin, it is apparently possible for even the spiritually innocent to become possessed—not as the result of sin or vice, but simply due to psychic trauma, which makes them vulnerable to demonic incursion.

This possibility raises certain questions, however. Fr. Malachi Martin, in his masterpiece *Hostage to the Devil*, asserts that true possession always results from a decision on the part of the possessed to accept the influence of the demon; if so, then how can the innocent be possessed? In a taped interview Fr. Martin also speaks of a relatively new phenomenon: the possession of infants. Perhaps we need to posit the existence of a state of partial possession where the soul that lacks the positive help of religious forces, such as the sacrament of Baptism or life within a traditional sacred ambience, becomes occupied by demonic forces short of full possession. Traditional folklore, for example, speaks of "changlings"—of infants who, prior to their baptism, were believed to have been abducted by fairies, who would leave a fairy child in their stead, outwardly resembling the human infant but in some way uncanny. It may also happen that a soul that is damaged for whatever reason may become so obsessed and tormented by demons that it ultimately succumbs to the *temptation* of possession, since the demons offer it relief from their tortures (a relief that is always only temporary), if not actually a demonic form of pleasure, if only it will place its will firmly in their hands.

In view of the fact that damage to the psyche from whatever cause makes it vulnerable to demonic influence, and the further fact that any motion of the will toward sin and rebellion against God (which will necessarily be based on a willful turning of the inner Spiritual attention away from the Divine) is always immediately aided and abetted by demons, just as it was doubtless originally suggested by them, it is extremely difficult in practice to discern exactly where mental illness leaves off and demonic influence begins. Suffice it to say that both are always present in *any* psychic pathology, although the demonic element may manifest as anything from a negligible potential that can be safely ignored to a full-blown case of obsession or possession.

Given the various kinds of "energy-healing" now available in the alternative spirituality/New Age world, a clear distinction needs to be made between exorcism and "psychic detoxification". Exorcism neutralizes demonic activity, which operates on the psychic plane, by virtue of theurgic power emanating from the Spiritual plane; most forms of energy-healing, on the other hand, deal with dark psychic forces through the use of lighter and more beneficent forces from the psychic plane alone. Thus while energy-healing may have influence, exorcism possesses *authority*. Types of therapy such as Reiki may nonetheless be of real help in both physical and psychic healing due to their ability to dislodge toxic psychic residues from the subtle energy body, whether these residues have been produced by negative emotions of long standing or simply picked up from the client's psychic ambience. Such therapies may also be effective in banishing various vague psychic "entities" of a morally neutral character that have in one way or another become attached to the psyche of the client, though in this case things are less certain. Demonic entities, however, are far from neutral: they are acutely intelligent, extremely powerful, and actively evil, which makes "Spiritual combat" a better metaphor for traditional exorcism than "Spiritual healing"; for this reason it is ill-advised to attempt to deal with actual demonic possession by means of energy-healing therapies. And there is also the danger that certain of these therapies, particularly those which operate upon the "etheric" or subtle energy body, after an initial therapeutic success may leave that body more permeable than before to psychically toxic or even demonic influences, thus leading to the etheric equivalent of a post-operative infection. And anyone who is confirmed in a traditional spiritual Way should probably stay away from all types of psychic healing, concentrating instead on the canonical forms of his or her tradition (for Muslims, the *salat*; for traditional Christians, the sacraments), as well as on invocatory and petitionary prayer: when God is offering us something directly from Himself, to apply to intermediaries instead is the height of discourtesy.

It should be reiterated at this point that demonic influence is not always the result of sin. The possession, or at least the partial possession, of innocent souls is also possible; for example, children traumatized by physical or sexual abuse may sometimes become possessed as a result.

And there are certainly many recorded instances where saints, or those making real progress on the spiritual Path, are obsessed or temporarily deluded by demons, who are simply defending themselves against the great damage to their kingdom that sainthood represents. In view of the possibility that even the innocent may suffer possession, exorcism should never be characterized as a "judgment" upon the possessed person—an attitude that is sometimes exhibited in certain counterfeit and abusive "exorcisms" which are demonic in themselves. But in cases where possession is indeed the result of sin or accompanied by sin, success cannot be gained without sincere repentance on the part of the exorcee. And although the will of the possessed may be so deeply compromised that it has been unable to concentrate its powers to the point where true repentance becomes possible, or else has not had the strength to persist in the process of purgation even if it momentarily wills to repent, it will still likely possess the ability, in the presence of the grace and power of *traditional* exorcism, to either accept that exorcism or reject it. It is my belief, though I am open to correction by any experienced exorcist, that exorcism in itself restores the will of the person possessed by and through sin to its proper condition, so that it may freely choose to accept or reject the good; if this were not the case, repentance could not be a factor in the process, and the effects of sin cannot be overcome without repentance. (I emphasize the word "traditional" in view of the fact that Father Gabriele Amorth, chief exorcist of the Diocese of Rome, has recently declared that the new Catholic rite of exorcism is no longer effective.) It may also be true that once the subject who was originally disposed to possession through sin is freed from demonic influence, he is then equally free to examine his conscience, to determine what past actions and choices opened him to demonic possession in the first place, to become convicted of the sinfulness of them, and finally to repent of them and be forgiven for them.

Malachi Martin also speaks of a condition known as perfect possession (see Dante's *Inferno*, Canto XXXIII) where the will of the subject is so completely in the power of the demonic that he or she exhibits no violent reaction, as most possessed persons will, to the presence of sacred objects or the power of Grace operating through exorcism itself. In this case it would appear that exorcism does not restore the will to its original freedom. On the other hand, the "intrinsic" rejection of Grace by a lost soul may legitimately be considered to be a renewal of that soul's willful rejection of God, a rejection that will only deepen its damnation. Every opportunity to repent that the soul does not take, every offer of Mercy that the soul does not accept, only intensifies the darkness of that soul. Thus we can say that the soul which rejects the Mercy of exorcism thereby transforms that Mercy into the Wrath of God. The Eastern

Orthodox Christians say that God, of Himself, manifests only Love and Mercy, because that is His intrinsic nature; likewise the highest Name of God in Islam is either the familiar *Allah*, or else *al-Rahman*, "the All-Merciful". God offers only Mercy; it is we who, by our rejection of it, turn that Mercy into Wrath.

Whenever a mental illness is diagnosed that also suggests the possibility of demonic possession—Multiple Personality Disorder for example (now called Dissociative Identity Disorder), or any condition in which the patient exhibits preternatural psychic abilities such as telepathy, clairvoyance, sudden knowledge of an unfamiliar language or the ability to predict the future, etc.—traditional exorcism should be considered. This does not mean that the various personalities exhibited by a person with MPD/DID are necessarily demons, only that some or all of them might be; diagnosis in such cases will therefore also include an evaluation of whatever preternatural physical manifestations may be in evidence, such as unexplained displacement or destruction of physical objects, levitation, unnatural heaviness of the subject or the people around him, spontaneous physical wounds, etc. The presence of various psychic abilities does not in and of itself prove the existence of possession; psychic talents may be congenital, accidental, or the result of psychological or neurological trauma without being demonic. They may be deliberately produced through various ill-advised "courses of study" that may or may not in themselves open the student to demonic influence; they may also develop as peripheral manifestations of progress on the Spiritual Path, as in the case of the clairvoyant saints so well documented in Sufism and Eastern Orthodoxy. But demonic "help" is always a possibility in such cases, especially if the psyche of the patient is obviously disordered.

Short of actual intervention by an exorcist, various "little exorcisms" will also likely be helpful, in both therapeutic and prophylactic terms. On the psycho-physical level, "smudging" with certain aromatic herbs or resins like sage or cedar or frankincense may be useful, though in serious cases one should never rely on such methods, which are "adjunct" at best. "Sacramentals" such as (in Catholic terms) holy water or the St. Benedict's cross or the St. Michael Prayer will be more effective, as will (in Islamic terms) the recitation of various Qur'anic verses, such as the *Surah al-Falaq* and the *Surah an-Naas*—although the Qur'an, as the actual Word of God transmitted directly to Muhammad, is better described as a full sacrament than a mere sacramental.

Given that mental illness is due to injuries to the psyche that may have physical, psychic or Spiritual causes, or any combination of these, a wise and integrated approach to psychotherapy will deal with all three. On the physical level, it should be determined whether or not the client has any organic diseases or has suffered any physical traumas; exercise and good nutrition should be prescribed, with special attention to specific nutrients which when deficient have been shown to contribute to mental or emotional difficulties (certain B vitamins, for example); physical detoxification should probably also be carried out, by such means as herbs, colonics, chelation therapy, fasts and sweats. Forms of bodywork that act to dissolve emotional knots manifesting on the physical level may also be helpful. The use of psychopharmacological agents may be necessary in acute cases and on a temporary basis, but such drugs have definite drawbacks since, generally speaking, they block psychological insight as much as they facilitate it (if not more so), and are often physically toxic as well as actually addictive.

On the psychological level, therapies which provide insight into one's emotional condition, motives and mental processes and patterns of relationship should be employed, and healthier emotional, mental and interpersonal strategies taught and practiced. (Hypnotic suggestion or various forms of behavioristic "conditioning" should probably be avoided, since they weaken the will instead of strengthening it.) And in terms of the psychophysical or properly psychic dimension, certain types of energy-healing might be considered— but one needs to be very cautious here, since most energy-healers and Reiki practitioners are extremely eclectic, often working with various "spirit helpers" of uncertain pedigree; not all of them always know exactly what they are doing. A few well-meaning energy-healers may actually be working with demons without realizing it, though my own experience with this therapy has been almost entirely positive. Nonetheless, I once encountered a Reiki practitioner who had "innocently" incorporated elements of Voudoo into her therapeutic method! Such healers may also harbor various beliefs and attitudes that are ultimately inimical to the Spiritual life. (Acupuncture, t'ai chi, and qigong, since they deal with subtle psychophysical energies but do not radically open the energy body to the psychic environment, and are less involved with psychic "belief-systems", are generally more reliable, and are not fundamentally incompatible with any of the traditional spiritual Ways.) An ability to remember and interpret one's dreams is also of great value; the development of this skill requires an extensive knowledge of universal symbolism and mythopoetic literature, however, as well as the ability to experientially distinguish between messages directed to one's intuitive faculty, to one's feelings, or to one's rational mind respectively. Such interpretation will initially require the aid of a competent therapist, or simply someone more conversant with the language of dreams than the patient is.

On the Spiritual level—which will only come into play if the client is a person of religious faith—examination of conscience (with or without outside help) should be practiced, and if the person is convicted of this or that sin, he or she should implore God's forgiveness and make a firm intention to repent. If the person is a traditional Catholic or an Eastern Orthodox Christian, he should certainly also avail himself of the Grace of the sacraments; a Muslim should rely upon recitation of the appropriate verses of the Qu'ran. Feelings of guilt should be put to work for the purpose of discernment and repentance, but never indulged in, seeing that spiritual despair is a sin in itself, and that one of the most common ploys of the Adversary is to convince us that we are in fact too evil for God to forgive. Finally, if demonic possession is suspected, exorcism should be considered.

In conclusion, an integrated approach to mental illness, one that takes all the levels of the human being into account, physical, psychic and Spiritual, is the one most likely to succeed.

9

THE PSYCHOLOGY AND
METAPHYSICS OF SUFFERING

[A shorter form of this essay appeared
in the Spring 2011 issue of *Parabola*]

SUFFERING, INFERNAL AND PURGATORIAL

The word "suffer" means both "to undergo pain" and "to allow". In the world of suffering, inescapable pain confronts the ever-present possibility of submission to the Absolute, which—God willing—may open the door to self-transcendence.

Dante, in the *Divine Comedy*, presents us with two kind of suffering: the suffering of Purgatory, and the suffering of Hell; these represent not just two posthumous states, but two different possible attitudes toward suffering in this life. In Hell, suffering only corrupts the soul; pain there is used as a weapon against other souls, against oneself, and against God. The soul tries to escape its suffering and to wallow in it at the same time; the end result of this flight from pain, which is equally a flight from reality, is to be frozen, like Lucifer in the Lake of Cocytus in the Ninth Circle of Hell. It is to enter a state where one is petrified and pulverized at the same time, where paralysis generates chaos and chaos serves paralysis. Sometimes those who have despaired of realizing the Absolute as God or Liberation (a despair that is for the most part unconscious) will become attracted to the false and inverted "absolute" of Hell, where perfect detachment is replaced by a virtually "total" nihilism, and the total annihilation of the soul in God—which results in the perfect subsistence of that soul in its eternal integrity before the face of the Divine Witness—by an endlessly incomplete annihilation in a subhuman chaos, where no integrity is possible and where any remnant of integrity that the soul may still possess simply deepens its degradation. If only nihilism could really be total—if only absolute unreality could be attained—if only complete annihilation were possible in Hell! Unfortunately, this can never be; the God-given desire for reality, for integral existence, no matter how completely we have betrayed it, can never be entirely be snuffed out: this is "the worm [that] dies not", "the fire [that] is not quenched".

The suffering of Purgatory is quite otherwise. The souls undergoing purgation embrace their suffering instead of struggling to escape it; and instead of indulging in it, they fully experience their pain, as it were, from a point beyond it. If faith is "the presence of things hoped for, the evidence of things not seen", then we can say that the good souls in Purgatory suffer in faith, and hope. Since their salvation is assured, they suffer gladly; they understand by their pain both the gravity of the sin they have fallen into, and the great privilege represented by being allowed to suffer for the sake of their divine Beloved. Their suffering is sometimes even more acute than the suffering of Hell, since they do nothing to anesthetize themselves to it and do not turn away from it. But it does not degrade them like infernal suffering does; it purifies and ennobles them. And if we are seriously walking the spiritual Path, purgatorial suffering, even in this life, will be possible—in fact, it will be necessary.

Jean Cocteau once wrote, in his book *Opium*, "A tree must suffer from the rising of its sap and not feel the falling of its leaves." He understood the pain of his withdrawal from opium addiction as the suffering of a soul struggling to embrace greater life. Even those who are suffering *in extremis*, who are facing death, may understand their suffering as the failing attempt of a dying body to a embrace greater Life than any body, even the youngest and healthiest, can encompass or withstand. Purgatorial suffering is the suffering of an inexorable spiritual expansion, against all the fixations and ploys of the ego that wants to control everything and at the same time avoid everything; it teaches the soul, by its penetrating rigor, how to accept the tremendous Mercy of God.

Edgar Lee Masters, in his poem "Elijah Browning" from *Spoon River Anthology*, writes of the struggle to accept this Mercy:

I arose and ascended higher, but a mist as from an iceberg
Clouded my steps. I was cold and in pain.
Then the sun streamed on me again,
And I saw the mists below me hiding all below them.
And I, bent over my staff, knew myself
Silhouetted against the snow. And above me
Was soundless air, pierced by a cone of ice,
Over which hung a solitary star!
A shudder of ecstasy, a shudder of fear
Ran through me. But I could not return to the slopes—
Nay, I wished not to return.
For the spent waves of the symphony of freedom
Lapped the ethereal cliffs about me.
Therefore I climbed to the pinnacle.
I flung away my staff.
I touched the star
With my outstretched hand.
I vanished utterly.
For the mountain delivers to Infinite Truth
Whoever touches the star!

Here Masters, like Dante, uses a mountain as a symbol of the path of spiritual purgation.

On one occasion, when I was in my 20's, I underwent a difficult-to-describe experience in which I understood that all suffering is produced by the contraction of the ego in the face of a Life that is too great for it; that experience resulted in the following poem:

He reached down, picked up a handful of sand, and said:
"In each one of these grains of sand is all the pain of all the
worlds.
In this one grain is Famine, War, Pestilence and the Fear of Death.
and this"—
He poured out his handful of sand against the wind—
"is Joy."

The damned—in either this life or the next—curse their pain and use it to curse others. Souls undergoing purgation—in either this life or the next—can bear their pain because they know how to *allow* it. According to the *hadith qudsi* (a category of Prophetic Tradition within Islam where Allah speaks directly through the mouth of Muhammad), "My Mercy has precedence over My Wrath", which implies that His Wrath is ultimately the servant of His Mercy. Those who really understand this also know how to use the inevitable sufferings of life as a way of opening to Mercy, and extending it to others; their suffering does not congeal their souls, but opens their hearts.

How can we discern the parting of the ways between the Purgatorial road and the Infernal road in our own lives, our own suffering?

In either case, it is only the ego that suffers. As Beat Generation poet Lew Welch said, "There is no suffering unless we invent someone to suffer the suffering." Or, in the words of God to St. Catherine of Sienna,

> For I wish thee to know that all the sufferings which rational creatures endure depend on their will, because if their will were in accordance with Mine they would endure no suffering; not that they would have no labors on that account, but because labors cause no suffering to a will which gladly endures them, seeing that they are ordained by My Will.

The ego that resists and refuses suffering is in rebellion against God's will; as Frithjof Schuon pointed out, though we have a legitimate right to struggle against evil circumstances, the point comes where struggle against circumstances becomes a struggle against God. To do all one can to overcome misfortune, with will and intelligence on the one hand and prayer on the other, is both our right and our duty; no one who fatalistically submits to "the will of the situation" can submit to the will of God. But if the time comes when all our heroic efforts fail, what then? What good is a struggle that ultimately fails? Wouldn't capitulation have been better from the beginning? The answer is, "no". If "man's extremity is God's opportunity", then we have a duty to seek that extremity—to exhaust our powers, not simply to renounce them. But we will not be able to accept ultimate failure, which may actually be our greatest good fortune, unless we are resigned to God's will in the midst of struggle, not simply in the hour of defeat. In the words of Krishna to Arjuna from the *Bhagavad-Gita*, "Act, but dedicate the fruits of the action to Me"; in the words of the Prophet Muhammad, peace and blessings be upon him, "Even if you know that the world will end tomorrow, plant a tree." If you find yourself, rather than doing all you legitimately can to end your suffering, rebelling against the *fact* of suffering, then you have taken the wrong road. But if you are able to accept your suffering as an act of God without feeling persecuted by Him, and with at least the beginning of the kind of faith that can intuit a transformative mystery within the pain and rigor of the situation—if you can say, with Job, "though He slay me, yet will I trust in Him"—then you have begun to climb the mountain. If we see our suffering as produced by other people, we will take offense and struggle against it; if we see it as produced by blind fate, we will despair in the face of it. But if we see it as authored by God for a greater purpose, then we have a real chance both to accept it, and to begin to understand it. Meaningless suffering is unbearable; suffering in which we can at least begin to discern the intrinsic meaning is not a stone to which we are chained, but a path that lies before us.

One of the best way to train ourselves to accept inevitable suffering is to meet it half-way. As many teachers, including Javad Nurbakhsh, have said, in our time ascetical self-torture is of limited value; life in the modern world is hard enough, especially for those struggling to remain faithful to spiritual norms, without artificially creating further difficulties. We meet suffering half-way by consciously placing ourselves in the presence of God, even if it hurts—and very often it *will* hurt. The Eastern Orthodox Christians say that God is, and offers, only Love; all the sufferings of Hell, and the just wrath of the Deity, are invoked by the prideful and despairing resistance of ego-ridden souls to the fires of this Love. In Hell the ego is petrified by this fire, burned down to an incombustible cinder; it Purgatory it is progressively volatilized until it becomes pure light. And given that the world is the projection of the ego, just as the ego is the internalization of the world, to remain fully in (but not of) this world while invoking the full presence of God is the best way to consciously encounter, embrace, and ultimately transmute into Mercy, the sufferings of life, as well as to do what little one can to reduce the collective suffering of the world:

The Fire is kindled;
Hear it seethe and crackle.

Suffering is the Fire:
Dhikr fans the flames.

Dhikr is the Fire,
Suffering the fuel that feeds it.

My wandering attention
Lights like a fool on
This or that perishing thing—

Dhikr calls it home:
Home to the Fire.

My heart is the altar,
Dhikr the Fire,
My living flesh the sacrifice.

Every nest on this world's tree:
Thrown into the Fire.
No perch. No resting-place.
No home.

Don't let the Fire starve.
Never let it die.
Bring more suffering.
Bring more fuel.
What would not wish
To pass through that Fire
And become immortal?

Come, fear of death.
Come, terror of failure.
Come, grim loneliness.
Come, weight of the world.

To feel pain is to suffer;
To suffer is to bear;
To bear is to allow;

To allow is to prevail.

The Fire speaks the Name.
The Fire is the burning Name
Of Him Who speaks it.

Beaten on the anvil of it
I take the single shape
That is His will.
Sweet Fire. Pungent knowledge.
Fragrant wood-smoke
Leads the vigilant, listening world

Back to the Heart of the Fire.

VICARIOUS SUFFERING
AND TRANSPERSONAL COMPASSION

We usually think of suffering as afflicting the individual, and this is
a good thing; the suffering of a million people in some great disaster
ultimately comes down to the particular and unique suffering of
each one of them. If we start to look at suffering statistically instead
of individually, true compassion will become impossible to us. But
one of the afflictions of the individual is, precisely, the suffering of
the collective. As Edgar Allen Poe demonstrated in his story "The
Masque of the Red Death", no-one is ultimately immune to the suffering of others, the suffering of all life. One of the implications of
the First Noble Truth of Gautama Buddha, "all life is suffering"—in
light of the interpenetration of life and consciousness as expressed
in Buddhist doctrine of "Indra's net", the truth that all identity is
based on relationship, that *separate* identity does not and cannot
exist—is that the one who has transcended his or her own suffering
immediately "inherits" the suffering of all sentient beings. This is
another way of saying that the Bodhisattva Vow, which is usually
presented as the magnanimous decision of the *arhant* on the edge
of attaining Buddhahood to delay his entry into *Nirvana*, to remain
behind in the *samsara* so as to save all sentient beings, is intrinsic,
not chosen; as Buddhist doctrine maintains, the realization of Void-
ness, *shunyata*, is inseparable from the realization of Compassion,

karuna. To see all sentient beings as void of self-nature is to witness them suffering the illusion of self-nature; thus the vision of *shun-yata* both spontaneously produces compassion for their suffering and posits the *upaya* or "skillful means" that possess the power to overcome it.

And just as the Bodhisattva Vow in Buddhism is both intrinsic and freely chosen, so the same is true, in the Christian universe, of the crucifixion of Christ. Even though Christ's manifestation is a free act of God and an incomparable instance of Divine Mercy and condescension, it could never have happened, nor could it have been effective to save, if it were not in line with the nature of things. To follow the nature of things is to obey God, not first on the level of His commands and prohibitions, but on the level of His essential attributes, of which all things are reflections. Behind "not my will but Thine be done" lies "not my contingent nature, but Your Absolute Being, is the Real."

The central paradox of the Crucifixion is as follows: that since God is perfect, He could not suffer, given that suffering is imperfection and privation—but that, nonetheless, according to another perspective, God must necessarily suffer, both because mercy and compassion ("suffering with") are intrinsic to His nature as aspects of His perfection, and because He is immanent in all things, as the single essence of all things. If God suffers, it is both because He loves all beings, and because He is the ultimate Witness, and therefore the ultimate Experiencer, of the sufferings of all beings.

To declare exclusively that God is beyond suffering is to assert His Transcendence—which is most certainly true—but deny His Immanence. To declare exclusively that God, through Christ—or in His own nature, and not exclusively according to the Christic revelation—suffers the sufferings of all beings is to is to assert an "Immanence" that compromises the Divine perfection by involving God (as the process theologians and others have done) in the contingencies of His own creation, thus veiling the very Transcendence that gives Immanence its meaning, and making Him less than God. Only an intellective gnosis that understands Him as being both Transcendent and Immanent, without these two perspectives involving in any way a duality within the Divine nature, can grasp the intrinsic reality that Christ manifested by His suffering and death on the cross.

We know from our own experience that attachment to limited and perishable forms—our own, or those of the various things, persons and situations we have identified with—diminishes our capacity for suffering, and thus increases our pain. To the contracted soul, immersed in the world—that is, to the ego—the slightest irritation is too much to bear, which is to say, too much to be impassively witnessed. One implication of God's Transcendence is that He is beyond all contraction, identification and attachment. And it is this very Transcendence that gives Him the capacity to suffer without being diminished, fragmented and lost in this "experience". It is precisely because God transcends all things that He possesses the power to "suffer with" all things—a power that is inseparable from His Immanence. Thus His suffering is both infinitely greater than the suffering that any limited, created being is capable of, and also—in essence—no suffering. In this fact lies the mystery of compassion, of which Christ's death on the cross is the most concentrated instance of which we have knowledge. The self-sacrifice of Christ was, and is, an incomparable instance of God's compassion for the world; it is also perfectly in line with the nature of things, and thus inseparable from the intrinsic nature of God. It is unique, free, gratuitous and never-to-be-repeated; it is also inevitable: "The Lamb" is "slain from the foundation of the world."

The doctrine of the Immanence of God, and the suffering of the Divine for all things—a suffering which is, in essence, no suffering— also means that God suffers for the whole of creation *in us*. Traditional Catholics, for example, believe that it is possible for the living to suffer for the dead, and speak of the practice of "suffering for the good souls in Purgatory". In certain states of consciousness we are able to experience the after-death struggles of these souls, thus allowing them, as it were, to be purified *through us*, through our very experience of their posthumous suffering, as if we ourselves were their purgatory. At the same time, we may offer up our own sufferings to God in partial expiation of the temporal suffering of these souls. And these two sufferings, that of our own purgation in this life and that of the souls who are undergoing purgation in the next, are mysteriously one. This is possible because departed souls who are in an intermediate condition between earthly and heavenly life form part of the Psychic Plane, which is also the objective environment of the soul of the living individual. To work through our own sufferings and attachments is thus to aid the dead in working through theirs; this solidarity of all souls undergoing purgation is one aspect of "the communion of the saints".

Charles Williams, a member of the "Inklings" group at Oxford that included C. S. Lewis, J. R. R. Tolkien, and Owen Barfield, had his own rendition of the doctrine of Indra's Net, which he called "co-inherence", and of vicarious suffering, which he termed "exchange and substitution". In exchange and substitution, a person consciously takes on the mental, emotional or physical suffering of another by mutual consent, under the assumption that someone who is not beset by a specific type of suffering or disorder (though he may certainly be troubled by other difficulties and attachments) may more easily bear and work through that sort of suffering than the original sufferer, who is particularly weak and damaged in that area. This would appear to be an extension of the Catholic principle that the living can suffer for the dead into the dimension of things where one living human being can suffer for another—not simply in an obvious physical way, as in the case of the "good Samaritan" who risks his life to rescue another or the one who dedicates his life to caring for an invalid, but in an inner, spiritual sense. According to Charles Williams, a *mutual* exchange of burdens between the original two "contracting parties" is not necessary, since the one accepting help may discharge his or her debt by helping a third party later on. This practice of exchange and substitution is Williams' more modest, particular and concrete version of the Bodhisattva Vow, as well as of Christ's Atonement for the sins of humanity through His suffering on the cross: If the Christian is commanded to "take up your cross and follow Me", then we may profitably suffer for each other in the same way, though to a much lesser degree, that Christ suffered for all of us.

The dark side of this practice is, of course, co-dependency and a blurring of boundaries between one soul and another. Only someone with a real degree of self-realization and psycho-physical balance, a person capable of true respect, discretion, and self-respect, can consciously take on the psychic burdens of another without doing more harm than good. At the very least, he or she must be free from the tendency to take on other people's burdens *unconsciously.* If you become psychically infected with another person's pain, or are vulnerable to having someone else's suffering "dumped" on you, you will do no good for anyone. And the one capable of consciously taking on the suffering of another must also be able to consciously *release* it when the time comes. (Interestingly enough, there is a Tibetan Buddhist practice known as *Tonglen,* where the practitioner will visualize "breathing in" the pain and darkness of another, transmuting it within his or her soul, and then "breathing it back" as light; this would appear to be another, more traditional version of Williams' "exchange and substitution".)

The Holy Qur'an, on the other hand, clearly teaches that *no bearer of burdens can bear the burden of another*—particularly on the Day of Judgment—though it certainly commands Muslims to engage in acts of charity. Does this place Islam in opposition to the doctrine of vicarious suffering as it appears in Christianity and Buddhism (there are plenty of stories about the vicarious suffering of the Buddha in former lifetimes), as well as to Charles William's rather eccentric rendition of the same general idea? Not necessarily. It is true that Islam does not see God as suffering for the sins of man, but Sufism nonetheless embraces the idea that Allah "desires" man's company, and thus may in a sense be said to suffer the loss of him, which is why He "woos" him into returning; our intermittent sense of longing for God is actually a misperception of God's eternal longing for us. And the tradition of Muslim spiritual chivalry or *futuwwah* directs the chevalier to practice the sort of radical generosity that in many cases will inevitably result in personal suffering, as well as to take upon himself the burden of social obloquy in order to protect others who are less able to bear this burden. In any case, though it may be possible to bear the temporal suffering of another, it is certainly not possible to *repent* for another. In Christian terms, Christ alone can atone for human sin; effective human repentance and purgation happen only when the penitent avails himself of this Atonement. Likewise the Buddha can only save those sentient beings who are "ripe" for it and consequently *ask* for it; nor can Christ redeem those who, as in the case of Judas Iscariot, reject the offer of this redemption. The forgiveness of sins in Christianity does not contravene the Justice of God, any more than the Bodhisattva's vow to save all sentient beings overturns the law of *karma*. The one who repents and is saved by Christ's Atonement, and is consequently destined for glory, must still undergo purgation via temporal suffering in either this life or the next. The Grace of God operating through Christ's vicarious suffering may ease and speed the purgation of the penitent, sometimes immensely, just as the guru in Buddhism or Hinduism, or the Shaykh in Sufism, may "eat" his pupil's *karma* up to a certain point, but it cannot fit a redeemed but imperfect soul to join the company of the perfected *without* purgation. Likewise the one who, in Buddhist terms, reaches *samyak sambodhi* or Perfect Total Enlightenment is no longer generating *karma*, since the one to whom such *karma* would apply is seen to be non-existent (or rather, fundamentally without self-nature); nonetheless, the *karma* already accrued must still work itself out. In Islam, which has the virtue of greatly simplifying things in terms of its fundamental principles, while allowing for exquisite subtleties in its esoteric dimension (Sufism), he who repents is necessarily forgiven, since Allah is "the Beneficent, the Merciful". If the penitent takes one steps toward Him, Allah takes ten steps toward the penitent; if he travels toward Allah walking, Allah travels toward him running. When the Hour of Judgment or the day of one's death arrives, the moment of truth has come; in that Hour, no-one can bear the burdens of another. Christianity, Buddhism and Islam are in perfect agreement as to the fact that no-one can repent for another or avail him- or herself of the Grace of God, or the intrinsic Buddhahood or "awakenness" of things, on behalf of another; as Gautama put it, "work out your own salvation with diligence". Vicariously taking on the burdens of someone else in order to alleviate his or her suffering is a *psychic* act, though it may take place under the influence of spiritual inspiration; repentance is a *spiritual* act. And without true spiritual repentance, the best-intentioned and most powerful psychic aid and comfort is ultimately of no avail. And certainly no-one should attempt to suffer vicariously for others unless he is already capable of resisting the temptation to dump his burdens on them, to make others suffer for *him*. Not to add to the sufferings of the world through complaints and recriminations, but to bear one's own burdens in "cheerful" silence, is formidable enough task for any one of us.

The royal road to the transcendence of suffering is the existential realization of theodicy, the intimate vision of all events and conditions as acts of God, and of God as the Sovereign Good. And this is in many ways a terrible thought. It is easier for us to conceive of God as all-good if we turn half of existence over to the Devil, who we see as continually thwarting His plans. The idea that the horrendous sufferings of life could be the signs and effects of a Good too great for us to bear is a hard thing to bear in itself. And yet this is the simple truth. We want to experience pleasure and avoid pain, yet our very insistence upon this creates an ego to which pleasure becomes less and less possible, and pain increasingly inevitable: this is perhaps the central irony of human life, an irony and a self-contradiction that only suffering, faithfully endured, can expose and redress. The Buddha said: "I come to end suffering." Christ said, "take up your cross and follow me." The apparent contradiction between these two statements is resolved in a line from *The Gospel of Thomas*: "If you knew how to suffer, you would know how not to suffer." The realization that God is the Absolute Good, and that all our sufferings come from resistance to this Good, a resistance that is initially inevitable due to our very desire to maintain our physical lives on earth, but which can be overcome definitively by spiritual death, is so powerful that it can even produce, God willing, a love for the rigors of suffering itself. To submit to God's Will when it appears as a sentence of inevitable suffering and death is perhaps the hardest thing we are called upon to do in this life; but hidden within it is the mystery of a transcendental joy. And the joy which follows upon submission to God's will, in the consciousness that ultimately only He is the author of all events and the performer of all actions, is in no way selfish or self-enclosed joy: rather, it is the root and power of compassion. Only those immersed in the Divine Bliss can have perfect compassion for the suffering of those not so immersed—a compassion by which the pain of the suffering ones is fully experienced with no denial, no recoil, but one which remains at the same time, in its intrinsic nature, beyond suffering entirely. Pity for the suffering only increases their pain; a cold indifference in the face of that suffering, masquerading as *apatheia* or spiritual impassivity, increases it as well. Only a compassion that fully "feels with" the pain of the sufferer, but at the same time is totally beyond it and unaffected by it, has the power to alleviate that suffering, because it neither remains aloof from the other (false impassivity) nor identifies with the other (toxic pity); this is the suffering of one whose ego is annihilated, and also the sort of suffering by which it is annihilated. True compassion is of God—which is why, like God, it must be both immanent and transcendent.

CONCLUSION

Suffering is a universal experience of all human beings, of all sentient life forms. If we see it as a meaningless misfortune that science and social engineering will someday eradicate, we are deeply deluded, while if we realize the truth that the permanent eradication of suffering is manifestly impossible, but still see no *meaning* in it, what else can we do but despair? The massive use of "weapons of mass distraction" in the contemporary world—drugs, pornography, meaningless sex, the craziness of the electronic media, dangerous and/or degrading games and sports, fantastic and empty belief-systems—is clear evidence of the fact that suffering no longer has any meaning for us. And this loss of any sense of the purpose of suffering is further evidence that, although we are human beings, we no longer know what a human being *is*. If we see no purpose in suffering, how can we maintain our courage in the face of the hardships of life? Nothing is left for us then but to make a religion, as well as an industry, out of our need to deny reality. But if we are able by the Grace of God to come to a true sense of the ultimate goal of human life—self-transcendence, and the God-given duty to stand as a sign and mirror of the Deity in this world—then our suffering will be transformed from a misfortune into a teacher, from a degradation into a ennoblement, from an incitement to hatred and self-hatred and despair into a great power in the service of love. In the words of William Blake, from his poem *The Little Black Boy*, ". . . we are put on earth a little space/ That we may learn to bear the beams of Love"; in the words of W.B. Yeats, from *Crazy Jane Grown Old Looks at the Dancers*, "Love is like the lion's tooth".

10

THE END OF THIS WORLD

I

William Burroughs once wrote, in his "novel" *Nova Express*: "Junk is cooked-down image". By "image" he meant anything that appears that isn't real, that replaces reality, that lives as a parasite on reality and thereby destroys reality, whether it be a product of the psychic environment, or of society, or of the media, or of various forms of interpersonal seduction, or of the deluded psyche itself. And if junk (i.e. the opiates, either natural or synthetic) is *image*, then image is equally *junk*: an addictive drug.

Burroughs recounts that, after taking many "cures", the only thing that finally broke his addiction to the opiates was *apomorphine*, a chemically-altered form of morphine. He saw it as a kind of anti-junk, and claimed that it "activates the regulatory centers of the back-brain".

Apomorphine is an emetic; it produces nausea and vomiting.†

Gestalt psychology speaks of a process or state called "confluence", where the boundary between self and other, self and world, is blurred or erased. Confluence is an "oral" condition; the prototype of psychological confluence throughout life is the infant's oral confluence with its mother's breast. This confluence between infant and breast happens by a process of "projection" and "introjection". Projection, as we have seen above, is to falsely see something that is in the self as part of the outer world, or as the outer world as a whole; introjection is to falsely see something that is in the outer world as

---

† Apomorphine would thus be the equivalent of the herb *moly* in Homer's *Odyssey*, which gives Odysseus the power to overcome the spells of the witch Circe—who is This World.

being within the self, or as constituting the entire self. The infant fills itself with its mother's milk and so "becomes" the mother—identifies with the breast. As the French poet Arthur Rimbaud put it, "*I* is another".

Identification of the self with the world, or of the world with the self—the extraverted and introverted forms or poles of identification (which happen concurrently, the one being relatively visible—at least from the outside—and the other relatively invisible, depending upon whether we are extraverts or introverts)—is the process by which the ego is formed. And paradoxically (or ironically), to become identified with the world is to be alienated from it.

This identification is the basis of "worldliness", of the all-pervasive psychic principality or power known to Islam as *al-Dunya* and to Christian theology as "This World". We tend to believe nowadays that "otherworldliness" is unreal, an expression of fantasy-life, while worldliness is real, is reality itself. But the opposite is in fact the case: worldliness is fantasy, is false identification, is "image"—which is why worldliness acts exactly like an addictive drug; it is This World which is the real "opium of the people". The "other" world, not this one—the world of the intelligibles, of the metaphysical principles—is the real world; in order to understand these principles, the ego must be deconstructed; identification must end. (It is of course also possible to indulge in fantasies about the intelligible, metaphysical world, but such fantasies have nothing whatever to do with metaphysics, nor are their contents in any way intelligible. They are nothing but that "higher" form of worldliness which has come to be known, in the words of Chögyam Trungpa, as "spiritual materialism".)

Once your mother was the world; now the world is your mother. When Jesus said to his mother, "Woman, what have I to do with thee?", he was renouncing worldliness, renouncing the world. We renounce the world by deconstructing the ego, because the world is a projection of the ego, and the ego an introjection of the world. Instead of drinking in the world, we vomit it out, thus reversing the process of oral confluence. This is why ego-deconstruction often produces a profound sense of psychic, and sometimes even physical, disgust. William Burroughs' experience of overcoming his addiction to opiates through use of the nauseating "anti-drug" apomorphine was only a special case of the general process by which worldliness is overcome, which is fundamentally nauseating. Thus psychic nausea should in many cases be looked upon as a positive thing, as something to be accentuated, not suppressed. None of us like the feeling of being nauseated; we usually try to avoid vomiting if at all possible. But as soon as we do vomit, we invariably feel better.

For some, the process of investigating the destructive trends our world is presently subject to, the conspiracies of those who would enslave us, the plans and actions of evil men, can help overcome their unconscious identification with the world; it can work powerfully against an addiction to image, especially in view of the fact that such addiction is deliberately being engineered by our rulers so as to mystify and hide their actions. Every aspect of the world that we are unconscious of is equally an aspect of our ego; the terrifying plans and possibilities the world holds in store correspond to the most deeply repressed elements of that ego. As they rise into consciousness, one by one, our unconscious identification with them dissolves; they lose their power over us. Unconscious anxiety in the face of This World first enters consciousness as realistic fear and righteous anger—which, if our goal is *apatheia*, or spiritual impassivity, will ultimately (God willing) ripen into disgust; if we cannot save the world, at least we can be properly disgusted by it. (Fear and anger in the face of shocking revelations demonstrate that we have been unconsciously attached to these things all along, even before we knew what they were; disgust breaks this attachment.) This is why Dante in his *Divine Comedy* had to begin his spiritual journey by investigating the dark designs of Hell: even on the plane of the most infernal possibilities, "the truth shall make you free". If anything can make us disgusted with This World, it is the vision of the cruelty—and also the ultimate stupidity, for all its ingeniousness—of human evil.[†]

† Strangely enough, the work of investigating the evil of the world as a way of detaching from both world and ego is analogous in some ways—in basic intent and final goal, though certainly not on the plane of technique—to the Tibetan Buddhist *Chöd* rite, "the Yoga of the Mystic Sacrifice". In this rite the practitioner seeks out a lonely spot in the wilderness, draws a circle of power within which he yogically

So for the world to become nauseating to us is a good sign. It means that we have begun, by the Grace of God, to break our addiction to worldliness, to fantasy, to image; and once we have completely vomited the world out, we no longer identify with it. Through nausea, the boundary between self and world is re-established; self and world now form not an unconscious chaos of projection-and-introjection, but a conscious polarity—a condition of *mutual respect*. At this point a particular verse of the Qur'an, which has already been quoted above, becomes especially relevant because the situation it expresses is spontaneously recognized as the actual state of affairs, the true nature of reality: *I will show them My signs on the horizons and in their own souls until they are satisfied that this is the Truth. Is it not enough for you that I am Witness over all things?* In other words, the deconstruction of the ego, leading to the conscious polarity of self and world, posits the Transcendent God, and unveils Him. God *transcends* both self and world because He is *Witness over all things*; but He is equally *immanent* in both self and world because He shows *His signs on the horizons* (the outer world) and in our *own souls*. And if God is not only the Supreme but the *only* Being, the only One to Whom Being can be attributed intrinsically and not by participation, then not only the world of *the*

roots and centers himself, and then calls upon all the demons of the surrounding forests and mountains to come and devour him, to devour the subtle aspects of his body, speech and mind until nothing is left. All those things that threaten the so-called integrity of the ego, the things the ego is always trying to deny or repress or ward off, are now deliberately invoked, and embraced. It was the ego's very attempt to protect itself from these demons that gave them all their power to threaten it. Once the ego's defenses are let down, once we offer all we have held ourselves to be as a sacrifice to feed the hunger of the demons, and thereby satisfy the fundamental privation of being that is the principle and source of all unreality and evil, that evil is overcome. The *Chöd* rite may thus be characterized as the full yogic enactment of Christ's dictum "Resist not evil"; as such it is the equivalent of a crucifixion: "This is my body which is broken for you; this is my blood which is poured out for you." [See *Tibetan Yoga and Secret Doctrines* by W.Y. Evans-Wentz, Book V] Here we can see exactly how the primal act of self-definition, which constitutes the ego, makes that ego vulnerable to demonic forces that always both threaten it and work to maintain it. The demonic threat to the ego's integrity tempts us to sacrifice all other aspects of life to preserve it—and yet the ego's very struggle to maintain itself against dissolution is, ironically, the very thing that makes it vulnerable to disorder and chaos.

horizons, but that of our *own souls* as well, is objective to this Witness. When Meister Eckhart said "my truest 'I' is God", he implied thereby that my contingent, psychic "I" is not really *I*, but *he. He* does not witness God; God witnesses *him.* Consequently when Arthur Rimbaud said "*I* is another", certainly he was positing the ego as parasite, a foreign body occupying and damaging the psyche, but he was also positing God as the Witness of the psyche. When we are disgusted with the world and disgusted with ourselves, this is a sign that God is calling us—calling us to die to the world and ourselves too, these two deaths being one and the same.

Jesus said, "What profit it a man if he gain the whole world (introjection), but lose his soul (projection)"?; He also said, "He who seeks to keep his life shall lose it, but he who loses his life, for My sake, shall find it." This is *the end of the world.*

II

Worldliness is complacency, and complacency is inseparable from fear, though it seems to be the exact opposite of fear. When children are afraid, they run to their mother—who is This World. The complacency of worldliness is a rejection of vigilance; its function, in part, is to imply that such vigilance is unnecessary because all is safe and secure. Sometimes we take the most foolish chances in dangerous situations as a way of denying our fear, of saying in effect: "Only in a situation of total safety and security would anyone dare to act as stupidly as I just have." Here we can see how courting danger and denying danger can be one and the same thing. Everyone knows that the world is dangerous, that if the world is our mother it can sometimes be a terrible mother. In the face of this danger, we can be either vigilant or complacent; we can either awaken to the reality of the world—not as This World, the system of collective egotism and unreality, but as the actual circumstances that confront us—respecting it and thus earning its respect, or we can fall asleep in it as upon our mother's breast, in which case it becomes This World indeed. In the first course, our fear leads to true security; in the second, a false security leads to an entirely justified fear.

Complacency is a strange passion. It seizes upon any evidence of the stability of the world or the psyche, no matter how slim, in order to indulge itself in a headlong flight from fear—a flight that appears, to oneself and others, as the most complete repose. "That tree outside my window; it's still there. It didn't die or disappear overnight, so I guess that the world is basically OK." "That fantasy I go into when I feel afraid; it's still available. I can call upon it whenever I need to, and fall into its dream. So I guess that my psyche is basically OK." All this ego-identification with the inner and outer worlds only goes to destroy vigilance, responsibility and respect, only makes the outer world that much more dangerous and the inner one that much more unstable. And under the worldly complacency such identification produces, fear grows. As the poet Jack Spicer put it: "Thanatos, the death-plant in the skull/ Grows wings and grows enormous:/ The herb of the whole system". And the entire process is deeply unconscious. As Carl Jung correctly stated, "whatever is repressed is projected." If a psychic content is partially repressed, it is projected as our experience of this or that thing, person or situation in the outer world; if it is totally repressed, it becomes the world *in toto*. And what is more likely to be repressed, what calls for repression more insistently, than fear?

But what are we *really* afraid of? If repressed fear becomes the world, what is the nature of that fear *before* it is repressed? It is here that we should remember, and soberly consider, the well-known Biblical proverb, "the fear of the Lord is the beginning of Wisdom".

More than one saint has taught us that "those who keep the fear of God in their hearts have no place therein for any other fear." The fear of God is our initial response to the undeniable Reality of God—a Reality we find that we cannot escape, try as we might. If worldliness is the unconscious complacency we indulge in so as to hide from fear, the fear of God is the conscious awe and vigilance we experience, and enact, so as to overcome that worldliness, to cut through the worldly dream. The fear of the Lord is the beginning of the emergence of the Witness, of Him Who is *Witness over all things*. Since we have been hiding ourselves, like Adam and Eve did after they disobeyed God, of course we fear to be seen! If our first parents had allowed themselves to be seen by God, if they had returned to their original nakedness, their transgression would have been overcome and redressed and forgiven. Instead they hid themselves from the Witness, hid themselves in the darkness of the ego—which is why they had to leave the Garden of Eden and go out *into the world*.

We fear to be seen because we identify with the ego, with the world, and we somehow imperfectly intuit that if we ever allow ourselves to be fully witnessed by God, both the ego and the world will die—which, since we are now totally identified with the ego and the world it projects, we interpret as literal physical death, the literal end of the world. Consequently we are terrified—and only the love of God, which is inseparable from metaphysical objectivity, can overcome this terror. "Perfect love casts out fear"; perfect objectivity also casts it out. Perfect objectivity is to know with certainty that we are seen; perfect love is to know with certainty that we are loved. These are the fruits of Faith. When Faith is perfected in us, it ripens into certainty. In the darkness of the ego, the darkness of This World, we see "as in a glass, darkly"; in the light of Faith, we see "face to face"— we know *even as we are known*.

III

Martin Buber, in his classic *I and Thou*, has this to say about the nature of the ego as projection-and-introjection, about the desire of the self to either devour the world or be devoured by it, in order to seek refuge from existential anxiety:

At times the man, shuddering at the alienation between the *I* and the world, comes to reflect that something is to be done. . . . He calls thought, in which he rightly has great confidence, to his aid; it shall make good everything for him again. It is, in truth, the high art of thought to paint a reliable picture of the world that is even worthy of belief. So this man says to his thought, "You see this thing stretched out here with the cruel eyes—was it not my playfellow once? . . . Will you make it up between me and it so that it leaves off and I recover?" And thought, ready with its service and its art, paints with its well-known speed one—no, two rows of pictures, on the right wall and on the left. On the one there is (or rather, there takes place, for the world-pictures of thought are reliable cinematography) the universe. The tiny earth plunges from the whirling stars, tiny man from the teeming earth, and now history bears him further through the ages, to rebuild persistently the ant-hill of the cultures which history crushes underfoot. Beneath the row of pictures is written "One and all". On the other wall there takes place the soul. A spinner is spinning the orbits of all stars and the life of all creation and the history of the universe; everything is woven on one thread and is no longer called stars and creation and universe, but sensations and imaginings, or even experiences, and conditions of the soul. And beneath the row of pictures is written "One and all."

Thenceforth, if ever the man shudders at the alienation, and the world strikes terror in his heart, he looks up (to right or left, just as it may chance) and sees a picture. There he sees that the *I* is embedded in the world and that there really is no *I* at all—so the world can do nothing to the *I*, and he is put at ease; or he sees that the world is embedded in the *I*, and that there really is no world at all—so the world can do nothing to the *I*, and he is put at ease. Another time, if the man shudders at the alienation, and the *I* strikes terror in his heart, he looks up and sees a picture; which picture he sees does not matter, the empty *I* is stuffed full with the world or the stream of the world flows over it, and he is put at ease.

But a moment comes, and it is near, when the shuddering man looks up and sees both pictures in a flash together. And a deeper shudder seizes him.

What exactly is this "deeper shudder"? It is the shudder of the shock, the awe, the terror of finding no refuge for oneself in either the darkness of the ego or the darkness of the world. It is the confrontation between the intrinsic nothingness of the ego within and the intrinsic nothingness of the world without—the nothingness of the world behind which lies the incandescent face of God; the nothingness of the ego behind which lies the only Witness who can witness that Face and not be burned to cinders: who can witness It with impunity, because It is He!

11

THE ISOLATION AND TRANSFORMATION OF THE *NAFS*

Sufism, in practice, is the constant attention to God—the awareness that He *is*, and that He is *here, nearer to you than your jugular vein.* And in order to practice this kind of attention, you must be able to differentiate between the "Heart" and the "soul", between *al-Qalb* and *an-nafs*. The *nafs* is whatever you identify with, whatever you think you are, whatever you think the world is—anything other than the presence of God in the Heart. In the simplest terms, the Heart is that in us which attends to God, while the *nafs* is that which blocks or interrupts this attention; so it behooves us to be able to identify the *nafs* when it appears. How can we do this?

The first thing we need is a set of moral and ritual standards, such as is provided by the Islamic *shari'ah*. It's not that obedience to these standards by itself will necessarily advance us on the Sufi path—but without standards like this we will not be able to catch the *nafs* in action. The *shari'ah* is God's command that we do this and avoid that—and whatever wants to make us *do what we should avoid* or *neglect what we should do* is the *nafs*. The *shari'ah* is the line; the *nafs* is whatever crosses the line. Without the line we will not be able to pinpoint the *nafs*, to recognize its own particular quality.

It's also important that the rules we follow come from an objective source outside us. We might be able to invent ethical rules for ourselves that, from one point of view, are very wise and very practical. But if *we* are the authority that enforces them, then—for all their wisdom and practicality—they are at least partially an expression of the *nafs*, which means that they can't be reliably used to discover and isolate the *nafs*.

The *nafs* is that which tempts us, through threats or enticements or distractions, to violate the *shari'ah*. But it also tempts us to betray the *tariqa*. Certainly it pressures us to transgress moral rules. But once we have begun the practice of *dhikr* or constant attention to the presence of God, it also influences us to let our attention wander away from God through every sort of obsession and distraction, every imaginable negative emotion or self-indulgent mental pleasure, including false fantasies of so-called "heavenly" realities. We begin the work of isolating the *nafs* through watching for whatever tempts us to disobey moral rules, but we *develop and refine* our understanding of it by watching for whatever distracts us from the constant remembrance of God. And *dhikr* not only provides a more sensitive gauge for the activities of the *nafs* than moral standards do; it also begins to establish a more objective standpoint in us from which we can spy on the *nafs'* antics without being observed. God is Objective Reality; the more real God is to us, the more objective we ourselves become.

To begin with, the *nafs* blocks the influx of the Spirit into the Heart. Later, it falsifies this influx, diverting it from its true goal. It either makes us obsessed with moral purity or spiritual practice, or leads us to indulge in emotional states and imaginary experiences we falsely believe to be angelic or Divine. And when it finds that it can no longer block the Spirit from entering the Heart, or divert it in various false and useless directions, it learns how to *abduct* the Spirit, to claim It for its own.

You can't fight the *nafs* hand-to-hand; it's too strong, too cunning. The *nafs* that influences us, or all but forces us, to do evil is called the *nafs al-ammara*, the "commanding self"; the *nafs* that struggles against itself is the *nafs al-lawwama*, "the accusing self". It does little good to say, "I WILL be good, I WILL defeat the *nafs*"— and then when you fail, to cry "Damn me, I did it again! Why can't I control myself? I'm corrupt! I'm an evil man! (or woman)". You can't fight the *nafs* through self-will, because self-will *is* the *nafs*. And if you claim that you are corrupt, then you will be corrupt. The real use of the accusing *nafs* is not to fight commanding *nafs*, but to establish the *mark* by which the action of the commanding *nafs*— and later, the accusing *nafs* itself—can be detected. You still might have to kick yourself from time to time, force yourself to do what so much of you doesn't want to do and refuses to do—but this kind of struggle ultimately cannot be won, because it is a struggle against yourself. Will-power must ultimately give way to submission; forcing yourself to do something or avoid something must develop into *islam*, surrender to God: and there can be no surrender without love (*mahabbah*). Instead of standing behind yourself and whipping yourself forward, you must learn (God willing) to look ahead, to Him—to *al-Hadi*, the Guide—and joyfully follow His lead.

So if you can't oppose the *nafs* directly and expect to win the battle, what can you do? What you can do is to watch it, discern it, understand it. (The one who watches, discerns and understands is essentially the Heart.) The time will come when the action of the *nafs* will appear to you in its true guise—and when it does, when you can confidently say, whenever it rears its head: "There! That's the *nafs* again, I'd know it anywhere"—whether or not you can always overcome it—then the battle is already half won. And perfect awareness of the *nafs* does in fact overcome it, because the *nafs* can only overpower you when you identify with it, and when you identify with it, it disappears as a separate entity: you start to think it's you. The veil of the *nafs* has fallen over the Heart.

But perfect awareness of the *nafs* cannot come until it is pacified, and the best way to pacify it is to make a bargain with it. Don't fight the *nafs*—just temporarily put it aside, and let the influx of the Spirit enter the Heart. And when the *nafs* protests, simply explain to her: "What you really want is the Spirit, but you can't have that just yet. If you try to grab for the Spirit on your own, you will drive It away. And if the Spirit enters the Heart, and then you show up at the Heart's table uninvited and ready for a hearty meal, you will eat up all the Spirit in one gulp, go into an imbalanced ecstasy, and wake up the next day with a bad headache and no memory of what happened the night before. If you want your share of the Spirit, you need to hold back until it fully enters the Heart and becomes established there. Then (and only then) can you have your share of it. Certainly you want to be satisfied and spiritualized and pacified;

God wants that too. But you can't be pacified if you want to grab the Spirit and possess it. First you'll need to stand back, take a breather, and let the Heart do its work. Rest assured that when the Spirit is fully established there, you will receive your invitation." The *nafs* that is willing to accept this bargain has begun to be transformed into the *nafs al-mutma'inna*, the "self at peace".

And once the Spirit is fully established in the Heart, the *nafs* WILL catch its overflow. From the veil that hides the Spirit it will be transformed into the mirror that reveals it, until it is ultimately indistinguishable from the Heart itself. Every one of its impulses will become a virtue; every one of its attacks, a protection; every one of its wiles, a wisdom; every one of its twists and contortions, a reflection of one of the Names of God in the mirror of the human form. The end of the first phase of the Sufi path is the *gnosis* or *ma'rifa* of God, which lies under the sign of *tanzih*, the divine Transcendence. The second phase culminates in the *ma'rifa* of the *nafs*, which is the site of *tashbih*, the divine Immanence.

[NOTE: Perhaps you've noticed that I have said next to nothing about the spiritual states that Sufism is famous for, the *ahwal*. That's because those states are none of our business. We cannot produce them and we should train ourselves not even to ask for them. They are God's business, not ours; they are gifts, not acquisitions. Our job is to do our job. God's job—is to do what He will.]

12

THE MYSTERY
OF FORGIVENESS

For Rasheed Mesco

Love is like the lion's tooth.
W. B. Yeats

Forgiveness is the least sentimental thing in the world. Forgiveness is objectivity. To see someone for who they are, with all their strengths and weaknesses, and yourself for who you are in the same way, is to forgive. Forgiveness is the end of your attempt to change others, also the end of your attempt to re-create yourself, as if you were a second God. The objective truth of any situation is God Himself; the power to see things objectively is the presence of God. That presence breaks the chains of all your demands upon others, all your demands upon yourself. To admit that others are who they are is not to judge them; it is to respect them. To admit that you are as you are, with all your weaknesses, is to respect yourself. It is to be objective with regard to yourself, neither to presume that you are better than you are, nor to despair because you are not omnipotent, because you are not God. It is also to open yourself to the Power by which you *can* change—not through self-will, but through submission to, and conscious cooperation with, the Will of God.

Unforgiveness is to see another person as having all the power in a situation, and to attempt to assert your power against his or her power. It is to treat another person as God, and yourself as a candidate for that position, as someone who might be able to *become* God if things would only go your way for once. It is arrogance. It is idolatry. It is bondage to unreality.

To soberly and objectively see a confessed, convicted and proven murderer as a murderer is to forgive him: not to make excuses for him, which is an entirely different proposition, but simply no longer to *judge* him—to depart from judgment, in his case, and arrive at certainty. There is no certainty as to whether or not he is damned, but there *is* certainty as to his being a murderer. To pretend he is somehow not a murderer, or to think that if you are good enough and caring enough and self-sacrificing enough you can make him other than a murderer, is to treat him as God, or yourself as God. And at the same time, it is to *judge* him. Your outrage at the murderer's crime is only arrogance, based on the belief that this outrage might change him, might somehow make him not a murderer. Likewise to hate yourself when you fail to make him other than he is, to believe you have "failed" in this because you were not good enough or self-sacrificing enough, because you were not God, is also arrogance; at the same time, it is self-destruction. To despair that the murderer is indeed a murderer it is to turn him into a tyrannical god demanding human sacrifice, and yourself into an oppressed devotee of a merciless idol. Between "I am God!" and "I *would* be God if only I weren't so weak and so evil" there is not much to choose. Negative pride is still pride and nothing else.

To judge someone as evil (as if you could know his secret with God) is not the only way of judging him; to judge him as *better* than he appears (as if you could know his secret with God), to judge him in any way as *other than he is*—that is to say, to project anything on him, good or bad—is to arrogantly put yourself in the place of God. "Judge not lest you be judged" means: Don't pretend that *you* are the judge, or some day you will find out in no uncertain terms, and to your great dismay, Who the Judge really is. *Your* judgment is all subjectivity and attachment and conjecture, but forgiveness is objectivity and detachment and true knowledge: *apatheia*. Only God can judge with objective justice—not you. To forgive, then, is to know God Alone as the Judge, and to see yourself, and the other person, and all existing things, as equally subject to His judgment—right now, in this very moment.

All attachment, like all sin, is based on pride. In your pride you believe that you can change people into something other than they are by attaching to them, by identifying with them, by possessing them and/or letting them possess you. All this is pure illusion: things are as they are, which means: people are as God knows them to be, not as you wish them to be or fear them to be or think you can make them be. To know this is objectivity; objectivity is freedom; and freedom is forgiveness. Until we stop wishing that people were other than they are, we cannot wish them well.

Forgiveness has nothing to do with "generating good feelings" for someone. We hate someone; we feel bad about hating them; we try to call up good feelings for them to counter and deny this hatred; we finally end up making excuses for them (which is really nothing but making excuses for ourselves), etc., etc. All of this is meaningless, destructive, barren, unreal. They stand under the judgment of God, and so do we. They rest under the mercy of God, and so do we. God is the Judge; God is the Physician; we wait on His good pleasure; we stand on the same ground as the other in this, the ground of our common humanity. And in doing so we realize, God willing, that one of the most destructive things we can do, and one of the most futile things, is to try and come between another and God's destiny for him. This is manifestly impossible—and if we place ourselves on the highway of another's secret with God when God's power elects to move upon it, we will be crushed like a bug. At the same time, when God's destiny for *us* arrives, we won't be there to receive it; we will miss it, this time around—and we do not know how many "times around" we might have, only that their number is certainly not infinite. In doing this we will only place ourselves under our own "judgment" and our own "mercy", not God's; we will subject ourselves not to His Justice but to the injustice of our own foolishness, not to His Mercy but to the cruelty of our own self-will.

"Forgive us our debts as we forgive our debtors". This clearly means, on one level, that if we forgive others as we are commanded, God will forgive us as He has promised. But beyond this, to forgive another, by the power of God (and this is a very important point: *only God forgives*) is to forgive oneself by the same power. To forgive another for being God (in our insane estimation of things) is to forgive ourselves for not being God. We believe that the other owes us that he or she be like God, both all-powerful and all-good, and treat us accordingly: this is the debt we foolishly hope that the other will repay to us, the debt we are commanded to forgive. We have lent to the other—usually at a high rate of interest—the right and thus the duty to be God. But this is something that was not ours to lend in the first place, something we owe to God alone, not another human being. God has freely given us His Justice and His Mercy, which nonetheless He will require back from us in the person of ourselves, our immortal souls, obedient and sanctified. But if we have lent this gift to another, we are now in debt to God—and equally to ourselves, since the debt we owe to God *is* ourselves, and we have lost ourselves by lending ourselves to another through our projections and our obsessive attention, negative or positive. In lending God's Power and Mercy freely given to us to another who doesn't deserve it and cannot use it (he has his own gift from God which we, by our false gift, have attempted to steal from him and, if he is foolish enough to play our game, have succeeded in concealing from him), we have turned that other into an idol, and ourselves into idolaters. We have made him God for us, and have come to believe that if we succeed in overturning this idol we have set up we may become God ourselves.

The only way out of this vicious circle, is forgiveness. If we forgive the other for not being God, we cancel his debt to us. We realize that he is as poor as we are, and so he owes us nothing. Only God is the Rich. And if we forgive him for not being God, then we are forgiven for *wanting* to be God; the burden of trying to save and control the universe is lifted from our shoulders. And so we owe him nothing.

Only God is the Rich; only God is the Judge; only God is the Merciful. Whatever we feel or don't feel, whatever we try or don't try, this is the objective Truth. On the ground of this objective Truth, all debts are canceled; our presumptuous belief that we might change the situation, as well as our despair in not being able to change it (and these two always go together), are wiped out.

And when we can do this—by the power of God and our faith in Him, not by the power of self-will—then the situation *does* change. How it changes we can neither predict or control. But we can be absolutely certain than when the tangled spiderweb of debt and judgment and manipulation and projection and hatred and self-hatred and presumption and despair is brushed aside, the over-whelming light and power of God's Truth and Justice and Mercy will radiate into the whole situation, inevitably and immediately, to the very root of it. We may not see this light, or we may sometimes see a bit of it; no matter. In the words of St. Paul, "Faith is the presence of things hoped for, the evidence of things not seen". In the words of the Prophet Muhammad, "Pray to God as if you saw Him—because even if you don't see Him, He sees you."

SHIFTING THE LINES OF ATTENTION

One of the best ways to overcome an obsession with another's offenses is, in the presence of God, to consider your own. Certainly you must avoid the temptation to blame yourself for the offenses of another against you; to do so is to claim, in effect, that you are the only real person in existence, to imply that you are God—and a rather ineffectual God at that! But if you succeed in avoiding this temptation and applying yourself to the business at hand, which in this case is repentance, then the "lines of attention" will shift from the horizontal plane of interpersonal attraction-and-repulsion to the vertical plane of direct relationship with God. The felt presence of God shrinks the significance of the other, and oneself as well, to negligible proportions. If the other is negligible, how can his offense affect you? And if you are negligible, how can an offense offered to such a negligible entity really matter? This too is forgiveness.

But repentance for one's transgressions is not the actual center here; the true center is repentance for letting one's attention wander to other-than-God. The idea is to attend to God, not to the world, by any means necessary. If your repentance takes the form of "I guess I'm partly to blame, really; maybe I'm *entirely* to blame. But no! Forget it! No way! It's not *my* fault, it's *their* fault!", then no good will come of it. This is what the Sufis call the "accusing self", the troubled conscience, which is still considered blameworthy; if you are always accusing yourself, it's not much of a jump for you to start accusing other people too. At this point the Sufis speak of the need to "repent of repentance". Certainly God is wrathful against trans-gressors, and the person with the kind of arrogance and foolishness

that tells him he has a right to transgress and that no negative consequences will come of it—the one dominated by the "commanding
self"—will taste that wrath, and justly so. But since "My Mercy has
precedence over My wrath", a deeper insight will reveal that God's
wrath is the servant of His Mercy. God is also *al-Rahman*, the All-
Merciful—a Name that is higher and more comprehensive than the
Names of Wrath, one that is actually synonymous (according to the
Qur'an) with *Allah* itself. So another way of shifting the lines of
attention from horizontal to vertical is to recognize God's present
Mercy and Generosity—a Mercy that is always there, though often
hidden by the feeling of personal offense and the narrow-minded
idolatry it presupposes—as if a petty or even a serious offense on the
part of a mere human being could have the power to dominate and
banish the tremendous Mercy of God.

Egos can be "negative" as well as "positive"; they are just as likely
to appear as self-hatred (especially in these times!) as they are to
manifest as arrogance. And arrogance can certainly *become* self-
hatred through obsessive guilt over it, just as self-hatred will often
turn into arrogance in an attempt to overcome itself by projection
upon another. The medicine for the positive ego is repentance in the
face of God's Justice; the medicine for the negative one is trust in
God's Mercy. And the medicine for both is the living sense of God's
presence—the exquisite *delight*—the formidable *awe*. Whoever truly
commends himself to God automatically commends all others to
Him at the same time, and leaves them to their Secret. This is the
true essence of forgiveness.

THE ROLE OF THE FEELINGS

The feeling most intimately related to forgiveness, the sign that forgiveness is required, is anger—anger either against the other, or
against oneself, or both. And the feeling that is most directly expres-
sive of forgiveness itself, is love. Nonetheless, forgiveness is not primarily a matter of the feelings. If our forgiveness of another ripens
into a feeling of sincere love for him, then so much the better; but
this is not required. Forgiveness is first of the intelligence and the
will, not of the feelings. If we discern the true existential nature of

the human condition, as well as our own mass of attachments and reactions to the actions and/or omissions of others, then we will know that forgiveness is required. And if, by the grace of God, we intend what we know, then forgiveness exists. Anger may continue, but it will not become *hatred*. Hatred is *intended anger*, anger that affects the will. Anger at another for his perceived offense against us, or anger at ourselves for our shortcomings, is still a negative passion; but unless it infects the will and turns into hatred, it is not a sin. And if it hasn't infected the will—if we intend not to be angry, not to retaliate, not to hate—then, God willing, it will eventually wear itself out.

There is also such a thing as righteous anger—which is emphatically not the *passion* of anger attempting to justify itself by attaching itself to some supposedly worthy object. Righteous anger is the war against whatever would adulterate purity-of-soul in oneself or others; it is that which wills, by the command of God, the destruction of all the barriers to God. Righteous anger is the power of *jihad*, the *incensive faculty* of Plato and the Greek Fathers (Greek *thymikon*, Arabic *ghadhab*), the firm intention to right a wrong, either in an outer situation or in oneself. And if righteous anger is the Warrior, the General in this *jihad* is the "rational faculty" (Greek *logistikon*, Arabic *darraka*), the faculty capable of understanding the implications of divinely revealed moral laws, and applying them to particular situations, both individual and collective. Righteous anger may be accompanied by the feeling of anger, if God judges that in a given situation this feeling will serve, or it may be essentially without such feeling. In either case it will be an action based on the virtue of *apatheia* or spiritual detachment. As such, it will be the servant not of passion, or vanity, or bigotry, but of the love of God.

True love is far beyond the feeling of love. It is the purified form of the Platonic "appetitive faculty" (Greek *epithymitikon*, Arabic *shahwa*) transferred from the relative, contingent and perishing world to the Eternal Creator; it is *shahwa* become *ishk*. In the name and by the power of the love of God it is possible to intend respect for others and do them justice, but it is not possible to intend the feeling of love for them—or any feeling, for that matter. Feelings are not intended by us; they are given to us. Any feeling of love for another that is not based on respect for him, on the firm intent to deal justly with him and do him good, is not love, but a lie; a fantasy; a temptation; a curse. Better we should feel cold as ice than indulge ourselves in warm feelings for another based on nothing but our own self-indulgence and self-congratulation, or on an attempt to throw a veil of false good-feeling over the rigors of a hard situation. It is here that a phrase I've always loved, but never knew the author of, finds its place: "There is no such thing as love—only proofs of love". Sometimes we love best, in the true and transcendental sense of that slandered and damaged word, by acting against "positive" feelings that are out of place because they are without respect, without self-respect, without truth. Deep feelings of love are the crown of love—if the love is true. But they are not really necessary. Why grab for the crown? The crown of true love is given by another Hand. But if we will to practice respect and do justice, then the feelings will surely follow: Because God is just too; He is Justice itself. His reward for those who do justice, who show respect to others and who also respect themselves—not out of vanity, which is the satanic counterfeit of self-respect and the death of it, but because "the heart of my loving slave does contain Me"—is the fountains of wine and of camphor, the *gardens beneath which rivers flow*. And if the full flowering of love is delayed, this is only in order to break love's attraction to false objects, the illusion of their power over it. If we submit to the Will of God, this attraction *will* be broken; love *will* find its true Object; of this there can be no doubt. In the words of the Noble Qur'an, *Shall the reward for goodness be other than goodness?*

[NOTE: The incensive faculty, the appetitive faculty, and the rational faculty correspond to the Lion, the Bull and the Man in Ezekiel's vision of the Four Living Creatures surrounding the throne of Yahweh; the fourth Living Creature, the Eagle, corresponds to the Spiritual Intellect, the *Nous*.]

AFTERWORD

Seeking psychic experience, either through examining one's own subjectivity, or through exploring the Psychic Plane which is the surrounding environment of that subjectivity, is immensely *diverting*. One can certainly learn a great deal in such deep dives and high flights and wide excursions; but the danger of lethal distraction is also great. In running after psychic experience we run the risk of losing sight of the "one thing needful" for our true salvation and healing. Once the patriarch Jacob saw, in a dream in Haran, after he had fallen asleep with his head upon a stone, a Ladder that reached up to heaven, with angels ascending and descending upon it. That Ladder is the Human Form. If we place ourselves (our egos, that is) upon this ladder, the angels cannot travel because we are blocking their way. Neither can our prayers reach heaven, not can God's answers reach us; this is what may ultimately happen to us if we become attached to psychic experience. Our duty is not to impersonate the angels, but simply to establish the Ladder, then get out of the Way. We establish it by two things: by prayer, and by work—the union of which two is love. If we are faithful in prayer, and faithful also to the duties of our station in life, then our soul will become not a mysterious glistening underworld or luminous inner sky whose secrets we feel called upon to explore and possess, but a Path for the messengers of God; our only job is to get out of their Way and let them move. We may be aware of their journeys from time to time, or possibly never aware of them at all: no matter. If we let them pass through us as on a broad highway, not by the narrow thorny footpath we might turn ourselves into, if we don't watch out, in our curiosity and self-involvement, then all their missions will be accomplished, in God's own wisdom and in His own time. The turnings of the Heart are God's business; He holds it between His two fingers, and turns it however He will. Our job is simply to let Him do it, and concentrate on the business at hand: On prayer, and on work. These two occupations are enough, and more than enough, to fill out the shape of any life.

APPENDIX ONE

TRADITIONAL PSYCHOTHERAPY, A REVIEW OF

Mental Disorders and Spiritual Healing: Teachings from the Early Christian East
(by Jean-Claude Larchet, Sophia Perennis, 2006)

by Jennifer Doane Upton

[This review appeared in vol. 12, no. 1 of *Sophia: A Journal of Traditional Studies*]

Mental Disorders and Spiritual Healing presents the viewpoint on mental disorders held by the early Church Fathers, and in so doing provides a fresh "new" look at psychotherapy, as seen from the standpoint of a tradition which knows the human being as composed of body, soul and Spirit, and gives precedence to the Spirit. The author, Jean-Claude Larchet, is a practicing psychiatrist as well as an Eastern Orthodox Christian.

As moderns, we commonly hold to psychological assumptions based on the ideas of Freud, Jung, behaviorism etc., or on the belief that all consciousness is derived from physical processes within the human brain. This book cuts through many of these assumptions, which treat emotion and emotional energy as if they could be dealt with without reference to morality or the basic disposition of the will, and certainly without reference to the Spirit. For instance, Larchet posits the union of soul and body, but does so in a far different manner than many modern theorists. It is fashionable nowadays to say, in opposition to Cartesian dualism, that "soul and body are one," but many of our contemporaries who assert this do not seem to have any clear idea that the soul exists in its own right. "By affirming that a human is at once soul and body," the author says, "they [the Fathers] opposed every form of materialism and naturalism that denied the soul or reduced it to being an epiphenomenon of the body, or something derived from and determined by the body."

According to Larchet, in the union of soul and body, the soul takes precedence over the body; it is active, the body passive. He quotes St. Makarios as saying, "The soul, which is a subtle body, has enveloped and clothed itself in the members of our visible body, which is gross in substance."

Mental Disorders and Spiritual Healing maintains that mental illness is from three sources: the *somatic* (body), the *psychic* (soul), and the *spiritual*. The somatic level is related to our familiar idea of that mental illness is caused by imbalances in brain chemistry and physiology, if not by actual physical trauma. On the psychic level, mental illness is caused primarily by demonic influence, though it is pointed out that demons are attracted to pre-existing psychic dispositions. Mental illness resulting from the spiritual level is based on the perversion of human free will—sin, in other words—though the author makes it clear that the misuse of free will affects the other two levels as well, albeit not in as central a manner.

This places mental illnesses of a physical origin in a much different perspective than that adopted by modern psychology. Larchet takes issue with our assumption that medieval monks and the early Fathers posited demonic activity only because they were ignorant of the physical causes of mental illness. He quotes Gregory of Nyssa as maintaining that "We are aware that mental aberrations do not arise from heaviness of head [drunkenness] alone, but skilled physicians declare that our intellect is also weakened by the membranes that underlie the sides affected by the disease, when they call the disease frenzy [*phrenitis*], since the name given to those membranes is *phrenes*." However, Larchet points out that

In cases where an organic disorder is clear, the function of the physician is ... limited to the physiological level alone. [To affirm] that in such cases the soul in its very nature is not harmed, and hence preserves its autonomy, hampers the claim of a certain kind of medicine or psychiatry to take charge of the human soul through the body and dictate to it its own ideas and values. In cases where the origin of the disease is physical, it is only the soul's self-manifestation that is compromised; its essence is left intact." [NOTE: "The soul's self-manifestation" is termed "soul" or "psyche" above; the soul's "essence" is referred to as "Spirit".]

The author admits that it is often difficult to discern the true origin of mental illnesses, given that they can have three distinct etiologies, and a major element in this difficulty is the fact that appearances by their nature tend to lead us astray. This is certainly true when the illness is of demonic origin, particularly since our materialist assumptions do not even allow for this possibility. Larchet says:

If 'profane' or 'rational' medicine chooses to ignore such a demonic etiology, it is because it accepts phenomena as the only reality that can be objectively considered. . . . True, it is especially difficult to determine the presence of demonic influence, to define its manner of acting or to gauge its importance. Such an understanding escapes the eyes of the profane. Only those who have obtained the charism of the discerning of spirits from God are capable of exercising this spiritual discrimination.

This limitation of diagnostic skill to one possessing certain spiritual gifts posits an authority higher than materiality and profane human knowledge. Clearly a postmodern mindset resists accepting such authority. Consequently, in talking about healing from the effects of demonic activity, Larchet is led into a discussion the *charism* (sacrament) of Baptism. He says:

[T]he Christian, by the grace received in Baptism, is freed from the tyranny of the enemy and always retains the power of opposing demonic activity. According to St. Symeon the New Theologian, Baptism gives us 'freedom no longer to be held against our will in the devil's tyranny,' and 'the enemy cannot take any action against us unless we of our own will obey him.'

The author speaks of the appropriate treatment for mental illnesses of a psychic nature as the product of a collaboration between the patient and the healer(s). Thus, in addition to a reorientation of the will through prayer and fasting, which the Fathers recommend,

Larchet speaks of the spiritual intervention of the saints as a powerful form of treatment. It might be objected that, if psychic illnesses are partly based on the misuse of the will, and given that the will is free and that no-one can will for another, it is up to the patient to reorient his will to the Spirit and thus to heal himself. This would seem to deny any legitimate role to "outside" spiritual intervention, such as the prayer of a saint or of the patient's friends and family. I would answer that in the case of possession, the door to the demonic may have been opened by a misuse of the will, but by the time the possession has really taken hold, the illness is beyond the control of the will. It is now the will of the demon that must be subdued, and this can only be accomplished by theurgic means, such as exorcism:

> If the Fathers tried to have the possessed/insane participate as much as possible in their own deliverance, it is because the individual must, if he is to be delivered from demonic influence, turn his will from himself and orient it toward God. God, in effect, does not grant healing unless it is asked of him, for he has granted man free will and in all the cases respects his will and will not act against it. However, the will of the individual is not always fully at his disposal. . . . Those who are disturbed in a significant way cannot even ask for their own healing or give evidence of their faith. . . . And yet it is possible for such individuals to be delivered and healed thanks to the faith and the prayers of those around them or accompanying them, as well as to those of the saint to whom they are entrusted. But the power of the saint's intercession is so much stronger when the faith of those asking for the deliverance of the possessed is more ardent and their prayers more fervent.

Spiritual illness has precisely to do with a perversion of the individual's relationship to God. According to Eastern Orthodox tradition, the Fall affected both the Intellect and the will; consequently some spiritual illnesses (*acedia* in particular; see below) repeat and accentuate the darkening of the mind resulting from the Fall. According to the early Fathers, some (but not all) mental illnesses actually derive from the spiritual level, though their effects nonetheless appear on the level of the psyche *per se*:

Mental illnesses of spiritual origin should not be confused with the spiritual illnesses themselves. Spiritual illnesses are formed by a disorder or perversion of nature (more precisely of nature's mode of existence) in the personal relationship of the individual to God. On the psychic plane, mental illnesses correspond to somatic disorders on the plane of the body; mental illness has to do with difficulties in the psyche considered in itself, with a dysfunction of the psyche's nature considered within its natural order. . . . From the point of view of Patristic anthropology, such a distinction can only have a relative value, for nature can never be considered in isolation and is fundamentally defined by its relationship to God.

This is clearly not how we view mental illness in today's world; and equally foreign to the postmodern mindset is the idea expressed by the author that such things as *fear* and *sadness* are actually *passions*. We can easily understand anger and lust as passions, but it is harder for us to see fear and sadness as such, because they show the passions to be essentially "passive," whereas we like to think of them as vital and dynamic. According to the Fathers, the passions take control of our will and force us to *passively* act according to their agendas instead of being true to ourselves. Thus the cure for them is *action* in its truest sense. Pure act is to center in God—who, according to Aquinas, is Himself "Pure Act." The essence of pure action is prayer.

Not every passion gives even the appearance of an excess of vitality, such as anger or lust seem to do. Larchet deals at some length with the more negative passions of *acedia* (*accidia*) and *sadness*. Sadness is a direct and conscious feeling of loss, while acedia is more like a general deadening of all life; one has "lost the taste for life." (Since the author points out that some of the Fathers do not distinguish between acedia and sadness, I will use the term acedia alone from here on.)

Acedia is characterized by a deadness of the senses, and even more so by a deadness of the feelings. A person afflicted by acedia has great difficulty in finding any meaning in life. In an article entitled "A Requiem for Friendship" [*Touchstone: A Journal of Mere Christianity;* September, 2005) Anthony Esolen complains that the youth of today are no longer as alive and "youthful" as young people once were; this could certainly be classed as a form of acedia. Acedia is a passion that pervades the modern world. It lowers spiritual expectations and thus draws people into an acceptance of hopeless materialism. It pervades every aspect of life, and as such its origin is difficult to isolate. According to Larchet, it is in the very nature of acedia that its victim should be relatively unconscious of it, since it always produces a decrease in awareness, and even on occasion a physical sleepiness. It is clear that the term acedia covers much of what we would define today as depression.

Larchet maintains that acedia especially attacks hermits—those attempting to do spiritual struggle in solitude—though he makes clear that those living the active life are not exempt from it. If, as I believe, acedia is a particularly modern malaise, it may because we moderns are emotionally isolated by our conditions, whether or not we are spiritually struggling in a conscious way. Spiritual struggle, according to Larchet, is the key to the healing of this condition, not really its cause. The great temptation when confronting acedia is to distract oneself by seeking novelty. *Restlessness* is a major symptom of it—and who could be more restless than modern man? A special case of this restlessness is dissatisfaction with the place where one lives, which of course makes it difficult to establish domestic roots and thereby overcome social isolation. Jungian psychologist Marion Woodman, in a lecture given in the early 80's, commented on the tendency among many of her clients to spend their spare time in restaurants, bars, coffee shops—anywhere but at home. Part of the reason for this behavior is that such people are trying to heal their acedia through contact with others. Larchet, however, maintains that this condition can only be healed through solitary struggle. One must directly resist the tendency to sleepiness, lack of awareness and loss of energy, not simply run from it.

Another result of acedia is our inability to value our homes, our habit of considering them merely as places to "crash". Many of our contemporaries who groom themselves impeccably for the workplace allow their places of residence to fall into disarray and even squalor. If we could live content within our homes, we would be far less tempted to turn our houses into mere economic commodities.

Mental Disorders and Spiritual Healing concludes with a chapter on *simulated* mental illness: the tradition of the "Fool for Christ." The Fool for Christ is one who consciously takes folly upon himself for spiritual purposes. This phenomenon seems to have largely disappeared from the Christian tradition in our time, but it was of great importance in the early church, and this importance certainly continued, in Russia, at least up to the time of the revolution (if not later).

Anyone can be a saint, and this includes the illiterate, the simple and the innocent—none of whom Larchet considers as Fools for Christ in the precise sense of this term. The simplicity of such people is related to a poverty of experience imposed by conditions. For example, the author does not consider Dostoevsky's character Prince Myshkin from *The Idiot* as a true Fool for Christ, since Myshkin's innocence is congenital, not adopted. The folly of the true Fool for Christ, on the other hand, is consciously simulated:

> He pretends to be a fool, has chosen to appear the fool, and does everything he can to seem to be so in the eyes of others, so that he is really believed to be a fool. He controls every act and word, precisely calculating their effect. For certain individuals who have discovered his secret or he himself has chosen, he lays aside this mask of foolishness, just as he does whenever he is alone, and reveals himself to be perfectly sound of mind.

The Fool for Christ deals with the realm of appearance as precisely that: *appearance*. Christians often squirm at what they consider to be the "Eastern idea" that this world is in some respects illusory. But the Fool for Christ acts within the world as if it were in fact an illusion—and how can any Christian claim to believe that this world is real in the same sense that God is real, given the otherworldliness of Christ Himself, whose "kingdom is not of this world"? When Satan, "the Prince of This World," is called "the father of lies," this is a way of indicating that the fallen world in which we live is not entirely what it seems—or at least what it seems to *us* in our fallen condition. Eve, who precipitated the fall of Mankind, brought about a darkening of the human intellect, while the Theotokos, through her receptivity to the Holy Spirit, brought salvation to mankind in the Incarnation of Jesus Christ—and this salvation entails a *metanoia*, a *renewing* of the mind. But if our minds are to be renewed, we must confront the illusions that dominate us, not run from them. If, according to the Patristic dictum, "God became man that man might become God," we might say that the Fool for Christ becomes an illusion so that those in a state of illusion might come to Reality. Clearly this is a vocation that one must be called to, and one that should not be attempted without great spiritual maturity. Larchet recounts an instance of spiritually advanced monk who was considering taking on the responsibilities of a Fool for Christ, but was cautioned against this by his spiritual director. After all, the world of illusion is by its very nature tricky and deceitful, and to enter into this world is necessarily to take on some of this quality of trickery, either consciously or unconsciously. There have been those who have attempted to mimic insanity, who in so doing have lost their grip on reality, and slipped into insanity itself.

Mental Disorders and Spiritual Healing clearly reveals dimensions of patristic psychology that are not what most of us would have expected. It is a book that should be of interest to people in many fields, laymen as well as professionals. Its unique insights will be of benefit to anyone sincerely seeking a greater self-knowledge—the sort of knowledge that is based on the true, but now largely forgotten, stature of humanity.

APPENDIX TWO

THE LIMITATIONS OF PSYCHICAL
RESEARCH, A REVIEW OF
The End of Materialism

(by Charles T. Tart, Ph.D., New Harbinger Publications, 2009)

In *The End of Materialism*, Charles Tart presents a comprehensive overview of the most convincing psychical research in telepathy, clairvoyance, precognition, psychokinesis and psychic healing, as well as out-of-body experiences, near death experiences and evidence for the human personality's survival of bodily death, including reincarnation. In doing so, however, he presents us with a view of "spirituality" that only a materialist could maintain. The book is definitely worth reading, but only if the reader is already well defended against the errors of scientism, knows the difference between psychic and spiritual realities, and has a good idea what a *religion* is, and thus is not likely to be swayed by the author's blanket dismissal of "organized" religion, based solely upon the kind of ignorance that would be obvious in the case of, say, a chess master who believed that his knowledge of chess also made him an expert in astronomy.

Like many nowadays, Tart speaks highly of "spirituality" and denigrates "religion". He appeals to "Direct" or "Primary Spiritual Experience" against traditional religious authority, which he identifies, in line with the conventional assumptions of our time, almost exclusively with narrow dogmatism, persecution of heretics etc.; religions grow out of the primary spiritual experiences of their founders, but later degenerate into mere systems of social control. To this degree he accepts revelation of a kind, but defines it, in more or less Buddhist terms, not as an action on the part of God to establish a Way of knowing Him, but as an intellective experience on the part of the founder, the expression of which later becomes authoritative for his followers. He accepts as Primary Spiritual Experience the state of "cosmic consciousness" spontaneously experienced by Canadian psychiatrist R.M. Bucke, but has no inkling that any organized religion (outside of Buddhism, presumably) might include *sciences* relating to higher states of consciousness, sciences not based on empirical experimentation starting from sense data or psychic impressions, but nonetheless possessing their own methodology and objective criteria for validating results. The upshot is that Tart includes both spontaneous mystical or psychic experience (between which he is unable to differentiate), and the data resulting from parapsychological experimentation, as Primary Spiritual Experience, simply because both occur outside the control of traditional religious authority.

Ironically, Tart has his own critique of "scientism". For him, scientism defines a set of prejudices held by most scientists that prevent them from applying empirical research to certain areas of reality, particularly those dealt with by parapsychology. For Huston Smith, however, scientism is an ideology according to which *only* empirical research, investigating material reality alone, can arrive at truth; revelation and *intellection* (i.e., *gnosis* or *ma'rifa*) are disallowed from the outset. Thus Tart's ideal of a science without scientism—a science whose findings, according to him, might well replace the dogmas of organized religion—is a perfect image of the *triumph* of scientism according to Huston Smith's definition.

Nonetheless, Tart's critique of his own kind of scientism is valuable; he proves to our satisfaction that the "materialistic" prejudices of the scientific community are in no way scientific. And yet he accepts no systematic way of knowing as valid outside of empirical experimentation operating on sense data, thereby imprisoning his worldview within the very materialistic paradigm that he intends to refute. This is the basic contradiction in his approach, a contradiction he shares with experimental parapsychology or psychical research as a whole. We are periodically informed by psychic researchers that if their findings were accepted as valid by the scientific community, and communicated as such to the public, *everything would change*; the materialistic worldview would be overthrown. Unfortunately, this never seems to happen; the public and the scientific establishment can apparently become ever more open, year after year, to the occult and the uncanny without ever breaking free from the materialistic paradigm. Dr. Tart's findings on out-of-body experiences, remote viewing, psychokinesis are "convincing"; J.B. Rhine's similar experiments in the 1930's at Duke University were equally convincing, as were those of the Society for Psychical Research in Britain, beginning in the late 19th century. Yet there is never any sense of real breakthrough. Like the attempt to explain human love in terms of pheromones or brain chemistry, the findings of parapsychology are not entirely devoid of relevance to a full understanding of the psyche, just largely devoid. Out-of-body experiences suggest that the life we call "posthumous" is also a present reality that can be experienced in this life; clairvoyance suggests omniscience; telekinesis, omnipotence. Yet all we actually experience are rather ghostly impressions, and all that experimental science can tell us about them for sure is that these experiences are "real" only in the sense that they are highly unlikely according to the laws of probability, though striking "anecdotal" evidence abounds.

Psychical experiences approached in a materialistic manner, once one gets over one's initial surprise at their occurrence, tend to be terribly boring—at least they are to me; they promise new worlds but deliver little more than the pale ghosts of materiality. And the apparatus of scientific psychical research only makes them more boring still. (I must admit however that earlier in my life I sought and found various psychic signs and wonders: out-of-body experiences, precognitive dreams, the powers of the Philippine psychic surgeons, various phenomena apparently springing from do-it-yourself "sorcery" of the Castaneda variety, etc.; in those days of little faith I needed to convince myself, through *phenomena*, that there was something beyond the material world.)

But it will be objected—and rightly so—that psychical research does not aim to be entertaining, but to establish truth. The truth it can and does establish is, however, only a faint reflection of the wonders the psyche is capable of revealing and experiencing when it recognizes its Source in the Spiritual domain that transcends it. Intellection—the direct perception of Spiritual truth, unmediated by either rationality or imagination—is capable of expressing itself via the most brilliant rational discourse and the most inspiring symbolic images and mythopoetic dramas. It is these that the human psyche is designed, on one end of its spectrum, to receive and contemplate—just as, on the other end, it exists to "make sense" of sense experience. In comparison with these, the psyche's proper functions, those aspects or the psyche capable of being validated by psychical research resemble nothing so much as a painted masterpiece used to wrap an order of fish and chips. This is not to say, of course, that psychic powers under the control of the Spirit cannot produce wonders if the Divine economy requires them, only that empirical investigation based on sense data can only detect the faintest echo of such miraculous or "theurgic" events. If a given faculty of the soul is not viewed in terms of its proper use and function, but only from the vantage point of something ontologically inferior to it—matter being inferior to psyche, as psyche is to Spirit—then it is in danger of being fundamentally misunderstood. Even if it happens to be valid in its own terms, a knowledge that is inadequate to its object is in great danger of spreading darkness rather than light.

TART'S VIEW OF RELIGION

According to Dr. Tart, religious theology is not by-and-large derived from Primary Spiritual Experience, but is merely a distorted overlay upon it based on childish wishes and fears on the one hand and cynical political power motives on the other. And while he will allow that religion may support Primary Spiritual Experience for some, his basic characterization of organized religion, as opposed to science, is as follows:

> Has there been any progress in spirituality in the last few centuries?
>
> I don't mean surface things like spiritual ideas being more widely available or the number of believers in particular religions increasing; I have a practical orientation. Are spiritual or religious training systems significantly more efficient than they used to be in making people more intelligent, wise and compassionate?

If you asked this kind of question about medicine, for example, or just about any other field where essential science has been applied, the answer is a resounding yes! Diseases that were fatal a century or two ago are now routinely cured, for example. But are there any spiritual systems that can say something like, "It used to be that N percent of our students reached such and such levels of performance, enlightenment, or salvation, and now it's three times as high"? You hear a lot of complaints in spiritual circles about the degenerate times we live in—certainly that's part of reality—but that kind of thinking, regardless of what truth value it has, can also serve as an excellent way of not facing up to a lack of progress.

In almost every traditional religious context, however, "the degeneracy of the times" is not simply a lame excuse for the lack of a progress that is expected but not in fact realized, but is understood as an inescapable aspect of the nature of things. It is degeneracy that is expected, not progress; the degeneracy of a particular religion is most often predicted by the founder himself. (Such expectations are not "pessimistic", but are simply based on the vast difference in scale between time and Eternity, on the realistic understanding that earthly life is, in the words of Chuang Tzu, "like a galloping white colt glimpsed for a moment through a crack in the rock.") The assertion that Christianity will degenerate in the latter days is well known from the New Testament; the Prophet Muhammad, peace and blessings be upon him, said "no generation will come upon you that is not followed by a worse"; the decay of Hinduism in the latter days is predicted in some of the oldest Hindu scriptures, the Puranas; Buddhism speaks of "the last 500 years of the Dharma" when evil and ignorance will abound. If religions were created by men, we might expect them to "progress", at least at certain periods, according to human standards. But the fact is that a revealed religion represents a breakthrough of eternity into time, a breakthrough that could not continue in its initial purity and intensity without terminating, and reabsorbing into the Unseen, the very world, or universe, it is designed to guide and enlighten. A religion is at its most perfect the moment it dawns upon the world; as soon as it appears, as soon as it departs from Eternity and enters time (in terms of temporal manifestation, that is, not in terms of its eternal essence), it has already begun to die. As with the primordial sacrifice and dismemberment of the Hindu Purusha or the Norse Ymir to create the universe, the religion in question must be "broken" and "scattered" in order to manifest itself in space and time; this is one of the things Jesus meant when, in instituting the Holy Eucharist, he said "This is My Body which is broken for you." History, in the traditional view, is fundamentally entropic, not progressive. A cycle of manifestation emerges from the Unseen like a star being born, after which it slowly decreases in order, slowly burns out. Revealed religions are like lesser creations within the greater cycle; they too emerge fully-fledged from the invisible world, only to begin their downward course; creation and revelation, in the traditional view, follow paths analogous to that predicted for the material world by the Second Law of Thermodynamics: "Things fall apart/The center cannot hold."

As for why science, as opposed to religion, apparently exhibits such great progress, the first thing to note is that religion, while it certainly recognizes lesser instances of "progress", various "revivals" or "redresses" within the context of overall degeneration, can only define progress in terms of the openness of the human race to salvation, liberation, enlightenment; and according to this criterion, it is science (which in practical, socio-historical terms is inseparable from scientism, at least in the post-Renaissance West) which has progressively destroyed religious faith by deliberately positing itself as an alternative worldview to that of religion, one that can prove its worth in the most concrete terms through impressive progress and innovation—progress and innovation in *the technical field alone*; consequently our technocratic culture is more accurately described, in spiritual terms, as degeneration rather than as progress. And the fact is that technology seems to have absorbed whatever progressive tendencies and hopes the human race might once have entertained; we no longer dream of social progress, moral progress, progress in the arts; all we can imagine any more is technical progress, to which all other forms of progress seem to have been sacrificed. Consequently our most common image of the future is not some social utopia, but a post-apocalyptic wasteland—the ultimate consequence, we fear, of technology itself.

Someone who characterizes organized religion as Dr. Tart has done might be compared to a person who says of science: "Science is responsible for global warming and nuclear weapons, for the pollution of our rivers and streams and air, for the thinning of the ozone layer, for unleashing a worldwide plague of obesity and diabetes by making us afraid to go outside and exercise for fear that the sunlight will give us cancer, and by sticking all of us in front of computer screens, thus making possible the near-universal surveillance of everyone, and consequently destroying our freedoms. And science seems hell-bent on reducing us, through bionics and genetic engineering, to bio-technological devices, mere industrial products, thus destroying our very humanity." Is this a fair characterization of science? What about the great strides against infectious diseases, the ease of travel, the universal availability of information, the comfort and safety of our homes? By the same token, is it fair to limit organized religion to narrow-mindedness and bigotry, social control through indoctrination, religious warfare and persecution of heretics, tempered by a bit of benign moralizing? What of the power of the revealed religions to create whole civilizations lasting many centuries, filled with profound philosophies, great art, refined social mores, and those paragons of the human form, the saints of God? That Dr. Tart could ignore all of this without a second thought is one the best examples I can imagine of the terrible blinding and constricting effects of the scientistic outlook.

In other passages, Dr. Tart provides further proof of his massive ignorance of the nature and history of the world's religions:

> By the time John Everyman [the founder of the imagined religion 'Angelicusism' revealed to him by the spiritual being 'Angelicus'] has been dead for a few generations, his original teachings . . . have been worked over to various degrees (lots of committee meetings and politics), and Angelicusism is now a distinct religion, with its own theology, rites, customs, political affiliations, and social agenda. Non-approved interpretations of John Everyman's visions are called heresy and condemned.

As a generic picture of religion, this implies that rites are never instituted by the founder of a religion, which is false; that heresy is always "non-approved" for socio-political motives alone, not because it can be shown as either self-contradictory or opposed to revealed or inspired scripture and tradition; and ultimately that objectively true statements, or even "spiritually useful" statements according to the Buddhist concept of *upaya* or "skillful means", cannot be made about God, since all theology is ultimately motivated by socio-political concerns.

[... genuine] science [shows] that a wide variety of traditional religious views about reality are factually wrong; they just don't stand up to empirical tests.

After such a sweeping statement, Dr. Tart gives not a single example. I challenge him to name *one* traditional religious view that has been disproved by empirical means; I am confident that he can't, because religious truth is only established by non-empirical means, the logical consequence being that it can't be empirically disproved.

By applying essential scientific method to the phenomena of religion and spirituality, could we separate the wheat from the chaff—any real important essence of spirituality from the superstitions and distortions of the ages? Could we thus create a refined spirituality and religion that would continue to give us a basis for human values, while leaving the superstitions, outmoded ideas and psychopathologies behind?

In other words, religious revelations are not sent by God; religions are man-made affairs. And all those aspects of religion not susceptible to scientific evaluation, research and development are necessarily pathological.

... by 'spiritual' I refer to a realm of values, experiences, realities, and insights that goes beyond the ordinary material world.

Here Dr. Tart demonstrates zero ability to discriminate between the psychic and the spiritual, between the Divine and the angelic, or between the angelic and the demonic—a lack of the most rudimentary degree of "spiritual literacy".

If people say to me, 'my religion R teaches such and such, and therefore, you must be wrong in what you say about X, even if you seem convincing', I can accept that as their honest position. We can openly agree to disagree, but we're not fooling ourselves or anyone else about the nature of our disagreement. We're not doing science; we're doing personal beliefs.

If all disagreements in the field of religion can be defined as differences in "personal beliefs", why can't we say the same for disagreements in the field of science? Because science deals with objective reality, while religion is all subjective; there is no objective reality to which it refers—in other word, no God.

I'm not making any absolute statement about the ultimate nature of reality. How would I know?

If Dr. Tart really means "how would *anyone* know?" he is denying that the Absolute is in any way intelligible, thus invalidating *all* theological statements. It is true that the Absolute *is* unintelligible in the apophatic sense; the intuition of this unintelligibility is not the negation of all spiritual knowledge, however, but is in itself an aspect of such knowledge: if the Absolute is "One without a second", It must be beyond the subject/object dichotomy; if It is beyond the subject/object dichotomy, it must transcend experience. And yet, seeing that the Absolute is by definition the only Reality, every experience must in some imperfect way be an experience of It, the corollary being that the realm of experience mediated by the subject/object dichotomy must be unreal in one sense, since it can neither grasp nor be the Only Reality, and relatively real in another, since it in fact appears. This is the metaphysical doctrine that God is both transcendent and immanent—or, in Islamic terms, both incomparable with and comparable to created things—a notion analogous to the Hindu doctrine of *Maya*. Note also how this doctrine can be expressed in strictly logical terms.

Dr. Tart is quite conscientious and competent when it comes to the scientific method—well-informed, balanced, intelligent, objective—but as we have already seen, when he turns to religion, he immediately appears as ill-informed, filled with poorly-considered emotional reactions, incapable of logical inference, and infected with many of the biases of the very scientism he claims to reject:

1) *Ill-informed.* Dr. Tart is either simply unfamiliar with much of the available literature on the world religions, their doctrines and their histories (for example, he attributes St. Ignatius Loyola's "pray as if it were all up to God and work as if it were all up to you" to G. I. Gurdjieff, which is like attributing the equation e = mc² not to Einstein but to the writer of an ephemeral paperback popularizing relativity theory)—or, though familiar with it, generally unable to make sense of it. Why do scientists so often believe that they understand everything about religion when they have *never systematically studied it*? Is it in any way logical or "scientific" to believe oneself an expert on something simply because one has dismissed it?

2) *Emotionally reactive.* "Passions are not feelings per se", says spiritual writer Marty Glass in his *Eastern Light in Western Eyes* [Sophia Perennis, 2003], but simply "feelings that we immediately identify with." Passionate and unbalanced emotional reactions are often simply the behavioral reverberations of ideas or insights we recognize on some level to be of crucial importance, but which are not yet clearly formed in our minds. And this appears to be the case with Dr. Tart's passionate hatred of organized religion, which he expresses as follows:

> I'm really angry at the people who have such a petty and warped conception of God that they made him into a blown-up version of an insecure petty tyrant, ruling by force and needing to be praised all the time to soothe his insecure ego. All the useless psychological suffering such ideas have created! Okay, there have probably been lots of kings and despots who were like that, and, unfortunately, lots of parents who were like that, but let's not confuse them with the idea of a truly superior being.

But who, exactly, sees God in these terms? Certainly not most traditional believers; they see Him as all-powerful, just, all-merciful, and in no way in need of us, while we are in total need of Him. Tart's image of God is a lot closer to the inaccurate notion that *secular humanists* or *atheists* have of how traditional believers view God, the straw man they use to debunk religious faith; Dr. Tart seems unaware that he is speaking more of himself than of the faiths in this characterization of the Almighty. This is due to the fact that he has not succeeded in viewing his emotions objectively and dispassionately (admittedly a very hard thing to achieve), so as to determine whether their assertions are rationally consistent, and—whether consistent or not—what they are trying to tell him.

And if this is a false image of God, what would be a truer one? Tart's "best bet" (his own considered term) is that God probably exists, or at least some higher realm of spiritual beings, and that this Being or beings are probably benevolent, but he has little or nothing to say about their actual nature. That he does believe certain things about the nature of God and the metaphysical order can, however, be deduced from other statements he makes. For example, he asks what would happen "if we developed sciences that were not only open to spirituality but also wanted to help *advance* spirituality, and spiritual systems that were not only open to science but also wanted to help *advance* science, where might this openness take us?" Implied in this seemingly neutral question is the belief that man, not God, creates religions and/or spiritual systems, which further implies that "God" is neither conscious nor active, that He might be a reality accessible to human research, but not one that can either speak to us or have intentions regarding us. And this is an increasingly common view of God in these scientistic times: like atoms or stars or nuclear energy, God is something we can study, and possibly use, but He is certainly not studying *us*, nor has He any real use for us. He is the passive reality, we the active. Needless to say, this places God on a lower level of reality than man, reducing Him to a merely conjectural entity that no longer fulfills the definition of a Supreme Being.

3) *Illogical.* In terms of science, if one wished to establish the validity and the mathematical expression of a given natural law, would it be in any way logical to systematically ignore almost the entire body of literature, going back thousands of years, authored by those individuals, institutions, and entire civilizations that not only believed in and lucidly described the nature and operation of the law in question, but knew how to employ that law to achieve practical results? If not, then how is it logical to ignore, if not debunk,

almost the entire written and otherwise-transmitted corpus of doctrine and experience of the organized religions having to do with
telepathy, clairvoyance, precognition, psychokinesis and psychic
healing—realities which have been recognized for thousands of
years by all of the world's religions, though usually considered sec-
ondary to (if not in some cases serious distractions from) the prep-
aration of one's soul for the afterlife, or the attainment of mystical
union with the Absolute in this life—as well as out-of-body experiences, posthumous existence, and communication with the dead?
Talk about reinventing the wheel! Furthermore, Tart characterizes
his own lack of mystical experience as an "advantage" because it
allows him to maintain his scientific objectivity. He doesn't seem to
realize that in identifying a *lack* of the Primary Spiritual Experience
upon which he bases his life's work, and which he accepts as more
authoritative than religious tradition, with "objectivity", he is defining Primary Spiritual Experience itself as subjective, and thus as
inherently incapable of establishing objective truth.

Tart posits Primary Spiritual Experience, including spontaneous
mystical experiences like that of R.M. Bucke, as a major component
of what he calls "spirituality"—which, like so many people nowadays, he opposes to "religion." He says: "I was forcibly brainwashed
by being taught my religion when I was too young to really understand and make choices... 'spirituality', on the other hand, has
been a matter of relatively conscious choice on my part as an
adult...." But if a major aspect of this "spirituality" is spontaneous
mystical or psychic experience, which Bucke describes as having
come to him while he was in a "passive" state, how can such spirituality be defined in terms of conscious choice? Tart's mind is admira-
bly logical in designing and evaluating experiments, but when it
comes to the larger context in which these experiments are conducted, and according to which his assertions about the nature of
reality are made, logic deserts him—undoubtedly because we are
taught today, by scientism, to identify logic with materialism alone;
when we say "there must be a logical explanation" for such and such
an event, what we really mean is "there must be a materialistic
explanation." The idea that logic can apply to non-material
matters—that theology, for example, can and must employ logic in

its doctrinal formulations—is inconceivable to us. This is largely due to the historical revisionism imposed (for example) on scholastic philosophy, whose strictly logical arguments have been reduced in the popular mind by scientistic propaganda to "angels dancing on the head of a pin."

4) *Subjective.* Most of Dr. Tart's section on the nature of God is limited to a kind of psychological introspection whereby he attempts to make sense of his own beliefs and/or prejudices; this is an honest attempt to reach objectivity, but since his approach is based entirely on his own and others subjective experience, not on any notion that God can and does reveal Himself, or aspects of Himself, on His own initiative, any objective certainty as to the reality of God and the metaphysical order remains elusive. It is true of course that no stable understanding of spiritual reality can be born and develop without spiritual experience—and yet no approach to this reality that is *limited* to experience can ever be stable or complete. As Beat Generation poet Lew Welch said: "I seek union with what goes on whether I look at it or not." God and the metaphysical order are objectively real; they cannot be limited to our subjective, psychic impressions of them; consequently psychical research is inherently incapable of establishing their reality. The faculty capable of reaching certainty as to this reality is not clairvoyance or automatic writing but Intellection—including the virtual Intellection known as Faith. Tart says, "we want evidence, not faith." St. Paul says, "Faith is the presence of things hoped for, the evidence of things not seen"; it is not subjective experience; it is a way of knowing objective Truth. But when Tart characterizes human consciousness not as a necessarily limited but nonetheless valid view of objective facts, physical or metaphysical, but as a "bio-psychological virtual reality", an individual/collective dream, he reduces God and the spiritual world to mere human beliefs and experiences, about which it is impossible to say anything more than that human beings have held these beliefs and had these experiences. But as Frithjof Schuon points out, the world may be a dream, but it is not my dream—nor, by the same token, a collective dream—but a "dream" of the Absolute. In terms of our common psychophysical world, we are woven into the fabric of that dream; we are dreams, not dreamers.

To conduct a scientific experiment based on faith rather than empiricism could only be a corruption of scientific objectivity by subjective considerations, a delusion, a fraud, a contradiction in terms; valid science, as Tart demonstrates, operates by empirical means alone. But materialistic science, even if it attempts to investigate psychic realities, has absolutely nothing to do with the realities that Intellection and/or Faith can reveal; it is simply not designed to either access or understand them. And it is the failure to grasp this simple fact that defines the spiritually constricting scientism of our time.

MORE ON TART'S VIEW OF SCIENCE AND SCIENTISM

Dr. Tart's characterization of "essential science" is much more reliable than his picture of religion, since science is his area of expertise. Unfortunately, like most of us, he is quite clear on what he does know, but rather foggy when it comes to what he does not know; he is more aware of his knowledge than his ignorance. He epitomizes the scientific method as follows: *Observe phenomena; theorize or generalize on the basis of these observations; make predictions on the basis of a given theory and then carry out experiments to determine whether our theory is valid—that is, whether or not the results of our experiment match the predictions we have based upon it—and refine our theory accordingly; constantly communicate our findings to our colleagues, and seriously listen to their input, criticisms and suggestions.* He goes on to say: "While I've described this formal process as essential and genuine science, need I say that it's also a quite sensible way of proceeding in most areas of life?" Here we see with painful clarity the tendency of science to cut out whole areas of universal human experience; as someone once remarked, "if your only tool is a hammer, you may start to see everything as a nail." To take only one example out of many possible, this scientific, clinical approach is only secondarily applicable to any of the arts. And it should obviously never play a central role in human relations, lest we descend into: "I observe the girl; on the basis of my observations I theorize that she is a good girl, not prone to jealousy; I test this theory by trying to make her jealous, thus either confirming or denying my theory; and I gossip about this 'experiment' of mine to all my buddies". How much longer will we allow the scientistic paradigm to shrink our lives and our souls till they are no more than the pitiful remnants of what we are capable of, what we are?

Dr. Tart is nonetheless clearly aware of many of the psychological compulsions and unconscious reactions upon which scientism (and dishonest religion) is based. In one highly useful section, he lists various "Pathologies of Knowing and Learning": *Compulsive need for certainty; premature generalization; compulsive attachment to a generalization; the need to appear decisive, certain, confident; an inflexible, neurotic need to be tough; lack of balance between our masculine and feminine sides; rationalization; intolerance of ambiguity; social factors biasing the search for knowledge; grandiosity; pathological humility; overrespect and underrespect for authority; overrespect for the intellectual powers of the mind; intellectualization; one-upmanship; fear of the truth; rubricizing; compulsive dichotomizing; compulsive need for novelty.* I agree that most of these are truly pathological—most, but not all:

1) Our need for certainty cannot be limited to a pathological compulsiveness, though such compulsiveness certainly exists. The human being was designed for certainty. Without certainty that a dropped rock will fall and that the sun will rise tomorrow, we couldn't function. Furthermore, certainty as to spiritual truth is not only attainable, but is in fact the very *raison d'être* for God's creation of the human form. Speaking in traditional Catholic language, we humans are made "to know, love and serve Him"—and what we can know, we also can embody; as St. Thomas Aquinas put it, "the knower becomes the thing known." Empirical knowledge however, while certainly valid, can never bring us to this kind of certainty; it is here that the quest for certainty becomes a "compulsive need", and therefore pathological. On the other hand, if science did not believe that certainty of a kind is possible according to its methods, would it ever dare to enunciate scientific "laws"? And if it begins to lose the belief that empirical methods can reach certainty on their own plane, may we not expect it to eventually deconstruct itself by denying, in line with the postmodern worldview, the validity of *all* scientific laws?

2) Under the pathology he calls "the neurotic need to be tough", Tart includes the desire to be *strong*. Strength, however, is not a sickness, but a virtue; if we are intelligent and of good will, we will try our best to attain strength and help others to attain it. Even receptivity—of the mind, of the emotions, of the will—requires strength.

3) Dichotomizing certainly can become compulsive; yet when Tart says "Buddhism . . . sees this automatic compulsive duality as a primary cause of our suffering. At times reality may be good or bad, good and bad, neither good nor bad, or something in between, something else altogether," he is in danger of denying the use and necessity of dichotomizing—not compulsive, but conscious and deliberate—on its own level. When Gautama enunciated the "Noble Eightfold Path", including "right view, right livelihood, right mindfulness," etc., he was saying that certain views, certain ways of making a living, and a general mental scatteredness are simply *wrong* from the standpoint of the work of attaining Enlightenment. And while Buddhism certainly has an explicit set of moral rules—known as *sila*—the tendency of Western Buddhists and New Agers to demonize all dichotomies, valid or otherwise—while still harboring plenty of *unconscious* dichotomies of their own—recently led one blogster to write, "Buddhism is my favorite religion because it has no morality."

And speaking of morality, one further disturbing element in *The End of Materialism*, which points out the dangers of a science or scientism that attempts to become self-sufficient unto itself, is Dr. Tart's entire willingness to participate in CIA-backed remote viewing experiments at the Stanford Research Institute. Now that we know the horrendous nature of the CIA's infamous MK-Ultra mind control program, where experiments every bit as vicious as the medical experiments conducted in the Nazi death camps were performed upon helpless prisoners, hospital inmates and members of the general public (see the research of Peter Levenda and David McGowan), to admit that one worked under CIA direction on psychic experiments is equivalent to claiming death camp doctor Josef Mengele as a respected colleague! This underscores the need for scientists to adopt moral values from realms outside science per se, since the only ethical rule proper to "pure science" seems to be that against falsifying experimental data. (The hippies too were surprisingly blasé when informed that their precious LSD was first distributed to them by the CIA. "Sure we were a CIA experiment," they said—"an experiment that got out of control!" What they didn't seem to realize is that the experiment wasn't over; it isn't over yet.)

CONCLUSION

Those who spend their lives trying to prove to themselves and others that music exists will never become competent musicians, or even aficionados of the art, even if their proofs are valid and convincing. Music is to be played, to be learned, to be enjoyed; whoever approaches it in any other spirit and for any other purpose has never come into the world of music, never really heard it. And the same goes for the attempt to materially prove the reality of non-material realms.

Take for example the evidence for the human personality's survival of bodily death. If life after death is a reality as Tart seems to think, then societies that know this, or knew it, would not spend vast resources in an attempt to prove this rather rudimentary notion, but would take the next logical step of determining how to prepare a *positive* afterlife, as every religious society has done. But Tart, because he rejects religion, never addresses this obvious and practical step—consequently his approach represents a clear regression in comparison to the religious worldview. Who would be likely to build a better boat—someone who knew that viable boats could be built, or someone who spent his life trying to prove that boats exist? The primitive gropings of parapsychology, when compared to the resources for the full development of the spiritual life available in ages of faith, are like the atomic theory of Democritus in comparison to the work of Albert Einstein and Niels Bohr, which resulted in the actual splitting of the atom and the release of its power.

It is nonetheless true that no one ignorant of the phenomenology of the psychic plane, an important piece of which has been re-established in our time by the discipline of parapsychology, can claim to be *trismegistus*: fully conversant with the material, the psychic and the Spiritual worlds. And *The End of Materialism* is a very good place to begin a study of psychic realities; its findings are striking, and quite convincing. But unless we realize that the psychic plane is a reflection of the Spiritual plane which transcends it and holds sovereignty over it, the most impressive and well-documented anecdotes and scientific findings relating to the psychic world will progressively lose credibility until we are compelled to define it—falsely—as a mere epiphenomenon of matter.

Materialism as a dominant worldview cannot be ended by materialistic means. It will end either by the opening of the faculty of Intellection by the grace of God—an event that, in the present age, can happen only in the case of individuals—or, in collective terms, by the dawning of the ultimate consequences of the materialistic paradigm: in other words, by the end of the "This World".

APPENDIX THREE

THE LEGEND OF THE TOLLHOUSES

by Jennifer Doane Upton
[This article appeared in Issue 21 of *Sacred Web*]

I

In the Eastern Orthodox Church there is a tradition regarding the "aerial tollhouses" which the soul encounters after death. Though it does not have the force of dogma, it is recounted by such Church Fathers as St. John Chrysostom, St. Athanasius the Great and St. Ephraim the Syrian. (The Orthodox Church maintains a certain dogmatic silence on matters such as eschatology, since these realities cannot be fully expressed in human language.)

In the late 20th century it was Fr. Seraphim Rose who, in his book *The Soul After Death*, re-introduced the tradition of the tollhouses to the English-speaking world—though he is a suspect figure to many Orthodox Christians in the West due to his counterculture background. According to this tradition, the soul after death encounters realms in the "air"—the psychic plane—that are ruled by demons, who tempt it according to various sins, particularly those it had a special affinity for during life. If it passes through those realms without yielding to temptation, it ascends to Paradise. If not, it may reside in Hell for a period, to be purged of those sins. The damned do not encounter the tollhouses, however, but go to Hell directly. Seraphim Rose quotes the following passages from Eastern Orthodox fathers and saints with regard to this tradition:

St. Athanasius the Great, describing a visionary experience of St. Anthony:

At the approach of the ninth hour, after beginning to pray before eating food, [he] was suddenly seized by the Spirit and raised up by the angels into the heights. The aerial demons opposed his progress: the angels, disputing with them, demanded that the reasons of their opposition be set forth, because Anthony has no sins at all. The demons strove to set forth the sins committed by him from his very birth; but the angels closed the mouths of the slanderers, telling them that they should not count the sins from his birth which had already been blotted out by the grace of Christ; but let them present—if they have any—the sins he committed after he entered into monasticism and dedicated himself to God. In their accusation the demons uttered many brazen lies; but since their slanders were wanting in proof, a free path was opened for Anthony. Immediately he came to himself and saw that he was standing in the same place where he had stood up for prayer. Forgetting about food, he spent the whole night in tears and groaning, reflecting on the multitude of man's enemies, on the battle against such an army, on the difficulty of the path to heaven through the air, and on the words of the Apostle, who said: *Our wrestling is not against flesh and blood, but against the principalities and powers of the air* (Eph. 6:12; Eph. 2:2). The Apostle, knowing that the aerial powers are seeking only one thing, are concerned over it with all fervor, exert themselves to deprive us of a free passage to heaven, exhorts: *Take up the whole armor of God, that ye may be able to withstand in the evil day* (Eph. 6:13), *that the adversary may be put to shame, having no evil thing to say of us* (Titus 2:8).

St. John Chrysostom, describing the hour of death:

Then we will need many prayers, many helpers, many good deeds, a greater intercession from angels on the journey through the spaces of the air. If when traveling in a strange land or a strange city we are in need of a guide, how much more necessary for us are guides and helpers to guide us past the invisible dignities and powers and world-rulers of this air, who are called persecutors and publicans and tax-collectors.

St. Macarius the Great:

When you hear that there are rivers of dragons, and mouths of lions, and the dark powers under the heavens, and fire that burns and crackles in the members, you think nothing of it, not know-ing that unless you receive *the earnest of the Holy Spirit* (II Cor. 1:22), they hold your soul as it departs from the body, and do not suffer you to rise to heaven.

St. Ephraim the Syrian:

When the fearful hosts come, when the divine takers-away com-mand the soul to be translated from the body, when they draw us away by force and lead us away to the unavoidable judgment place—then, seeing them, the poor man . . . comes all into a shak-ing as if from an earthquake, all in trembling. . . . The divine tak-ers-away, having taken the soul, ascend in the air where stand the chiefs, the authorities and world-rulers of the opposing powers. These are our accusers, the fearful publicans, registrars, tax-collec-tors; they meet it on the way, register, examine, and count out the sins and debts of this man—the sins of youth and old age, volun-tary and involuntary, committed in deed, word and thought. Great is the fear here, great the trembling of the poor soul, indescribable the want which it suffers then from the incalculable multitudes of its enemies surrounding it there in myriads, slandering it so as not to allow it to ascend to heaven, to dwell in the light of the living, to enter the land of life. But the holy angels, taking the soul, lead it away.

St. John Damascene, from the Divine Liturgy:

O Virgin, in the hour of death rescue me from the hands of the demons, and the judgment, and the accusation, and the frightful testing, and the bitter toll-houses, and the fierce prince, and the eternal condemnation, O Mother of God.

St. Cyril of Alexandria:

What fear and trembling await you, O soul, in the day of death! You will see frightful, wild, cruel, unmerciful and shameless demons, like dark Ethiopians, standing before you. The very sight of them is worse than any torment. The soul, seeing them, becomes agitated, is disturbed, hastens to the angels of God. The holy angels hold the soul; passing with them through the air and rising, it encounters the toll-houses which guard the path from earth to heaven, detaining the soul and hindering it from ascending further. Each toll-house tests the sins corresponding to it; each sin, each passion has its tax-collectors and testers.

II

The reality which the Orthodox tradition of the tollhouses unveils is not fundamentally other than the Catholic doctrine of Purgatory. According Bishop Kallistos Ware, we don't change ontologically simply through death, and so if our love still needs to be perfected, this happens in the afterlife. This is the truth behind both Purgatory and the legend of the tollhouses.

Many Orthodox however, unwilling or unable to take a symbolic leap, are appalled by the idea of the tollhouses, which they consider to be rank superstition—an attitude due in part to the tendency of many modern Orthodox to define themselves primarily as "not Roman Catholic", making them highly suspicious of any doctrine that resembles the Catholic Purgatory. Also, the contemporary "Protestantizing" of Eastern Orthodoxy, in North America at least, makes many Orthodox wary of any doctrine of after-death purgation, though such traditions are as much Orthodox as Catholic. Kallistos Ware, for one, de-emphasizes the difference between the Eastern and Western concepts. (Whether or not Hell and Purgatory are two different "places", there is obviously a great difference between posthumous suffering accompanied by hope, and such suffering when it is totally without hope; this is the crux of the matter.) And a third reason for Orthodox suspicion of this tradition among many Orthodox Christians is the mistaken idea that the concept of aerial tollhouses implies that the soul, if it fails to pass these obstacles, might actually be damned. Such a doctrine would certainly go a long way toward denying the efficacy of Christ's Atonement. But as we have seen, Orthodox tradition associates the tollhouses with the purgation of the saved, not the punishment of the lost.

It is only believing Christians who encounter the tollhouses after death. The unbeliever gave up his soul long before his death. He saw no value in his Spirit; therefore when the Evil One offered him worldly gain in return for his giving evil something like a spiritual valuation, he accepted the bargain without hesitation. And so, at the moment of his death, this man has nothing in his soul which can ascend even as far as the psychic realm, the only place where choice can be made, the only realm in which evil could possibly tempt him. Consequently he falls below the earth, below the human state, into the infra-psychic realm, where he finally sees all those demonic worlds which he was mercifully forbidden to see during his terrestrial life.

The believing Christian, however, has kept the Spirit alive in his soul to a greater or a lesser degree, and that Spirit longs to ascend homeward to Paradise. The Spirit flies away toward Paradise, its one true love, with seeming unconcern for the soul it carries in its wake. The soul which had the single life-task of conforming itself to that Spirit, has nonetheless spent a lifetime trying to hold on to its worldly attachments and to the passions which seemed to give this world such richness and stability.

At the moment of death, however, this world is gone. If the soul is pure, the Spirit enfolds the soul within itself, and becomes like a golden arrow which delivers the soul in an instant to its true home.

The soul with worldly attachments, however, is left hanging in the air as it were. It can't follow with simplicity the Spirit in its ascent. The soul's passions keep reaching for a world that is no longer there. And the demons, who can move about with greater suppleness in the psychic realm (which the soul has just now entered) than they could in the physical one, offer themselves to the soul in lieu of the world it has lost. Here, if the soul does not listen to the angels which have been sent to it as helpers, it will not see that the demons are in fact offering it nothing, but are instead trying to take away its eternal life. It is now more than ever that the soul needs to understand the ways of the Spirit. In life it far too often followed the ways of this world because that is all it could see through its passional vision. Had it only raised its vision higher it would have seen the comings and goings of the Spirit creating a multitude of paths, which fall like a golden web upon everything the soul had taken to be merely "this world." It is here, in a world of higher vision, that the awakened soul wishes it had willed to follow the Spirit long ago.

APPENDIX FOUR

THREE PSYCHIC DREAMS

Some years ago I and a Muslim colleague posted a call on the internet for accounts of dreams dreamt by Muslims; over the years we received such accounts from many parts of the world. During the time of the great South Asian tsunami in 2004, I received the following three dream-records, which ought to prove to anyone's satisfaction—unless he or she believes that I or the dreamers themselves have practiced deliberate deception—that clairvoyance and/or precognition are true psychic talents, and that they may sometimes manifest in the dream state:

FIRST DREAM

I dreamt of a tidal wave hitting a country. And I tried to save myself by finding a safer place by running in a panic state. That time I was unprepared to die because I felt I had not taken my *wajib* bath. I passed a shophouse and saw some Muslims learning some things related to Islam. Suddenly I saw a big mosque and so many people were there who were Indians and Southeast Asians all doing some kind of prayers in a strange way. I try to join them but I can't because I'm not clean yet. The wave is getting closer then I woke. I say it was just a dream. The next day, the news says that there's a tsunami wave happening at the counties of the Indian Ocean.

SECOND DREAM

I had a dream that I was driving with my little brother we were speeding away from a huge tidal wave and there was a earthquake also and when the ground began to split I woke up. I had this dream the morning in which the earthquake hit Asia and I didn't even find out it happened till I woke up.

THIRD DREAM

I saw Jesus walking on the water and he was guiding me past large harsh waves. Behind him was a pinky orange sky where the clouds had something written on the sky, I couldn't make out what it spelled out. He gave me a boxed toy and I ended up in a large warehouse full of toys. The atmosphere of people felt like I was going to the hajj which was at a beach to see Jesus. [09/22/2004]

[NOTE: To the Muslim psyche the Prophet Jesus has particularly to do with the end of the world; His Second Coming, during which he will battle and slay al-Dajjal, the Antichrist, is one of the major signs of the Hour.]

A CONCISE BIBLIOGRAPHY
OF PRINCIPIAL PSYCHOLOGY

TRADITIONAL SUFI PSYCHOLOGY

Chittick, William, *Imaginal Worlds: Ibn 'Arabi and the Problem of Religious Diversity*, New York: State University of New York Press, 1994.

al-Ghazali, Muhammad, *Al-Ghazali on Disciplining the Soul and on Breaking the Two Desires: Books XXII and XXIII of the Revival of the Religious Science*s, Louisville: Islamic Texts Society, 1997.

Nurbakhsh, Javad, *The Psychology of Sufism (Del wa Nafs)*, London & New York: Khaniqahi-Nimatullahi Publications, 1993.

_____. *Sufism II: Fear and Hope, Contraction and Expansion, Gathering and Dispersion, Intoxication and Sobriety, Annihilation and Subsistence*, London & New York: Khaniqahi-Nimatullahi Publications, 1982.

_____. *Sufism III: Submission, Contentment, Absence, Presence, Intimacy, Awe, Tranquility, Serenity, Fluctuation, Stability*, London & New York: Khaniqahi- Nimatullahi Publications, 1985.

_____. *Sufism IV: Repentance, Abstinence, Renunciation, Wariness, Humility, Sincerity, Constancy, Courtesy*, London & New York: Khaniqahi- Nimatullahi Publications, 1988.

_____. *Sufism V: Gratitude, Patience, Trust-In-God, Aspiration, Veracity, Zeal, Altruism, Shame* London & New York: Khaniqahi-Nimatullahi Publications, 1991.

Rumi, Jalaluddin, *The Quatrains of Rumi: Ruba'iyat-é Jalaluddin Muhammad Balkhi-Rumi*, trans. Ibrahim W. Gamard and A.G. Rawan Farhadi, San Rafael: Sufi Dari Books (an imprint of Sophia Perennis), 2008.

TRADITIONAL CHRISTIAN
PSYCHOLOGY AND ITS ORIGINS

Aquinas, St. Thomas, *The Soul: A Translation of Thomas Aquinas' De Anima*, trans. John Patrick Rowan, Eugene: Wipf and Stock, 2008.

Aristotle, *De Anima*, trans. R.D. Hicks, New York: Cosimo Classics, 2008.

Climacus, St. John, *The Ladder of Divine Ascent*, Mahwah: The Paulist Press, 1982.

Larchet, Jean-Claude: *The Theology of Illness*, Redondo Beach: Oakwood Publications, 2002.

———. *Mental Disorders and Spiritual Healing: Texts from the Early Christian East*, Hillsdale: Sophia Perennis, 2005.

St. Nikodimos of the Holy Mountain and St. Makarios of Corinth, *The Philokalia: The Complete Text, Vol. 1*, trans. G.E.H. Palmer, Philip Sherrard, and Kallistos Ware, London: *Faber and Faber,* 1979.

———. *The Philokalia: The Complete Text, Vol. 2*, trans. G.E.H. Palmer, Philip Sherrard, and Kallistos Ware, London: Faber and Faber, 1981.

———. *The Philokalia: The Complete Text, Vol. 3*, trans. G.E.H. Palmer, Philip Sherrard, and Kallistos Ware, London: Faber and Faber, 1984.

———. *The Philokalia: The Complete Text, Vol. 4*, trans. G.E.H. Palmer, Philip Sherrard, and Kallistos Ware, London: Faber and Faber, 1991.

Roney, Lois, *Chaucer's Knight's Tale and Theories of Scholastic Psychology,* Tampa: University of South Florida, 1991.

Scupoli, Lorenzo, Theophan the Recluse and Nicodemus of the Holy Mountain: *Unseen Warfare: The Spiritual Combat and Path to Paradise, Revised Edition,* Yonkers: St. Vladimir's Seminary Press, 1997.

Suarez, Francisco, *Opera Omnia, Tractatus Tertius: "De Anima"*, Paris: Apud Ludovicum *Vives*, 1856–1878. [See also http://www.sydneypenner.ca/suarez.html]

TRADITIONAL HINDU PSYCHOLOGY

Akhilananda, Swami, *Mental Health and Hindu Psychology*, New Delhi: Munshiram Manoharlal Publishers, 2005.

Iyengar, B.K.S., *Light on the Yoga Sutras of Patanjali*, London & San Francisco: Thorson's (an imprint of HarperCollins), 1993.

TRADITIONAL AND
CONTEMPORARY BUDDHIST PSYCHOLOGY
The *Abidhamma/Abidharma*

Bodhi, Bhikku, *A Comprehensive Manual of Abhidhamma: Vipassana Meditation and the Buddha's Teachings,* Onalaska: Pariyatti Publishing, 2000.

Kornfield, Jack, *A Wise Heart: A Guide to the Universal Teachings of Buddhist Psychology*, New York: Bantam, 2009.

[Further texts available at http://www.abhidhamma.com]

DEMONOLOGY AND EXORCISM

Martin, Malachi, *Hostage to the Devil: The Possession and Exorcism of Five Contemporary Americans*, New York: HarperCollins, 1992.

ALCHEMY

Burkhardt, Titus, *Alchemy: Science of the Cosmos, Science of the Soul* (Revised Edition), Louisville: Fons Vitae, 1997.

Eberly, John, *Al-Kimia: The Mystical Islamic Essence of the Sacred Art of Alchemy*, Hillsdale: Sophia Perennis, 2005.

Made in United States
Orlando, FL
13 March 2024

44731332R00162